Transforming the Hong Kong Legal Machine

Man-Chung Chiu

Transforming the Hong Kong Legal Machine

Gender and Familial Law in Jurisprudence

Springer

Man-Chung Chiu
Law School
Beijing Normal University
Beijing, China

ISBN 978-981-19-1271-9 ISBN 978-981-19-1272-6 (eBook)
https://doi.org/10.1007/978-981-19-1272-6

This Springer imprint is published by the registered company Springer Nature Singapore Pte Ltd.
The registered company address is: 152 Beach Road, #21-01/04 Gateway East, Singapore 189721, Singapore

To my parents

Preface

I was supposed to finish this book in 2019. Unfortunately, the seriousness of the social violence in Hong Kong diverted all my attention, time and energy from writing philosophy to reflecting on life.

People who work with me know very well that I am very rigid with timelines. I rarely miss a deadline and always aim at arriving 15 minutes early for appointments. So failure to finish this book on schedule, to me, is something unimaginable. However, the unrest and related violence in my mother city, and more importantly, the subsequent need for reflection, have really rendered me unable to concentrate on my writing.

The 2014 Occupy Movement that took place in Hong Kong, as mentioned in my other book, *De/Sexing Hong Kong Law*, has already passed out of the imagination of the majority of HongKongians. Blindfolded by my very limited understanding of the pseudo-essentiality of HongKongians, I naively and unconsciously assumed the physical conflict in 2014 had already hit the ceiling of the scale of violence possible in Hong Kong and had challenged the extent of mass tolerance. So, during the 2019 Umbrella Movement, initiated by the failed proposal to revise the existing extradition law, when I saw the massive brutal images broadcast live on TV and the internet, to me, it was extremely shocking. The impact created was intensified by the stream of information, which was later proven untrue and fabricated. However, when being immersed in that contextual machine, no one was able to triple check the accuracy of news at the time, given the affect manufactured by the events, the scarcity of resources and the urgency of decision-making.

The 2019 event not only showed the multiplicities and novelty of resistance strategies but also opened a debate on the usefulness of philosophy and theory. Although some academics were very familiar with the theories, could they persuade frontline participants to slow down and reflect? Could anyone make any prompt decision, without possible future regret, given the very limited resources (including time and data)? When I saw the video clip, that circulated widely, showing the university teachers—on asking the students blocking the main entrance to a major hospital, to calm down and reflect, being scolded and sworn at, I, at that moment, felt absolutely powerless and disheartened. An acquaintance sympathetic with the students, said: 'Perhaps, we are now living in the age where theories are becoming useless'.

So, can philosophies and theories only be utilized in post-event analysis? Can they no longer (as surely they once did) offer tentative guidelines for instantaneous decision-making and simultaneous re/action, especially during the climaxes of social movements? Is this because it takes too much time to understand philosophies and theories? If true, would it, at the end of the day, reduce a society to an anti-intellectual organism?

Another question also arises: Is it perhaps not the philosophy or theory that people find dysfunctional, but the authorities that hold the power to interpret and apply those abstract ideas? There are a few, not many, online discussion forums that have generated quite a number of interesting ideological debates. I am not concerned to evaluate the quality of discussion; but whenever there were ideas that challenged the ideas supported by the majority of viewers or netizens (on the forum), they would be criticized severely, not in a rational mode, but in a very emotionally provocative way. If the one who posted the views in question attempted to elaborate or defend the arguments further, s/he would only attract more and more streams of bullies; even her/his personal data would be revealed publicly. It seemed no one cared anymore if it was a kind of censorship or infringement of privacy.

Amid the storm of violence and confrontations (physical or online, philosophical or anti-theoretical), I find that justice is present and absent at the same time: We can have a whole society arguing as to whether a decision or an action is just or not, with little attempt to define what they actually mean by justice. Can law and court procedure still be a means to re-construct and restore justice? What does justice mean? Does justice simply mean a reflection of majority emotion?

The violence and conflicts died down gradually after the District Board election in 2019; when people could enjoy a moment of peace, Hong Kong was, and still is, ravaged by COVID-19. The pandemic started in late February 2020. The very serious shortage of face masks and the refusal to close the northern border again put the Hong Kong SAR Government under attack. The lack of support made the anti-pandemic measures once extremely difficult to implement—the policy of setting up designated clinics (for patients with slight symptoms but who might not be infected) was once shelved after a certain number of clinics were set on fire or petrol bombed—I always wondered if those people who initiated these attacks understood that violation against medical neutrality is a war crime.

The motivation for the attack was disability discrimination—the opposition camp argued that the locations of clinics were too close to residential areas—although those clinics were also used during the 2009 swine flu outbreak; and numerous experts had explained again and again that the facilities were well-enough equipped to avoid any possible spread of the virus and that they were not close to any households, medically speaking. The opposition camp still resisted these ideas. This was not the only instance of discrimination—there were cases where restaurants and shops refused Mainland Chinese/people who spoke PuTongHua. Again, medical experts explained that the virus was not discriminatory and would not only attack a particular race of people. The discriminators simply did not listen.

I am not saying that the ruling authority was fault-less during the crises: in hindsight, more consultations, more elaborations of policy, more equal-footing discussions and dialogues, more responsive and more accurate reactions could definitely have created more peaceful and efficient solutions to the problems. What I am wondering is: Can a resistance movement, which relies on a view of society lacking in any coherent theoretical foundation, genuinely bring about a better future?

Those are the questions that haunted me when I was trying to finish this book. I did not respond to those questions directly and explicitly: Perhaps those are the essential steps in the multiple and diverse constructions of new Master Signifers, processes of re/de-territorialization, or sanguinary jouissance. Nonetheless, I wish the three themes that permeate the chapters of this book can be applied to the search for the settlement of future conflicts in Hong Kong. These themes are:

1. While equality is the starting point for reproducing justice, critical self-reflection and acceptance of different opinions will form a stronger foundation for the re-constitution of justice;
2. The transplantation of foreign ideas (including legal concepts and political ideology) without proper modification (e.g. localization) will only bring more conflict and violence (e.g. postcolonialism) and
3. Law is still an effective way to represent justice.

A society can never be stable and static, but if it is ruled only by the Real and its Symbolic Order constantly collapses, when we are becoming self-centred, non-critical against ourselves, discrimination-tolerant, law-ignorant, are we distancing ourselves from Dao 道, nirvāṇa 涅盘 and justice? In lay terms, can a society where people believe in a concept of righteousness that has been reduced to the emotional judgement of the majority, and where legal procedure is no longer taken to be a reliable way to settle social conflicts, still survive?

I want to take this opportunity to thank Nigel Bruce for his editorial assistance. Special thank also goes to Lawrence Lau, discussion with him, academically and non-academically, is always enlightening.

Beijing, China

Man-chung Chiu

Introduction

Re/Conceptualizing Transformation

This book is a collection of articles published between 2008 and 2017, which have all been revised and rewritten. Revision and rewriting are essential not only because, since they were first written, there have been new laws and new consultations, but also because I want to more fully elaborate on the issues discussed, making reference to new interpretations and developments of relevant theories (especially those derived and reinterpreted by Slavoj Žižek—given how prolific he is).

I tell my law students that the focus of studying law is not learning the court decisions and memorizing the provisions of statutes, but developing a critical mindset. At the end of the day, when they graduate, there will be new legislation and new cases, and many existing laws and decisions may have been repealed or overruled. Even if there have been no new actual developments, new concepts or additional perspectives would have been tabled through the issuance of consultation papers and research reports. Critical thinking, hence, is becoming more and more vital in evaluating the practicality and influence of those innovative ideas and related legal techniques.

Themes of the Book

This book investigates how Buddhism and Daoism constitute a platform that could facilitate intercultural articulation, i.e. the (legal) transplantation of Rawlsian/Deleuzian/Žižekian notions of justice. While understanding how the assemblages of transplantation that generates/transforms justice in the recipient culture operates, this book also profiles how concepts, that are not locally originated, could also be modified through this process of osmosis, as I argue in Chap. 3. Even if the transplantation is not intentional, such modification still happens—is Mahāyāna 大乘 Buddhism (including Vijñānamatra 唯识 and Mādhyamika 中观), itself not an indigenous Han-Chinese cultural product, modified during the establishment of Han-Chinese School of Vinaya-Discipline 律宗? Does such transformation lead to a non-stop development of a (more) sophisticated Buddhist jurisprudence, which in turn helps epitomize poststructuralist theories of unstable subjectivities and desire during transplantation (Chaps. 4, 5, 6 and 7)? In short, local culture is not simply a transplantation machine (Chap. 8). Intercultural transplantation can also be taken as a continual dialogue between different (aboriginal and overseas, newer and older) philosophical analyses—we cannot imagine, once Desexualization, Degenderization and De-ageing are realized in Hong Kong, that the interaction between different theories of justice would come to an end.

The problem of transplantation is created by Hong Kong's historical reliance on laws enacted and cases decided in other common law jurisdictions. The Hong Kong Law Reform Commission, during consultations and collections of opinions, has always relied heavily on statutes and cases in other common law jurisdictions. This practice has created two fatal problems. First, although Hong Kong is using the common law system, statutes and cases developed in other common law jurisdictions are the products of foreign cultures and traditions; therefore, would the transplantation of the related provisions and case decisions to Hong Kong, a predominately Han-Chinese society, create any possible socio-cultural conflicts, i.e. postcolonial violence? Second, is it appropriate to neglect laws and related legal developments in civil jurisdictions, including laws in Mainland China, Macao and Taiwan, which are significant domains of (Han-)Chinese 汉族华人 civilization? The question that underlies the above problems is: Is law not a socio-cultural product?

The problems of cross-cultural transplantation outlined above have created obstacles, perhaps unconsciously, during the process of legal transplantation and transformation. Same sex marriage/partnership is a good example. Same sex marriage was legally recognized by the Constitutional Court of Taiwan in 2018—since Taiwan is a civil law jurisdiction, the case would seem to have no relevance to Hong Kong.[1] Same sex marriage or partnership is also legally acceptable in a number of Euro-American jurisdictions, but because their cultures are so different from traditional Hong Kong culture, their laws should have no direct and legal impact upon Hong Kong.[2] Any attempt to transplant such reforms to Hong Kong and transform existing laws accordingly is very likely to be adjudged as not compatible to local (Han-)Chinese culture. Following this analogy, does it mean that same sex marriage/partnership should never be lawfully recognized in Hong Kong?[3] (Whether it is essential to transform the related law and transplant the concept is another issue.) That also explains why legal reform proposals that are related to gender/sexual culture (including suggestions related to child sexual abuse and rape law), are usually shelved, sometimes

[1] For details, please see Chiu (2019).

[2] *Navarro Luigi Recasa* v *The Commissioner of Correctional Services and the Commissioner of Police* HCAL 93/2015.

[3] A good example is the strong resistance to repealing the customary laws governing the New Territories, Hong Kong, which are clearly misogynistic. For details, please see, Chiu (2017).

even years after the final reports have been published. For details of these proposals and related analyses, please see Chaps. 7 and 8.

Possible Solutions

In order for legal and cultural transplantation to take place smoothly (whether successfully is another narrative), a new perspective and a meticulous machinic process have to be designed and manufactured. The construction of such assemblage must start with a critical understanding of local culture that is able to problematize the longstanding imagination of tradition, including the illusory equation of 'Confucianism = Harmony = Han-Chinese culture'. A possible transplantation machine, relying on Deleuzian theory and Hsiao-hung Chang's 'transcultural articulation', that is briefly discussed in Chap. 6 of *De/Sexing Hong Kong Law*, is elaborated in more detail in Part I of this book (in Chaps. 1, 2 and 3). The key point is the search for a zone of sim*u*larity, where the osmosis of cultures can be articulated.[4]

I decided to conduct research into legal-cultural transplantation as the non-stop redefinition of justice and anti-discrimination has been more sophisticated in Euro-American civilizations; so if we want to revise the existing notion of 'justice' and re-produce a new version of 'justice' in the context of Hong Kong, an easy way would be to transplant the concepts from overseas and transform the laws accordingly. I argue that justice, in a context where the transformation of local law/culture is projected, inevitably involves the construction of a Buddhist jurisprudence and a Daoist perspective on law, philosophies that are permeated with the concept of equality—the starting point of justice. While discussing Buddhist legal philosophy, besides Vijñānamatra and the School of Vinaya-discipline, Mādhyamika, the Buddhist philosophy of deconstruction, is also employed in this book to problematize the existence of intrinsic nature, the root of a hierarchal society (Chap. 2).

Even though the Rawlsian theory of Justice shares the same starting stance—equality—with Buddhist and Daoist notions of justice, it is critically examined in this book from the respective perspectives of Deleuzian philosophy and a Žižekian (re)interpretation of Lacanian psychoanalysis. The concepts of deterritorialization/lines of flight and 'Body without Organs', advocated by Gilles Deleuze (and Félix Guattari), effectively destabilize and reset the connections between machines (concepts), while Žižek's concept of 'act' signifies an attempt to create a new Master Signifier. Both theories, which can synchronize with Buddhism and Daoism, mark the instability and fluidity of common-sense realities and thus produce spaces for the redefinition of justice.

When redefining justice in issues like discrimination against same sex erotic relationships (Chap. 4), transsexuality (Chap. 6) and Mainland Chinese pregnant women (Chap. 5), child sexual abuse and law reform related to sexual offences in

[4] Please also see Chap. 6, Chiu (2017).

Hong Kong—as I advocated in *De/Sexing Hong Kong Law*—I firmly believe that the constructs of Desexualization, Degenderization and De-ageing can be efficient and effective in re-presenting justice. The problem is: As re/territorialization and de/territorialization is a repetitive loop and the search for object a is doomed to be a failure, reality is never static, new problems are generated in different formats, and the definition of justice thus has to be constantly questioned and subverted. Desexualization, Degenderization and De-ageing can never provide the answers to all socio-legal problems.

Schedule of Chapters

This book is divided into two inter-related parts. Part I contains three chapters, which focus on the transplantation and transformation of law. In these chapters, I attempt to produce a holistic philosophical perspective, elaborating why the interaction among theories (going beyond an overseas/local binarism) and the investigation of tradition are becoming vital.

Chapter 1 discusses why the transplantation of overseas theories is essential in engineering a localized theory of justice in the cultural context of a Han-Chinese civilization. This is not only because we lack a strong and powerful perspective of criticism in Han-Chinese traditional culture but also because we can take the related reform strategies and experiences as references for an indigenous exercise of resistance. In this chapter, the myth of Han-Chinese culture being harmony-centric is also challenged.

Chapter 2 continues the discussion of transplantation from a non-Orthodox perspective of Han-Chinese culture. I question whether harmony, under an imaginary hegemony of (Orthodox) Confucianism, is invariably the theme underlying the development of Han-Chinese (legal) culture. I conduct an in-depth investigation of the conflict between different schools of Confucianism and explore how Mādhyamika Buddhism can help with locating and exploring possible spaces of resistance and revolution within Han-Chinese jurisprudence.

After discussing why transplantation of theory is vital in constituting spaces of resistance and redefining justice within Han-Chinese culture, in Chap. 3, I detail a conceptual machine by which transplantation can be effectively conducted. I advocate that the recipient culture needs to create and locate a zone of sim*u*larity, by sustained reflection and self-examination. I argue that Buddhism and Daoism are jointly becoming a platform of transplantation.

In Part II, I propose different reform strategies, relying on the philosophical machines set out in Part 1, that can eliminate different types of discrimination. I argue that identity is always unstable, and elements like age and sexuality are becoming redundant and irrelevant in the exercise of justice, and therefore can be removed from the legal equations.

Chapter 4 discusses the ban on the influx of Mainland pregnant women, which was imposed in 2013. That policy re-confirmed the imaginary dichotomy between

Hong Kong and Mainland China. I argue that Rawlsian theory, in that context, can be effectively challenged by a Deleuzian strategy of 'becoming powerless', and that the Buddhist philosophy of justice—as subjectivity is always a repetitive becoming, initiated by unresting desire, any proposal to define (racial) identity is doomed to failure. Chapter 4 also uses that context to explain in detail how Vijñānamatra subverts the objectivity of images.

While debating whether a new anti domestic violence law should be enacted, opposition to such reform tends to argue that traditional Han-Chinese values, where familial harmony is (over-)emphasized, is still relevant in contemporary Hong Kong society, thus resisting any socio/legal intervention. In Chap. 5, relying on Deleuzian syntheses of time, I argue that the past and the future can be taken as mental constructions. In other words, new law and new concepts, i.e. line of flight, can be produced in the struggle between a molar past and a molecular future.

After *W* v *Registrar of Marriage*,[5] it seems that the marital rights of transgender people are well confirmed in Hong Kong. Nonetheless, the bill which aimed at reforming the current Marriage Ordinance (Cap 181, LHK) that can accommodate those rights has failed. Since then, all reform attempts have ceased. Chapter 6 cross-examines the reasons underlying this failure, stressing again that, from the perspectives of Žižek and Mahāyāna Buddhism, gender identity is never a universal concept, but a non-stop becoming, where differences are constantly being constructed. Only if (marriage) law is degenderized can justice, where multiple desires are respected, be manufactured.

In Chap. 7, using mainly the Deleuzian philosophy of deterritorialization, I argue that it is impossible to construct a rigid and monolithic notion of human subjecthood in law. While the Hong Kong Law Reform Commission proposed constructing a more comprehensive legal protection for children in the sexuality machine, the suggestions tabled simply relegate children to a more powerless position.

Although the Hong Kong Law Reform Commission has announced a series of reform proposals related to sexual offences since 2015, the law machine, even after engaging with the suggested revisions, has still failed to deterritorialize gender stereotypes, and further reterritorializes sexual injustice and the patriarchal social machine. Hence in Chap. 8, I argue that, in order to re-create justice, a multiple-faceted strategy, comprising the Žižekian 'act', Deleuzian deterritorialization and the Laozian theory of actionless-ness 无为, can be employed to explore the possibility of producing a new Master Signifier and subvert the dominating phallocentric assemblages.

So this book, though different from *De/Sexing Hong Kong Law* and not relying on Foucauldian theory in its analysis of different socio-legal problems, explores very similar issues relating to Hong Kong's legal machine and reaches the same conclusion and proposes the same solutions. People may ask: Why then do you have to use different routes simply to reach the same outcome? I certainly concur, given the fact that I am still relying on Buddhism (although a different school of thought—Mādhyamika, which together with Vijñānamatra, belongs to the Mahāyāna division of Buddhism—is also used) and poststructuralism (where Jacques Lacan, Žižek,

[5] [2013] 3 HKLRD 90.

Deleuze and Foucault are considered the most important figures). The strategy of becoming, the idea of 'Body without Organs', the Žižekian act and the Buddhist problematization of intrinsic nature, all strengthen the philosophical foundation of my proposed reform strategy and thus can withstand more powerful challenges. Although the reform process is definitely important, how it is carried out and the outcome generated may be influenced by unexpected events. In order to make sure the desired effects are achieved, it is essential that a comprehensive understanding of the underlying theories applied in this approach be manufactured by building a robust matrix of multiple interrelated paradigms.

Credits

All Chapters are either revised or rewritten versions of the following chapters and articles:

1. 'Going Beyond Globalization and Localization: Articulating a Theory of Justice in Han-Chinese Culture' [2010] 21 *Law and Critique* 93–110.
2. 'Development of an Indigenous Legal Theory of Sexual Justice in Hong Kong' [2007] 37(3) *Hong Kong Law Journal* 775–803.
3. 'Beyond Colonialism: Osmotic Reconstruction of Gender / Sexual Justice' [2009] 10(3) *Inter-Asia Cultural Studies* 399–421.
4. 'Desiring Justice, Acting Jnana' in Heather Shipley (ed), *Globalized Religion and Sexuality* Canada: Brill (2014); 40–61.
5. 'Simularizing Tradition and Foreign: Osmotic Production of Justice in the Milieu of Hong Kong Anti-Domestic Violence Law' in Piotr Pachuta, (ed), *New Knowledge in a New Era of Globalization* Vienna: InTech, (2011); 149–164.
6. 'Deterritorializing Sexuality, Act(less)ing Justice' in Man-chung Chiu, (ed) Resisting and Reproducing: Reconstructing the matrix of sexual politics in Greater China and Singapore 15.2 *Reconstruction* (2015).
7. 'Un/Controlling Desire, Becoming Others: Negotiating Justice in the Hong Kong milieu of Mainland Pregnant Women Influx [2012]'3(3) *Beijing Law Review* 92–102.
8. 'Confession of Law' [2012] 33(1) *Liverpool Law Review* 46–66. (Special Issue: Sexuality/Gender Justice in Greater China and Singapore).

References

Chiu, Man-chung, (2017) *De/Sexing Hong Kong Law*. Hong Kong: Red Publish.

Chiu, Man-chung, (2019) '"Can Overman Bring Justice to Her/His Body and Romance?" Investigation of Recent Cases of Non-traditional Different-Sex Marriage and Recognition of Transsexual's Newly Acquired Gender Identities from a Nietzschean Justice Perspective' 54 *Hong Kong Journal of Social Sciences* 97–127.

Contents

Part II Becoming Justice, Desiring Transformation

Part I
Transplanting Concepts, Engaging the Local

Chapter 1
Beyond Colonialism (1): Destablization of Han-Chinese Traditional Socio-legal Culture

1.1 Introduction

In 2005, the court in *Leung William Roy* v *Secretary for Justice*[1] decided that the legal control of (man with man) sodomy in Hong Kong violates the Basic Law (the mini constitution of Hong Kong) and the Bill of Rights Ordinance (Cap LHK, 383); and in 2008, it was ruled that the determination published by the Hong Kong Broadcasting Authority, which declared that the TV programme 'Gay Lovers' had violated the broadcasting code of practice, was itself a breach of freedom of speech.[2] It seemed that the move towards an era of total gender/sexual justice Hong Kong, a predominately Han-Chinese 汉族华人 society, which started in 1978 (when the sex work industry was again regulated), continues. However, when scrutinising the local context, a different conclusion begins to appear: The Hong Kong SAR Government still refuses to review the New Territories Small House Policy[3] and to discuss the

This chapter is derived in part from an article published in *Law and Critique* (2010) Routledge.

[1] HCAL 160/2005.

[2] *Cho Man-kit* v *Broadcasting Authority* HCAL 69/2007.

[3] The Small House policy is designed to allow any indigenous male resident of a village which has been in existence in the New Territories, Hong Kong since 1 July 1898, who has reached the age of 18, to apply for permission to build a house for his own habitation. The Small House policy is entrenched in Section 13(1), New Territories Ordinance (Cap 97, LHK), which maintains the usage of Han-Chinese land customs in the area. In *Kwok Cheuk-kin* v *Directors of Lands* [2019] HKCFI 867, the first ever court case in Hong Kong to discuss extensively and comprehensively the legal status of the Small House policy, Mr. Justice Anderson Chow ruled that: (1) The policy is discriminatory in nature; (para 24) (2) part of the policy (the part in the form of Free Building Licence) is 'a lawful traditional right and interest of the New Territories indigenous inhabitants', and is thus well entrenched by Article 40 of the Basic Law of Hong Kong, which writes: 'The lawful traditional rights and interests of the indigenous inhabitants of the 'New Territories' shall be protected by the Hong Kong Administrative Region.' The Court of Appeal, however, overturned the decision on 13 January 2020. Mr. Justice Jeremy Poon ruled that: (1) The long-held custom to build houses in the village of indigenous residents in the New Territories for their own occupation had been recognized by the Colonial Government; (paras 51, 53, 56 and 67); (2) The Small House

M.-C. Chiu, *Transforming the Hong Kong Legal Machine*,
https://doi.org/10.1007/978-981-19-1272-6_1

possibility of introducing same sex partnership/marriage, degenderizing rape law, or enacting any law against sexual-orientation discrimination.[4]

The refusal to countenance further reforms can be attributed to the alleged possible conflict between the Euro-American model of gender/sexual justice and the 'indigenous' Han-Chinese civilization in Hong Kong. The opposition to reform camp insists that the transplantation of Euro-American gender/sexual politics and the related legal reforms into Hong Kong will manufacture legal-cultural colonialism that would marginalize interpersonal harmony, a core tenet of Han-Chinese philosophy. The implementation of gender/sexual equality since the 1990s, in short, reproduces a series of dichotomies: Indigenous residents vs British; aboriginals (early settlers) vs immigrants (latecomers); authentic Han-Chinese vs contaminated Han-Chinese; Han-Chinese culture vs Euro-American culture; Han-Chinese patriarchal custom vs Euro-American human rights; colonized locals vs foreign colonizers; and local resistance vs foreign colonisation.

These crude dichotomies only serve to reinforce the imaginary monolithic definition of Han-Chinese culture. Take wife abuse and sexual orientation discrimination as examples: While 'wife' was not respected in the (Orthodox) Confucian 儒家 li 礼, in the social context where harmony between families is emphasized, 'extreme wife abuse' could not be tolerated, this therefore constructs the theoretical basis where mandatory counselling is accepted in Hong Kong. Also, whenever the issue of sexual orientation discrimination is raised in the Legislative Council, lawmakers also argue that Han-Chinese tradition has to be considered and respected.[5] But, sexual orientation discrimination did not always exist and same-sex erotic desire was not pathologized in ancient Chinese history and literature—this thus shows that the Han-Chinese culture proposed/reconstituted by people who oppose anti-sexual orientation discrimination law is only an illusion.[6]

This chapter attempts to further problematize and politicize the fossilized and monolithic reading of Han-Chinese socio-legal culture, put forward by people who object to further legal reform. It asks a series of questions that critically investigate the Hong Kong Han-Chinese socio-legal culture: Why did/does harmony become the metaphysics of Han-Chinese socio-legal culture? How does Han-Chinese socio-legal culture re-constitute human nature/subjectivity? Can Han-Chinese socio-legal culture engage with overseas resistance politics and strategies in reproducing gender/sexual justice?

---

policy therefore was based on that recognition; (para 69) and (3) The Basic Law intends to protect the 'essence' of the right, despite 'some occasional gaps or disruption' (para 91). In sum, the Small House policy, without any exception, is fully protected and recognized by the Law of Hong Kong. ([2021] HKCA 54) For details, please also see Jin Yuan Yuan (trans., original: 金圆圆) (ed) (2011); Chiu Man-chung (2017).

[4] 'Most say gays are ok, as long as they're not family', *South China Morning Post*, 14 Feb 2006, CITY 1.

[5] *Report of the Panel on Home Affairs for submission to the Legislative Council 2000–2001*, para 8.

[6] Chiu (2017).

1.2 Reconstruction of Indigenous Han-Chinese Socio-legal Traditions in Contemporary Hong Kong

A question is often asked: 'Is indigenous Han-Chinese socio-legal traditional philosophy still relevant in contemporary Hong Kong society—a former colony of British Empire which only became part of PR China in 1997?'. It is not surprising to find that the imagination and representation of Han-Chinese tradition exists in the reconstruction of current Hong Kong culture. Not only in their daily language do Hong Kong Han-Chinese still use the traditional philosophical perspective and knowledge, like FengShui 風水 (the usage of YIN-YANG 阴陽 and five elements 五行 in traditional environmental science) and Han-Chinese medical knowledge (where the paradigm YIN-YANG and five elements is used to understand and nurture the human body)[7] in everyday life, Han-Chinese patriarchal traditions are also widely believed to be a major factor leading to the increase in divorce and wife abuse. Customary law in colonial Hong Kong, which is deeply influenced by the Qing 清 Dynasty (1644–1911), is still firmly in place after the handover of Hong Kong in 1997.[8] Also, traditional marriage (polygamous marriage formed before 1971) is still recognised by the Hong Kong common law system. In the 2006–2007 Policy Address, titled *Proactive Pragmatic: Always People First*, Donald Tsang, the then Chief Executive of the Hong Kong SAR Government, adopted 'Harmony', in both family and society, as one of the cornerstones of his government policy: '[C]herishing the family is a core value of our community, and family harmony is the foundation of social harmony.'[9] He then pledged to allocate more resources to providing support to families and to the control of domestic violence. Please note: Harmonious society and family are the principal ideologies of Confucianism.[10]

The above facts demonstrate how Han-Chinese traditions influence and permeate the interactive re-formation of different discourses in Hong Kong, including the legal system and gender/sexual politics. To quote Ambrose King:

> Although Hong Kong is very Westernized, Chinese still preserve their particular racial and cultural consciousness…57% of the [Hong Kong Chinese] people insist that they are Chinese because they still preserve the traditional Chinese values of filial piety, being thrifty and respecting their seniors.[11] (trans., original: 尽管香港已相当西化, 但中国人仍保持着其特有的文化意识…57%的人坚持说他们是中国人, 因为他们仍保持着像孝敬父母、勤俭节约和尊敬师长等中国传统的价值观。).

[7] Kuang (1998).

[8] Samuels (1997), at 712, 717, 724.

[9] *The 2006–2007 Policy Address: Proactive Pragmatic: Always People First* available at: https://www.policyaddress.gov.hk/06-07/eng/pdf/speech.pdf (visited 5 April 2022), at 13.

[10] For more discussion on Confucianism, please see below.

[11] King, Ambrose, 'A Cultural Interpretation of Economic Development in East Asia' (trans., original: 东亚经济发展的一个文化诠释), (1987) 11 (8), *Hong Kong Economic Journal Monthly,* at 54, 56.

Siu-kai Lau argues that through utilitarian familialism, Han-Chinese traditional culture permeates the construction of Hong Kong contemporary society.[12] Put simply, no one can deny that the Han-Chinese tradition has always formulated and formatted Hong Kong contemporary culture.

The problem is: Is there an authentic Han-Chinese culture? Is there a binarism of Han-Chinese tradition and current Hong Kong (Han-Chinese) culture? Gilles Deleuze effectively points out that no one can have experience without referring to the synthesis of past, present and future: '[T]he present is not purely in itself, self contained.'[13] In other words, a present is also a past/future, since it is accompanied with all the past events/future; and the past, in fact, also accompanies every instance of the present/future:

> [T]he condition for the lived present is the passive synthesis of time where the past is synthesized, or contracted, in the present as a behaviour towards the future.[14]

The reproduction and representation of historic tradition thus always exists together with contemporaneousness.[15] In short, the present always engages with the past which engages with the present. We can only understand and represent the past/tradition with reference to a simultaneous reproduction of present and future. In other words, 'whenever we remember, there will be two main aspects to this: Firstly, the "actual" memory of that past; but also a representation of the present (or the self) as itself being engaged in remembering.'[16] Claire Colebrook also writes:

> Looking at history, then, is not looking at a series of ideas that follow each other in time; it is looking at the different ways in which time takes eventful turns.[17]

If, as Deleuze argues and Arif Dirlik agrees, tradition is only a simulant representation of culture repetitively reproduced (and discussed) by contemporary society,[18] then can we destablize and problematize the simulant yet powerful notion of 'traditional Han-Chinese (socio-legal) culture' through critically investigating its non-stop political representation?[19] When discussing (Hong Kong) Han-Chinese socio-legal culture, a number of academics tend to essentialize/equate the concept with (Orthodox) Confucianism,[20] assuming that there is an authentic and essential Confucianism which marginalizes law, reproduces the grand narrative of 'harmony politics'

---

[12] Lau (1982); Lee (2003), at 7.

[13] Grosz (2000), at 223. For more discussion, please see Chap. 5.

[14] Williams (2003), at 87.

[15] Lo (1997), at 6.

[16] Reynolds, Jack, 'Derrida and Deleuze on time, the future, and politics' (2004) 3(1) *Borderlands*, para 35, available at: http://www.borderlands.net.au/vol3no1_2004/reynolds_time.htm (visited 20 Apr 2008).

[17] Colebrook (2002), at 64.

[18] Dirlik (2000), at 133; Lo (1997), at 6.

[19] Chang (2007), at 20; China Society of Legal History (ed) (2007), at 20.

[20] Peerenboom, Randall, 'Toward a Methodology for Successful Legal Transplant', Paper presented at the 'International Conference of Chinese Experience of the Law and Development', Organized by RenMin University of PR China, held in BeiJing, on 10 May 2008.

and is represented by Confucius 孔子 and Mencius 孟子.[21] But, do the socio-legal ideologies developed by Confucianism amount to an authentic representation of Han-Chinese socio-legal culture? Is there an essential notion of Confucian socio-legal culture? And the most significant question is: How would the (simulant) representation of traditional Han-Chinese socio-legal culture articulate the re-constitution of human nature/subjectivity[22] and the discourse of law?

1.3 Differences Within (Orthodox) Confucian-Centric Harmonious Han-Chinese Socio-legal Culture

1.3.1 YIN-YANG Interaction: Historicizing the Politics of Harmony

Scholars often argue that the socio-legal culture in (traditional) China is essentially formulated and constituted in the aura of harmony politics. They often neglect to examine why harmony politics becomes the metanarrative of Han-Chinese socio-legal culture. YIN-YANG interacts with the five elements (Metal, Wood, Water, Earth and Fire) and constructs the universal order (i.e. nature), which is also the guiding principle of human behaviour.[23] In other words, nature, to Han-Chinese, means both natural science (including weather and landscape) and the highest order of the universe, TIAN-Dao 天道.[24]

Han-Chinese tend to take TIAN-Dao and the human world, REN-Dao 人道 (Way of Human),[25] as a 'continuum'.[26] It was in this context that the cosmology of YIN-YANG and five elements was constructed and engineered: Han-Chinese, from the lengthy observation of nature, tried to reproduce the formulae of YIN-YANG and the five elements, by which the natural order and the interaction between nature/TIAN-Dao and human/REN-Dao could be understood and predicted. YIN-YANG cosmology is not merely a kind of ontological binary opposition, but a duality of mutual interdependence.[27] YIN and YANG are the dual cosmic forces that permeate every sector of the universe (including human and law).[28]

---

[21] He (1998), at 247, 258; Lin (1994), at 72.

[22] There are always debates on whether human/nature in the discourse of Han-Chinese philosophy shares the same meaning of 'subjectivity' in the Euro-American academic context. Jin-bao Ye investigates the question in detail and argues that the definition of human (nature) in Han-Chinese culture, though it does not exactly mean 'subjectivity', the term can share the same meaning from the perspective of agency. Ye (2006), at 54, 191.

[23] Ma (2005), at 23; Liu (2003), at 98.

[24] Jiang (2005), at 240.

[25] Ma (2004), at 57.

[26] Huang (1999), at 37.

[27] Chou (2000).

[28] He (2006), at 190.

The five elements, like YIN-YANG, are also products of nature; they are related to different combinations of locations, natural materials, seasons and human biological organs (East–Wood–Spring–Liver, West–Metal–Autumn–Lung, North–Water–Winter–Kidney, South–Fire–Summer–Fire and Centre–Earth–End of Summer/Start of Autumn–Spleen).[29] The arrangement, assembling the model of TIAN-Dao~REN-Dao, shows that the universe and human are in fact part of a continuum. The principle of supplement/destruction (opposition) also applies among the five elements; the interactive relationship can best be summarized and elaborated by two cycles, productive and destructive, shown below:

Diagram 1 Productive Cycle

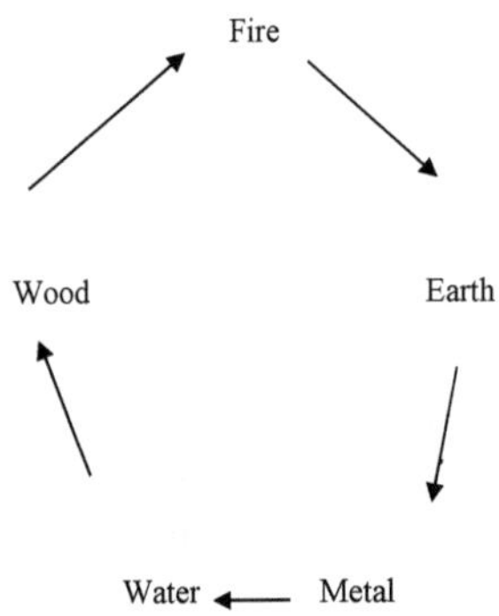

Diagram 2 Destructive Cycle

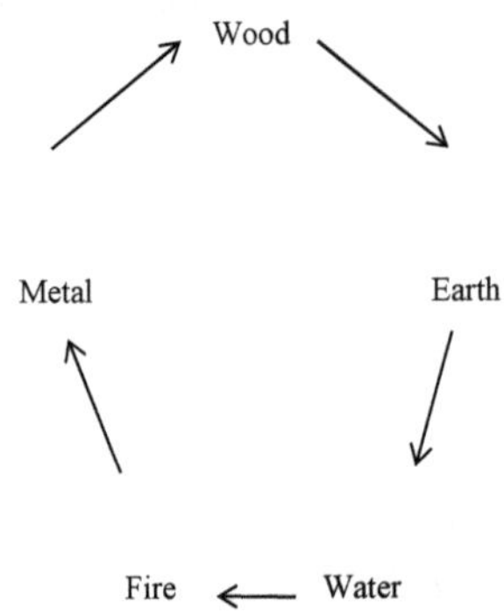

The constitution of li offers the best illustration elaborating the significant effect of YIN–YANG and five elements in (ancient) Han-Chinese society. li, in Zhou 周 Dynasty (1029 BC–221 BC) started as a set of religious rituals; it related the duties of people in their rituals with reference to their respective positions in the familial-social-political hierarchy, and thus reproduced hierarchical class differences.[30] According to Book Eight of *liJi 礼记 (Book of Rites)*, YIN-YANG and five elements were the guiding principles of li.[31] The influence of YIN-YANG and five elements on Han-Chinese socio-legal culture is further exemplified during the Han 汉 Dynasty (206 BC–220). Zhong-zhu Dong 董仲舒 believed YIN-YANG cosmology

29 Kuang (1998), at 24. According to, Xiao-hong Liu the arrangement has its own particular underlying theory—the sun rises from the east and signifies the nurture of wood; sunset in the west implies the death of life, i.e. the opposite of wood (metal); in Northern China, there is the icy area (water) and in the southern China, it is much hotter (fire); in the middle, it is the country, the centre, the most important location (note: China was called the Middle State ('中' '国'), the stable earth. Please see Liu (2003), at 10, 13.

30 Huang (1999), at 45.

31 Book 7, 礼器 *liJi (trans., original: 礼记),* available at: http://www.sacred-texts.com/cfu/liki/liki08.htm (visited 5 Jun 2006).

was the origin of the world and incorporated the theory with the principles of five elements and argued that the latter are subordinate to the former.[32]

Through representing a historic perspective on the development of YIN-YANG and the five elements, I am not trying to present an authentic notion of Han-Chinese harmony, since the definition of harmony keeps on changing with the destablization of discourses.[33] However, by contextualizing the construction of Han-Chinese harmony, we can reproduce a cultural-sensitive perspective to investigate and represent that philosophical concept.

1.3.2 From li (Social Moral Order) to fa 法 (Law): Construction of Confucius's and Mencius's Politics of Harmony

The ideologies of YIN-YANG and the five elements have long influenced and permeated the development of Han-Chinese civilization, including Confucianism.[34] Confucianism views interpersonal harmony as an analogy of YIN-YANG—only if YIN-YANG and TIAN-Dao~REN-Dao are in a harmonious and balanced state, can the human world develop positively and productively.[35]

Humans then need to develop the principles which people can follow so as to synchronize with TIAN-Dao. TIAN-Dao in Confucianism means human morality, so there should be no difference between TIAN-Dao and REN-Dao.[36] In this context, Confucians advocate the importance of 'personality perfection' and 'morality enhancement',[37] and the need to develop rules, regulations and guidelines for people to practice so as to achieve the ultimate standard of TIAN-Dao and finally harmonize themselves with it.[38]

In this context, the principle of ren 仁—good being/benevolence—is formulated and considered as the guiding principle of Confucian interpersonal politics, since the concept of harmonious interpersonal relationships enjoys the highest status in the

---

[32] Ma (2001), at 59. For details, please see Chiu (2017).

[33] Zhao (2007), at 26.

[34] Kuang (1998), at 1.

[35] Chapter 1 尧典, Book 1 虞书, *ShangShu 尚书 (Book of Documents)*, available at: http://www.chinaknowledge.de/Literature/Classics/shangshu.html (visited 5 Jun 2006); Chap. 8 泰伯, *The Analects of Confucius*, available at: http://www.analects.org/analects/analectschaptereight.html (visited 11 Apr 2008).

[36] Ma (2004), at 59.

[37] Jiang (2005), at 55.

[38] Gong-Pi (2004), at 128.

context of Confucian philosophy.[39] ren implies a mutual interdependence between people, a respect of others and an extension of oneself to others.[40] Familial relationships are always at the centre of the discourse of ren. Confucians formulated the five constant virtues (benevolence between father and son, righteousness between Emperor and ministers, differences between husband and wife, hierarchy between elder and the young, fidelity between friends) to monitor ren's smooth operation.[41]

Confucius and Mencius, the most renowned Confucian philosophers, related ren with li. In the eyes of Confucians, li hence becomes the most significant regulation of human life, as it polices interpersonal interactions.[42]

Confucian li hence assigned socio-familial duties with reference to different positions in interpersonal relationships; especially the five constant virtues. li, after the reconstruction conducted by Confucians, no longer referred to religious rituals only, but also meant the 'rules governing religious, social, diplomatic, and military ceremonies, rituals and rites…as well as rules and norms regarding proper behaviour, etiquette, manners, clothing, etc. for persons in different social classes or standings in particular familial or social relationships towards other persons.'[43] li therefore is the most powerful and influential 'social moral order',[44] and the harmony constructed does not mean equality, but a hierarchical interpersonal relationship, where women were relegated to secondary position in li. As (Orthodox) Confucianism permeates the socio-legal structure, its codification thus becomes natural and necessary. ren and li become more influential after engaging with fa 法 (law).[45] Confucian culture, nonetheless, prefers an ideal society which is free of litigation and internal conflicts,[46] such that interpersonal harmony would be better preserved:[47]

> In hearing lawsuits, I am no better than anyone else. What we need is to have no lawsuits.[48] (trans., original: 听讼, 吾犹人也. 必也, 使无讼乎!)

This does not mean that Confucius and Mencius totally ignore fa; however, moral education is always more important.[49] From an 'authentic' (Orthodox) Confucian perspective, if kindness and compassion, the pre-given qualities of human

---

[39] Please note that ren, like li, was not invented by Confucians. However, it was Confucius who transformed it into a virtue achievable by human beings, and broadened it to become 'a comprehensive virtue covering all individual Confucian virtues, and finally elevated it to become the centre of his philosophy.' (Ling 1995, at 73).

[40] Tang & Zhang (2003), at 169.

[41] Tang & Zhang (2003), at 76.

[42] Jiang & Sun (1999), at 15. Chapter 12 颜渊, *The Analects of Confucius,* available at: http://www.afpc.asso.fr/wengu/wg/wengu.php?l=Lunyu&no=294 (visited 5 Jun 2006).

[43] Chen (1999), at 508.

[44] Zhang (2001), at 44.

[45] Huang (1999), at 48.

[46] Lin (1994), at 29, 85.

[47] Pan (2006), at 110.

[48] Chapter 12 颜渊, *The Analects of Confucius,* available at: http://www.afpc.asso.fr/wengu/wg/wengu.php?l=Lunyu&no=294 (visited 5 Jun 2006).

[49] Ma (1995), at 59, 60.

nature/subjectivity, are enhanced by education, a perfect society can be constructed, with harmonious interpersonal relationships, avoiding adversarial lawsuits. Although Confucius did not state clearly his assumption of human nature/subjectivity underlying his view on education, Mencius filled this vacuum by pointing out that all humans are good, that people are born with the principles of ren:[50]

> The feeling of commiseration belongs to all men; so does that of shame and dislike; and that of reverence and respect; and that of approving and disapproving.[51] (trans., original: 恻隐之心, 人皆有之; 羞恶之心, 人皆有之; 恭敬之心, 人皆有之; 是非之心, 人皆有之。).

The paradigm on li and fa developed by Confucius and Mencius is regarded as an authentic and mainstream (Orthodox) Confucian principle; in the following sections I propose to destablize this illusory hegemony by representing and exploring the differences within Confucianism through a discussion of how (Orthodox) Confucian viewpoints on li and fa and assumption of prediscursive human nature/subjectivity have been challenged by Xun Zi 荀子, another influential 'Confucian' scholar and his follower, Han Fei Zi 韩非子, a faist 法家學者.[52]

1.3.3 Xun Zi's and Han Fei Zi's Emphasis of fa: Differences within Confucianism

Xun Zi is widely considered a 'different' Confucian—while Xun Zi believes that TIAN-Dao~REN-Dao harmony and the principle of ren are vital, he points out that it is impossible to assume that all humans are intrinsically good. From his point of view, inborn human desire can never be fulfilled, thus humans are essentially 'evil' 恶 in nature. He writes:

> Human nature is evil, and those acts of goodness are human-made.[53] (trans., original: 人之性恶, 其善者伪也。).

Xun Zi, however, agrees that human nature/subjectivity could be regulated. In order to control human desire and maintain a harmonious hierarchical social order, rules and regulations—li, its function as social moral order, not education (and fa within li)—were vital.[54] Xun Zi's view is believed to have set a strong basis for the further development of faist philosophy via his student, Han Fei Zi.[55]

---

[50] Zhao (1999), at 23, 36, 37; Tang & Zhang (2003), at 52.

[51] Chapter 6 A 告子上, *Mencius*, available at: https://ctext.org/mengzi/gaozi-i (visited 9 Jan 2021).

[52] faism is usually referred to as 'Legalism'. But in order to take account of the cultural specificity of this legal concept, I choose to use the term 'faism'.

[53] Chapter 23 性恶, *Xun Zi*. The translation is slightly modified from 'Xunzi; Human Nature is Evil (1)', available at: https://wangwenzheng.wordpress.com/2020/06/16/extract-xunzi-human-nature-is-evil%E3%80%8A%E8%8D%80%E5%AD%90%C2%B7%E6%80%A7%E6%81%B6%E3%80%8B1/ (visited 9 Jan 2021).

[54] Zhang (1997), at 16; Xia (2005), at 139. Chapter 19 礼论, *Xun Zi*.

[55] Lin (2004), at 1.

Han Fei Zi adapted Xun Zi's assumption of human nature/subjectivity that all humans are evil. Also, no one can change the adiscursive human nature/subjectivity or completely avoid all human conflicts,[56] especially where there is a scarcity of resources.[57] So the only effectual way of reconstructing harmony and governing a state is rule by fa/law.[58]

The theoretical perspectives developed by both Xun Zi and Han Fei Zi destabilize the 'authentic' and 'mainstream' Confucian perspective on fa/law and human nature/subjectivity. In other words, we cannot simply reduce traditional Han-Chinese socio-legal[59] culture into Confucianism: There is an absence of general and universal principles underlying the development and production of the Han-Chinese perspective on human nature/subjectivity and fa/law.

One of the problems, when critically representing Han-Chinese socio-legal philosophy, is the monolithic and prediscursive human nature/subjectivity devised by a number of jurists. While Mencius, Xun Zi, and Han Fei Zi always assumed the existence of an essential human subjectivity—Mencius assumed all human are kind and compassionate; and Xun Zi and Han Fei Zi supposed that human nature/subjectivity is essentially evil; my questions hence are: Why is there an essential ahistorical human nature/subjectivity? How is human nature/subjectivity re-constituted? We can find the answer by investigating another YIN-YANG cosmologic product, Daoism, has provided the answer.

1.4 Re-Interpretation of YIN-YANG Cosmology: Daoist Destabilization of Essential Human Subjectivity in Han-Chinese Socio-legal Philosophy

As I always emphasize, Han-Chinese socio-legal culture does not simply mean that (Orthodox) Confucianism is developed by Confucius and Mencius; but a hybridity of different schools of thought, including Daoism. Before the development of Daoism, although it was widely understood and accepted among the Han-Chinese that the harmonious philosophy of YIN-YANG and five elements had a close relationship with TIAN-Dao~REN-Dao, there was still a lack of systematic and scrupulous interrogation on the following vital questions: What is Dao? How does Dao relate to the theories of YIN-YANG and the five elements? And in the fa/legal context, how do those interactions intertwine with the development and understanding of fa? An attempt to respond to those questions was constructed by Daoism, another important and influential school of thought developed during the Zhou Dynasty.

---

[56] Chapter 19 饰邪, *Han Fei Zi.*

[57] Peerenboom (1993), at 155.

[58] Ma (2001), at 151, 152. Han Fei Zi's notion of fa philosophy does not work alone, it has to work with political purchase (势, Shi) and the art of rulership (术, Shu) in order for the ruler's power to materialize.

[59] For more discussion of the theories developed by Xun Zi and Han Fei Zi, please see Chap. 2.

According to Lao Zi 老子, the philosopher who is widely believed to be the founder of the school, Dao is the origin and reference of everything, including human, fa/law, society and culture.[60] Thus, Dao assumes the status of ultimate and transcendental metaphysics.[61] Dao permeates the entire common sense world.[62]

Daoism, after describing the nature of Dao, goes on to elaborate how Dao works with the cosmology of YIN-YANG. YIN and YANG both come from Dao and their interaction produces everything, including human and fa.[63] As the exercise of Dao maintains and permeates the world, different combinations of YIN and YANG are reproduced, and the universe (including human and fa/law) cannot stop evolving and changing.[64] The re-construction and the transformation of the universe follow the rule of Dao[65]—the rule of 'reversion' 反. Reversion has two meanings—opposition and return: Lao Zi points out that when the development (of everything) reaches the limit (say, peak), it would 'become' the opposite (say, lowest point of the other extreme), and vice versa.[66]

Since the principle of reversion and YIN-YANG mechanism can work continuously, Lao Zi advocates another ideology: actionless-ness 无为, i.e. 'letting things work to their perfection naturally.'[67] Actionless-ness merely means that everything can transform spontaneously as all things are reconstituted by Dao. So, being too obsessive with the value and pride reproduced by the human world is a violation of Dao. From the standpoint of actionless-ness, Daoism hence opposes any excessive regulations.[68]

1.5 Judicial Mechanism of Karmic Seeds: The Buddhist Jurisprudential Re-Construction of Contextual Subjectivity

Within Han-Chinese socio-legal culture, besides Daoism, Buddhism also constructs a sophisticated and complicated philosophical perspective on both subjectivity formation and fa. The prime principle of Buddhism is equality, which is emphasized by Buddha Śākyamuni:

> Within my Dhamma, the four clans—(1) priestly, (2) military and ruling, (3) farmers and traders, and (4) serfs…would all drop their original titles and are all called 'Shih' students

---

[60] Wang (2003a), at 98; Wang (2004), at 149.

[61] Ng (1998), at 2.

[62] Fu (1994), at 26.

[63] Verse 42, *Lao Zi*, available at: https://ctext.org/dao-de-jing (visited 10 Feb 2021).

[64] Wang (2003a), at 93.

[65] Ng (1998), at 30.

[66] Ng (1998), at 9; Wang (2004), at 217.

[67] Koller (2002), at 288.

[68] For more discussion on Daoism, please see Chap. 8.

of Buddha.[69] (trans., original: 于我法中。四种姓刹利婆罗门毘舍首陀。以信坚固从家捨家学道。灭本名皆称为沙门释子。).

Buddhism not only advocates equality among humans, but among all lives.[70] Academics like Xiang-ping Li and Li-ping Pan thus argue that Buddhist equality also makes equal harmony possible,[71] and destabilizes the Confucian hegemony of hierarchical interpersonal relationship. Vijñānamatra 唯识 (the doctrine of consciousness[72]-only)—the Buddhist ontological psychology—constructs a meticulous re-constitution of the universe, human life and human, which aims to challenge the concept of essentialism and insistent,[73] and has great impact on the development of Buddhist jurisprudence, a vital element of the Han-Chinese socio-legal tradition.

Vijñāna means consciousness (识, vijñāna) in (Han-Chinese) Buddhist philosophical discourse.[74] According to Vijñānamatra, the Buddhist ontological psycho-theory,[75] there are eight consciousnesses: The five consciousnesses in response to visual perception (眼识), auditory perception (耳识), olfactory perception (鼻识), gustatory perception (舌识), tactile perception (身识) (the five senses), mind-consciousness (sense-centred consciousness, 意识, Mano-vijñāna), ego-consciousness (末那识, Mana-vijñāna) and storehouse-consciousness (阿赖耶识, Alaya-vijñāna). The first five elements are indeed the consciousness constituting the biological senses (eyes, ear, nose, tongue and body). Mind-consciousness determines the moral value of biological actions.[76] Ego-consciousness always assumes that there is an essential and universal 'I'/subjectivity.[77]

Storehouse-consciousness continuously activates the exercise of the other seven consciousnesses. It is an unstable and forever-changing entity. It 'collects and stores

[69] Vol 22, Taishō Tripiṭaka Editorial Committee (1986).

[70] Yung Ming (1997), at 1.

[71] Li (2006), at 139; Pan (2006), at 31.

[72] Whether consciousness in the Buddhist philosophical context means exactly the same as consciousness in the Euro-American psychoanalytic discourse has been the subject of many debates. As John Suler argues, both concepts should be able to engage with each other: 'The psychoanalytic goal of exploring the unconscious, of letting ego be where id was, may correspond to the Zen 禅 intention of 'awakening' within the unconscious. The unconscious that is realized in these two disciplines [psychoanalysis and Buddhism] may differ in content, but the underlying process of awakening is similar.' Sular (1993), at 2. As Vijñānamatra and Zen Buddhism share the same goal, the argument should also apply in the discussion of Vijñānamatra.

[73] Yu (2019), at 1, 2, 177.

[74] Vijñāna has two connotations: '[W]aking, object-oriented cognitive awareness' and 'a persisting, underlying level of basic sentience.' (Waldron 2003, at xii).

[75] Zhou (1998), at 5.

[76] Yu (2019), at 134.

[77] Xu (1993); Fang (2008), at 137.

the effects or seeds (种子, Bīja) of experience until they mature and give rise to new experiences.'[78] Consciousness activities are initiated by seeds, which are reconstituted and influenced by the activities of the subject in the past (including past lives), i.e. 'karma'.[79] Karma, in short, is the 'power by virtue of which cause is followed by effect.'[80] The supply and the production of seeds never stops—seeds will be used in the consciousness activity; however, consciousness activity will re-create another set of seeds, which are stored in the storehouse-consciousness. The nature of seeds is determined by particular conditions 缘, which are in turn (pre)decided by the nature of subject/seed activities.[81] fa/law is constructed by the interactive exercise of consciousness seeds/karma.[82] From the perspective of Vijñānamatra, since the perceptions of oneself (i.e. human nature/subjectivity) and the material world (including fa/law) are only the consequences of mental mechanisms, which are motivated by a set of ever-changing seeds, there can never be any transcendental, fixed and universal notion of subjectivity.[83]

The destabilization of essential human subjectivity brought about by Vijñānamatra is deployed through its advocacy of 'selfless-ness' (无我, Anātman). 'Self' in this context does not mean 'a person', human nature or subjectivity, but '(self-centred) insistent attachment', which in terms of anti-essentialist politics, is a unitary and universal philosophical conception. Since the Buddhist philosophies of seeds, karma and selfless-ness, subjectivity/being and gender/sexuality identity are not pregiven and prediscurisve concepts, there is no eternal basis of hierarchical discrimination/inequality:[84]

> The Buddhist Path of anātman holds that there is neither soul nor any essential form that constitutes a human being…Secondly, anātman is not a denial of self as person but denial of self as self-centredness…the goal of anātman is to detach from our egocentricity in order to realize the interdependence and interconnectedness of all beings, sentient and insentient.[85]

The state of 'selfless-ness', in the discourse of Vijñānamatra, can be achieved by 'transmutation of consciousness (vijñāna) to wisdom (jñāna)' (转识成智).[86] According to *Vijnaptimatratasiddhi-sastra 成唯识论*, through this transmutation, consciousness can be changed into different kinds of wisdom, which are totally free from any attachment:

---

[78] Koller (2002), at 222.

[79] Hu (1999).

[80] Joe Tom Sun (1988), at 3–11.

[81] Faure (1998), at 20.

[82] Yin (2003), at 132.

[83] Yin (2003), at 132.

[84] Kulatissa Nanda Jayatilleke (undated), at 74.

[85] Chan (2005), at 25.

[86] For more discussion on the mechanism, please see Chap. 4 and Chiu (2017).

(1) Storehouse-consciousness → Wisdom of the Great Mirror (大圆镜智, Ādarśana-jñāna): The wisdom also advocates ignoring differences in physical appearances.[87]
(2) Ego-Consciousness → Wisdom of Equality (平等性智, Samatā-jñāna): This wisdom signifies the disappearance of 'I' (i.e. an individual subjectivity with insistent attachments) and self/others split. It emphasizes equality.[88]
(3) Mind-Consciousness → Wisdom of Wonderful Contemplation (妙观察智, Pratyavekṣaṇā-jñāna): This marks the ability of critical examination.[89]
(4) Five senses → Wisdom of Successful Performance (成所作智, Kṛtyānuṣṭhāna-jñāna): This wisdom allows the physical body to be equipped for assistance and help.

Put simply, Vijñānamatra challenges the possibility of constructing a hegemony of a particular moral perspective and universal subjectivity. But, how is the transmutation carried out? Can it be implemented within fa/legal discourse? As the seeds are 'Perfumed' (Vāsanā) by daily activities,[90] they can be affected by the implementation and following of fa/law. *Sifenlu Xingshi Chao 四分律行事钞* points out that since making, understanding, following and implementing fa/law is a kind of activity (karma) initiated by seeds/vijñāna, those activities themselves will also have their effect tattooed on the seeds (and finally the human subjects) which already exist—this influence is called the 'substance' 戒体;[91] that the nature of the seeds affected therefore changes. Substance is the psychological function which forbids people from making mistakes and encourages humans to act conscientiously.[92] The process also generates new seeds, which will then be stored in storehouse consciousness and will (re)format the subjectivities through the exercise of the other vijñāna. If fa/law can substantiate the principle of 'selfless-ness', i.e. advocate and realize the philosophies of anti-discrimination, justice and equality, through making, interpreting and following fa/law, the transmutation can be initiated and finally completed.

---

[87] Hong, De-ren (trans., original: 洪德仁), 'Buddhist Doctrine of Equality (trans., original: 佛教的平等观)' (2004) 7 (43) *BeiYe 贝叶 Hong Kong Society of Humanistic Philosophy*, available at: file://C\WINDOWS\TEMP\K0N3C66H.htm (visited 27 Jun 2004).

[88] Vol 31, Taishō Tripiṭaka Editorial Committee (1986). It is often argued that gender inequality permeates Buddhist organizations (e.g. nuns are always inferior to monks, no matter how junior the monks are) and therefore the substantial equality advocated by Buddhism is only a myth. Shih Chao Hwei however argues that the discriminatory practices were only the historical leftovers created by traditional male-dominated Indian societies. She therefore advocates the abolishment of all those misogynist rules and regulations. Shih Chao Hwei (2002).

[89] Zheng, Shi-yan (trans., original: 郑石岩), 'Vijñānamatra and Psycho-Health' (trans., original: 唯识法门与心理健康), available at: https://www.liaotuo.com/fjrw/jsrw/zsy1/111440.html (visited 8 Jan 2021).

[90] 'Perfume' means the effect brought by every action and thought on the seeds that are stored in alaya-vijñāna. Yu argues that the effect accumulated by perfume that has happened in each life manufactures one's current personality. Yu (2019), at 153, 215.

[91] Hu (2015), at 148.

[92] Miao (1999), at 108.

The problem is: How do we formulate fa/law which can bring forward equality and justice in the discourse of gender/sexual politics?

1.6 Challenges of a Monolithic Han-Chinese Socio-legal Culture

The above sections have demonstrated and reconstructed, through representing Han-Chinese cultural-philosophical discourse, how fa/law can be transformed and how human nature(s)/subjectivities can be destabilized and interactively re-constituted by YIN-YANG cosmology and consciousness/seeds mechanisms—hierarchical interpersonal harmony hence ceases to be the sole principle of Han-Chinese culture. Through repeatedly representing and investigating traditional culture, we have critically examined the culture and how it influences the re/production of the future.[93] In the case of Han-Chinese socio-legal culture, the lack of a powerful and mature legal-philosophical paradigm for the production of resistance/subversion is obvious and evident under critical scrutiny. As I argued in *De/Sexing Hong Kong Law*, there is a lack of critical perspective and related resistance strategy within Han-Chinese culture.[94] Change is accepted but the strategy has to be devised and conducted according to the grand narrative of harmony. This viewpoint is especially amplified due to the domination of YIN-YANG philosophy/harmony in the cultural construction of socio-legal perspectives. Under Buddhist discourses, changes and reforms are allowed and accepted, but again, where is the motivation for changes and reforms and what are the policies? The lack of a critical perspective has given rise to a vital question: Would the meta-narrative of Han-Chinese harmony become an excuse for continuing/reproducing suppression and discrimination?[95] Examples include: (1) For the sake of maintaining familial harmony, no one should report cases of domestic violence to the police or seek assistance from social service institutions, although familial harmony emphasized by Confucius and Mencius is patriarchal; (2) Before getting consensus from society and avoiding social diversification, demands for anti sexual orientation discrimination legislation should be put aside, even with meticulous historical scrutiny we can understand that homophobia did not always exist in ancient (Han-)Chinese history.[96] Harmony, advocated by the people objecting to further legal reform which may bring gender/sexual justice, nonetheless, can be a masquerade, covering inequality and suppression (faced by women and LesBiGayTransIntersexQueer/TongZhi).[97]

---

[93] Colebrook (2002), at 8.

[94] Chiu (2017).

[95] Liu (2007), at 7.

[96] Chiu (2017).

[97] In the vocabulary of Hong Kong Chinese, 'TongZhi' includes two words—(同) means the 'same' and 'Zhi' (志) connotes 'beliefs (of anti-heterosexism)'; 'TongZhi' therefore signifies all people who share and stand up for the destabilization of heterosexism. Chiu (2001b), at 185.

This is why I advocate that we need to engage Foucauldian socio-legal studies and the related legal reform scheme, which is capable of (1) engineering a critical perspective that is sensitive to ever-changing contexts and (2) constructing a legal policies that can achieve gender/sexual justice.[98] Incorporating Foucauldian philosophy with the revision and examination of Han-Chinese socio-legal tradition can therefore sensitize people to the unstable circulation of power and the possibilities/technologies to locate, explore and expend the spaces of resistances.

1.6.1 Foucauldian Desexualization and Degenderization—Possible Reform Strategies?

Foucauldian anti-essentialist study challenges and destabilizes the Enlightenment notion of universal, fixed and monolithic subjectivity, and proposes that subjectivity is a derivative product of such a contingent and specific set of linguistically infused socio-political-historical-cultural-legal practices. Foucauldian theory disturbs the mystified notion of an eternal and essential subjectivity (reproduced by the legal mechanism);[99] i.e. Wo/Men, LesBiGayTransIntersexQueer/straight are no longer universal in their definitions; and the legal system has played a vital role in the re-formation and reformat of sexual subjectivity.[100] Michel Foucault exposes the possible spaces for resistances within all kinds of hegemonies: 'If there are relations of power in every social field, this is because there is freedom everywhere.'[101] Resistance always exists, but, it does not promise any successful or complete subversion.[102] Whether resistance can destabilize a hegemony depends on the strategy deployed.[103] A strategy proposed by Foucault is Desexualization (of law).[104] He once wrote:

> It is the agency of sex that we must break away from, if we aim—through a tactical reversal of the various mechanism of sexuality—to counter the grips of power with the claims of bodies, pleasures, and knowledges, in their multiplicity and their possibility of resistance.[105]

This suggestion comes from Foucault's famous work, Volume 1 of the *History of Sexuality*. Foucauldian Desexualization aims at striving against the normalization of (hetero)sexuality in the reconstruction of subjectivity. In legal discourse, Desexualization does not simply mean the enactment of anti-discrimination legislation or sexuality-neutral law, but acceptance of individual multiple sexual choices. The

---

[98] Ho, Hsin-chuan, 'The Future of Confucian Political Philosophy, (trans., original: 儒家政治哲学的前景), available at: http://huang.cc.ntu.edu.tw/pdf/CCB2809.pdf (visited 9 Jan 2021).

[99] Douzinas (2005).

[100] Smart (1989).

[101] Foucault (1978), at 293.

[102] Brown (1995).

[103] Lloyd (2005), at 106.

[104] Xia (2005), at 12.

[105] Foucault (1978), at 157.

Desexualization of law therefore means different sexualities (not sexual actions, such as rape and harassment) under all circumstances are respected/protected and should not subject to any legal regulations; i.e. the law should accept multiplicities of sexuality. Desexualization does not mean the ignorance of sexuality in the formation of one's identity, but should free one from the preset, mandated and 'normalized' socio-legal script of supreme heterosexist domination.[106]

In short, phallocentric heterosexism, which marginalizes all non-penile-vaginal-penetrative (reproductive-centric) sexual activities, should cease to be the ultimate guiding philosophy of the legal system in Hong Kong. Adopting Desexualization as a perspective in analysing the current laws in Hong Kong, the following questions should be posed: Why would the validity of marriage, as a private contract between two people, be related to the sexual consummation and the ability to have sexual intercourse? Why would law intervene SM activities where all parties involved consented? Why would law only legalize the adult sexual activities, while putting up barriers for the sexual expression of the teenagers? Why should law develop and construct a particular category of law which regulates assault on a body organ (like the vagina), called rape? Why would the age of consent in the case of vaginal penetration be different from the age limit in contract formation? Why cannot sex work be a kind of occupation? From the insights brought by Desexualization, we may further ask why gender specificity exists/is re-constructed in the legal discourse: Why would marriage and the legal control of rape[107] be linked with the gender identities of the parties involved? Why does the Small House policy which benefits only male indigenous residents of the New Territories still exist after the enactment of Basic Law of Hong Kong SAR? The strategy of Degenderization, in this context, can hence be devised to remove gender as an element of subjectivity/identity formation in legal discourse[108]—for example, the removal of gender specific provisions in rape law, marriage law and the repeal of New Territories Small House policy.

Nonetheless, the possible consequence of implementing Desexualization and Degenderization, as advocated by local feminist activists, is the ignorance of power difference—male-dominating heterosexism still exists and women and LesBiGay-TransIntesexQueer/TongZhi are still marginalized in the current legal environment, as noted by Ralph Sandland. He rightly points out that Desexualization neglects the inequality of power already existing. He writes:

> It can (and has) be argued forcibly that the desexualization…as a strategy fails to consider the very real power differences between men and women. (emphasis added)[109]

[106] Cornell (1998), at xi.

[107] For more discussion, please see Chapter 8.

[108] Tan & Jiang (2007), at 3.

[109] Sandland (1995).

It is in this context that I argue that either Desexualizaton or Degenderization must go together with the development of a theory of justice in order to enhance the sensitivity of laws towards power differences among the multitude of society. But, what is justice?

1.6.2 Sensitizing a Theory of Justice Towards Gender/Sexual Politics

In *A Theory of Justice*, John Rawls argues that 'justice' merely means 'fairness'. But then, what is 'fairness'? Rawls derives two principles to qualify the concept: (a) the greatest equal liberty principle—this does not mean that there is no restriction on liberty, as one's liberty cannot infringe others' freedoms;[110] and (b) inequality is inevitable, but it cannot contradict two rules—(i) the difference principle, which means that a socially acceptable inequality must be able to benefit everyone; and (ii) the principle of fair equality of opportunity, which means that opportunities,[111] in the public context of economic competition, are open to everyone.[112] Only if the inequality is accepted by the most powerless in a society, can it be treated as positive and beneficial. The principles are in irreversible lexical order. Hence, in order to realize justice, fairness and equal distribution of primary goods (i.e. rights, freedom, power, income, resources and individual self-respect),[113] we need to substantiate the greatest equal liberty principle first, then the difference principle and finally, the principle of fair equality of opportunity. The order declaims the foundational belief of Rawls: Political freedom is the base of justice, and we cannot sacrifice it for any economic advantages.

Drucilla Cornell, in *The Imaginary Domain: Abortion, Pornography and Sexual Harassment*, engenders and sexualizes Rawlsian Theory of Justice, and relates the theory to the significance of the 'imaginary domain': According to Lacanian psychoanalysis, the imaginary relates to self projection/introjection of erotic desire, which is vital in the construction of individual subjectivity. In the imaginary domain, one can fantasize oneself having and being of indefinite gender/sexual identities:[114]

> The notion of imaginary domain recognizes that literal space cannot be conflated with psychic space and reveals that our sense of freedom is intimately tied to the renewal of the imagination as we come to terms with who we are and who we wish to be as sexual beings.[115]

[110] Rawls (1971), at 203.
[111] Rawls (1980), at 526.
[112] Rawls (1971), at 60.
[113] Rawls (1971), at 62, 95.
[114] Grosz (2005), at 73.
[115] Cornell (1995), at 8.

So, prohibiting people from imagining/representing their erotic desires or imposing a particular gender/sexual political model on others is an eradication of others' self-respect, a kind of oppression and dehumanization which is unjust. She writes in *Moral Images of Freedom: A Future for Critical Theory*:

> The [imaginary] domain is only bound by our respect for others as also in need for the space of play and for somatic freedom. Hence, the degradation prohibition. By the degradation prohibition I meant to indicate that not one of us could fall below the register of humanity and the respect for that humanity because of our sexual practices.[116]

1.6.3 Is Infiltration of Desexualization, Degenderization and Theory of Justice Possible?

The problem is: Even if Foucauldian Desexualization, Degenderization and Rawlsian Theory of Justice are valid and effective subversion strategies, can they, Euro-American cultural products, incorporate with Hong Kong socio-legal traditions smoothly without reconstituting any cultural colonialism? The question in fact assumes there is a universal and essential definition of culture, which constitutes a binarism of local/foreign culture. Since it is impossible to have a static meaning of culture as it is always discursive and changing, such a dichotomy cannot exist persistently. Further, what postcolonialism objects to is colonial hegemony, not foreign philosophical perspectives. Political representation of any local/indigenous culture, in the context of decolonialization, on one hand, resists the imperial hegemony/imposition of overseas culture, while on the other hand, does not mean any blindfolding exclusion of cultural impacts or stubborn insistence on self-developed ideologies.[117]

Han-Chinese culture is always a hybrid—Buddhism, which is a vital component of contemporary Han-Chinese culture is not a locally produced philosophy[118]—through meticulous examination and design, foreign cultures can smoothly engage with Han-Chinese culture. In fact, as I argue, any effective representation of (indigenous) culture must be critical and political;[119] and a substantial scrutiny is usually constructed and stimulated by the interaction between cultures (be they 'local' or 'foreign').[120]

---

[116] Cornell (2008), at 13.

[117] Gao (2007), at 128.

[118] Ito (2004). Please note: The inconsistencies between Confucianism, Daoism and Buddhism have always existed—Chu points out that the conflict between Confucianism and Daoism represented the competition between Northern Culture and Southern Culture during the Zhou Dynasty; during the Southern/Northern 南北朝 Dynasties (220–580), Daoism also resisted strongly the importation of Buddhism; and Confucianism always criticizes the Buddhist philosophy of equality for violating hierarchical interpersonal politics. For details, please see Chu (1994).

[119] Chiu (2017).

[120] Chen (2006).

Transplantation[121] is never a problem; a vital perspective, however, which must be considered when examining the possibility of immersing foreign theories and related anti-discrimination socio-legal policy (like a Foucauldian analysis of sexual politics and politics of Desexualization) within Hong Kong society, is the cultural element: Can such a framework—which is developed in a Euro-American context—work effectively in Hong Kong, a predominately Han-Chinese society?[122] If law and its underlying policies are always the products of a particular cultural discourse, then they cannot be applied universally—there have been a lot of examples in Chinese history demonstrating the failure of law transplantation.[123] What was missing in such an engagement of two legal-cultural products (e.g. a new legal model and an existing socio-legal culture) was usually a meticulous investigation of cultural similarities and differences.[124] Hong Kong, being at the margin of the PR Chinese political/cultural map (the dominant language in Hong Kong is a dialect (Cantonese) and Euro-American civilization (the legal system in the former British colony become localized)), hence provides a particularly powerful cultural context to examine whether transplantation of a foreign perspective on gender/sexual justice is possible.[125]

What we need to investigate is not whether any gender/sexual justice exists in authentic Han-Chinese civilisation (which does not exist), but, in terms of Hsiao-hung Chang's theory, if there are any cultural platforms for 'transcultural' articulation by which sim*u*larity between cultures can be located and reconstructed.[126] Through this transcultural sim*u*larity, overseas socio-legal theories of gender/sexual justice can infiltrate or osmose with the Hong Kong Han-Chinese culture (a non-authentic replica of traditional culture) and its common law legal system (another non-authentic replica).[127] A possible start is the search for the matching point(s) between the civilizations: The civilization into which the legal reform was first introduced, and the civilization into which the legal reform will be transplanted.[128] It is in this context that the question is raised: Is there any platform for Foucauldian Desexualization, Degenderization and a Rawlsian Theory of Justice on which to incorporate Hong Kong Han-Chinese philosophy?

---

[121] Some academics, like Gunther Teubner, argue that 'transplantation' is the wrong term and should be replaced by 'irritant', which can avoid the dichotomy of original/copycat. For details, please see Teubner (1998). Other terms and theories are also proposed, like legal translation and legal transportation. For details, please see Peerenboom, Randall, 'Toward a Methodology for Successful Legal Transplants', Paper presented at the 'International Conference on Chinese Experience of Law and Development', organized by RenMin University of PR China, held in BeiJing, on 10 May 2008.

[122] Xia (2004), at 33.

[123] Ma (2004), at 318, 319.

[124] Yu (1999), at 302; Pan (2006), at 195.

[125] Lee (2003), at 16; Chen (2006), at 14.

[126] Chang (2007), at 20.

[127] The next question this line of argument leads to is: Is there any such thing as a particular Chineseness/local culture? Please see Chiu (2017).

[128] He (1998), at 117.

1.6.4 Infiltration of Desexualization

Investigating the representations of different Han-Chinese socio-legal theories, sexuality did not play an important role in all their theorems of subjectivity formation and fa/law—the legal politics developed by Confucius, Mencius, Xun Zi, Han Fei Zi and Lao Zi do not put much emphasis on sexuality—sexuality is simply a kind of natural desire which people have to accept. They actually focus on harmony among people and harmony between the universe and humans—if one's (sexual) activity does not upset or disturb their harmonious social life, people can accept it.[129] Another rule which is related to harmony is yin 淫/over-obsessiveness (of sexual desire/activities, not YIN 阴) which upsets the social life, and thus has to be punished. Apart from these two rules, all kinds of sexual postures/positioning (e.g. anal sex) and the sexual identities involved in the activity are not problematic. Any rules, which unnecessarily sexualize human nature/subjectivity in the context of Han-Chinese socio-legal heritage, may then violate Dao and the principle of actionless-ness/simple regulation. In Buddhist discourse, sex is never an object of inquiry:

> Buddhism never treats sex in isolation, but always as an element of general discourses on desire or power.[130] (emphasis original)

Buddhist Vijñānamatra also does not incorporate sexuality in the engineering of subjectivity formation and the seeds mechanism. Desexualization can thus become the strategy of legal development by which transmutation of consciousness to wisdom can be conducted and fulfilled.

1.6.5 Infiltration of Degenderization

In the case of Degenderization, the problem is again, is there any cultural platform for the incorporation of such a policy? Although Confucianism does not specifically mention gender identity, the five constant virtues are heavily gender connotated and gender biased.[131] In Daoism, YIN-YANG dynamics has closely engaged with gender identities; Verse 28 of *Lao Zi* reads:

> Who knows his manhood's strength,
>
> Yet still his female feebleness maintains;
>
> As to one channel flow the many drains,
>
> All come to him, yea, all beneath the sky.
>
> Thus he the constant excellence retains;

---

[129] Chiu (2017).

[130] Faure (1998), at 10.

[131] Chiu (2017).

The simple child again, free from all stains.[132]
(trans., original: 知其雄, 守其雌, 为天下谿。为天下谿, 常德不离, 复归于婴儿。).

One of the possible matching points is, perhaps, Buddhism, since gender is not mentioned in the seeds mechanism. In fact, Buddhism also advocates the ideology of Degenderization—this can be illustrated by the outfitting and appearance of nuns (bhilsunī) and monks (bhiksu), which aims at blurring their gender identities.[133] Degenderization can also be a legal strategy to realize the transmutation of consciousness to wisdom.

1.6.6 *Infiltration of Theory of Justice*

When examining whether Han-Chinese socio-legal culture can accommodate a Rawlsian Theory of Justice and Cornell's perspective on gender/sexual justice, we need to ask a preliminary question: Can the Rawlsian Theory of Justice, which is translated as yi 义 in contemporary Han-Chinese language, engage with the Han-Chinese concept of yi? Li-li Huang, and Guo-yong Yang all equate yi with justice.[134] However, does yi mean justice?

Within Han-Chinese socio-legal culture, while Buddhism does not have a detailed discussion about the content and application of yi,[135] Daoism also holds that yi, as a human project, violates Dao;[136] however, Guu-ying Chen points that, in fact, Lao Zi does not object to yi, provided that it is derived from Dao.[137] In Confucianism, yi always assumes a vital role: 'The superior man considers yi as the most important.'[138] (君子义以为上) Both Confucius and Mencius provide an in-depth and influential analysis of yi—they started with the perspective of ren and li: yi is the product of ren and li which, as discussed above, mean harmonious hierarchical interpersonal dynamics. In other words, yi is devised to maintain the smooth operation of the hierarchical social structure.[139] Confucius therefore always advocates the idea of 'putting oneself in other shoes': 'What you do not want done to yourself, do not do to others'.[140] (trans., original: 己所不欲, 勿施于人) and when 'a man of perfect

[132] Verse 28, *Lao Zi*, available at: https://ctext.org/dao-de-jing (visited 9 Jan 2021).

[133] Cho (2021).

[134] Huang (1999), at 53; Yang (2005), at 150.

[135] Sung-taek Cho argues that the Buddhist concept of selfless-ness can engage with the Rawlsian Theory of Justice as it can go beyond the self/Others dichotomy. But the author does not elaborate that argument in detail. Cho (2021).

[136] Wang (2003a), at 23, 43.

[137] Chen (2001), at 43–44.

[138] The translation is slightly modified from Chap. 17 阳货, *The Analects of Confucius*, available at: https://ctext.org/analects/yang-huo (visited 9 Jan 2021).

[139] Pan (2006), at 45.

[140] Chapter 15 卫灵公, *The Analects of Confucius*, available at: https://ctext.org/analects/wei-ling-gong (visited 6 Jan 2021).

virtue, wishing to establish himself, seeks also to establish others; wishing to be enlarged himself, he seeks also to enlarge others.'[141] (trans., original: 己欲立而立人, 己欲达而达人) yi therefore means an extension of oneself to others; it does not merely go beyond a 'self vs others' binary, but is a reconstruction of a 'both-and' perspective. The mechanism on one hand recognizes the importance of individual subjectivity, while on the other, it appreciates the existence of others, so, like YIN-YANG cosmology, there is a politics of interdependence, and this inter-related matrix of personal relationships forms the foundation on which public political discourse is reproduced in a Han-Chinese context.[142]

As yi has to start with ren and li, Confucians expect every individual to fulfil the requirements of ren and li, before realizing the principles of yi: How can s/he appropriately put herself or himself into others' shoes and maintain/reconstruct harmony, if s/he does not know ren and li thoroughly?[143] So, ren and yi, like ren and li, are two sides of the same coin: Both aim at achieving harmony, even though the former starts with interpersonal politics, and the latter with individual practice.[144] Although yi starts with personal practice and the fulfilment of ren and li, it is not a self-centred concept, as the focus of ren and li is the reconstruction of a harmonious interpersonal relationship matrix; yi therefore despises selfishness.[145]

Mencius takes yi as the ultimate standard of human behaviour. He says: 'yi is their straight path.'[146] (trans., original: 义, 人之正路也) Xun Zi elaborates the interaction between rationality and the concept of yi: Whether an action is just and appropriate is determined by rationality. He writes, 'yi is following the inherent order of things'.[147] (trans., original: 义者循理。) ren and yi, in short, form and reproduce the foundation of harmonious interpersonal relationships. Juxtaposing Rawlsian theory and the Han-Chinese concept of yi, we find that both are using righteousness as the benchmark of human behaviour evaluation. Han-Chinese Confucianism emphasizes individual discipline (within a political discourse of interpersonal relationships) and Rawlsian respect of individual choice (in a liberal economy) can constitute an interesting and effective matching point of two theorems—does individual choice represent/decide individual discipline and respect? Especially, Cornell's respect of personal representation of (sexual) desire echoes the Confucian concept of 'putting oneself into other shoes': 'If you don't want others to impose their choice on you, should you not do the same to others?' Cornell's interpretation of the imaginary domain can also supplement Confucius's concept: Only if one can imagine what could happen to

[141] Chapter 6 雍也, *The Analects of Confucius*, available at: https://ctext.org/analects/yong-ye (visited 6 Jan 2021).

[142] Wang (2004), at 246.

[143] Li (2000), at 64, 65; Jiang (2005), at 90.

[144] Tang & Zhang (2003), at 179.

[145] Jiang (2005), at 270.

[146] The translation is slightly modified from Chap. 4A 离娄上, *Mencius*, available at: https://ctext.org/mengzi/li-lou-i (visited 9 Jan 2021).

[147] Chapter 15 议兵, *Xun Zi*. The translation is slightly modified from King, R A H, 'Along the Grain: yi (Justice) in the *Xun Zi*', available at: http://oriens-extremus.org/wp-content/uploads/2019/03/OE-55-3.pdf (visited 9 Jan 2021).

others, can s/he understand the importance of respect and acceptance; this technique can certainly help one to put oneself within the web of interpersonal politics and avoid imposing one's own perspective on others; in short, such a perspective can help build a more harmonious society in Hong Kong.

The problem, however, is that yi is used to restrengthen and reconstruct the social hierarchy (i.e. the five constant virtues) and hence social inequality. In other words, equality is not an element in the formation of yi in the Han-Chinese socio-legal culture. This lack of equality is exemplified throughout the development of Confucian dominating fa/law, which was developed to correspond with different assumptions about human nature / subjectivity, aiming at reinstating a hierarchical social structure. Buddhist Vijñānamatra and the theory of 'transmutation of consciousness into wisdom' can fix the problem, however—they describe in detail how subjectivity is reconstituted and deconstructed (in the discourse of fa/law), and advocate the importance and vitality of equality. Also, as Rawlsian theory also focuses on the welfare of peripheral powerlessness via the principle of fair equality of opportunity, it can remedy the resultant discrimination and suppression and help explore the possible space of equality, advocated by Buddhism.

1.7 The Story is Still Ongoing ...

Through the meticulous examination of different philosophical perspectives, it seems that it is possible to engage Foucauldian Desexualization, the strategy of Degenderization and a Rawlsian Theory of Justice with a simulant (Hong Kong) Han-Chinese socio-legal culture. Transplantation, or localization of the theories, inevitably means a rewriting of culture(s).[148] Desexualization and Degenderization can fully politicize the non-discriminatory practices which exist in Han-Chinese socio-legal culture, and sensitize the culture to the sexual politics. Any changes/reforms in law may inevitably bring more lawsuits and court cases and thus upset harmony in the society on the one hand, but on the other hand, might redefine social harmony, which is more accommodating and is more capable of accepting differences. In short, harmony and thus Hong Kong Han-Chinese socio-legal culture can be reconstructed.

However, even if such a transplantation is successful, whether the 'new' culture can subvert and politicize the discrimination and marginalization which are represented in the simulant Han-Chinese tradition in Hong Kong needs more in-depth observation and evaluation. A series of problems may remain: (1) In the process of engagement, due to the power differences between cultures, postcolonial violence may nonetheless re-occur. The argument put forward by this article seems to put

[148] Chen (2006), at 14.

much emphasis on the resistance/critical power of Euro-American cultural concepts (Desexualization, Degenderization and theory of justice); is it hence reproducing a notion of globalizaton where (a simulant) Euro-American culture is dominating? Can a reconstruction of a theory of yi/justice be able to manoeuvre the interaction between cultures so as to avoid such cultural over-domination?[149] (2) Can the grand narrative of harmony, which becomes very discriminatory after Dong hierarchized the system by making YANG (male, father, husband) superior to YIN (female, mother, wife),[150] be problematized if it sets the tone for the development and representation of the (simulant) Hong Kong Han-Chinese culture?[151] (3) Since the engagement among Buddhism, Daoism and Confucianism is never smooth and problem-free, how would that affect contemporary socio-legal and gender/sexual politics in Hong Kong? (4) Can we devise any effective model to evaluate whether the transplantation of these concepts and related legal reform have been successful?[152] In the context of globalization, where multiple modifications, interactions and re-definitions of cultures re-occur in different and conflicting discourses,[153] the questions raised will surely keep on lingering.

References

Brown, Wendy, *States of Injury: Power and Freedom in Late Modernity* (Princeton: Princeton University Press, 1995).

Chan, Stephen, 'Buddhism and Human Rights' in Rhona Smith & Christien Van Den Anker, (eds), *Human Rights* (Spain: Hodder Arnold, 2005), 25–31.

Chang, Hsiao-hung, *Fake Globalization*, (Taiwan: Unitas, 2007).

Chen, Albert, 'Confucian Legal Culture and its Modern Fate' in Raymond Wacks, (ed), *The New Legal Order in Hong* Kong (Hong Kong: Hong Kong University Press, 1999), 505–533.

Chen, Guu-ying, 'The perspective of *li* of Pre-*Qin* Daoism' (trans, original: 先秦道家之礼观) in Guu-ying Chen & Da-wen Feng (trans., original: 冯达文), (eds), *Daoist Philosophy and Daoist Religion (trans., original: 道家与道教)* (GuangZhou: GuangZhou People's Publishing House, 2001) 39–61.

Chen, Ding-jia, (ed), *Globalization and Identity Crisis (trans., original, 505–533: 全球化与身份危机)* (KaiFeng: HeNan People's Publishing House: 2003).

[149] Chen (ed) (2003), at 18.

[150] He (2006), at 217.

[151] Lim (2003), at 5, 6.

[152] Xu & Ren (2007), at 4.

[153] Hilsdon, Macintyre, Mackie & Stivens (2000).

Chen, Kuan-hsing, *Towards De-Imperializiation: Asian as Method* (TaiPei: Flaneur, 2006).
China Society of Legal History, (ed), *Chinese Culture and the Rule of Law (trans., original: 中国文化与法治)* (BeiJing: Social Sciences Academic Press, 2007).
Chiu, Man-chung, 'Tongzhi Dancing with the Law—Postmodern Discourse on Anti Sexual Orientation Discrimination Law in Hong Kong' (trans., original: 「同」法共舞) (2001b) *Con-temporary Monthly* 106–127.
Chiu, Man-chung, *De/Sexing Hong Kong Law* (Hong Kong: Red Publish, 2017).
Cho, Sung-taek, 'Selflessness: Toward a Buddhist Vision of Social Justice', 7 *Journal of Buddhist Ethics*, available at: https://them.polylog.org/3/fcs-en.htm (visited 9 Jan 2021).
Chou, Wah-shan, *Gender Transgression in China (trans., original: 性别越界在中国)* (Hong Kong: Hong Kong Queer Forum, 2000).
Chu, Yiu-wai, *Post-Orientalism* (BanCiao: LuoTuo 骆驼, 1994).
Colebrook, Claire, *Gilles Deleuze* (London & New York: Routledge, 2002).
Cornell, Drucilla, *The Imaginary Domain* (London: Routledge, 1995).
Cornell, Drucilla, *At the Heart of Freedom: Feminism, Sex, and Equality* (Princeton: Princeton University Press, 1998).
Cornell, Drucilla, *Moral Images of Freedom: A Future for Critical Theory* (New York: Rowman and Littlefield, 2008).
Dirlik, Arif, 'Reversals, Ironies, Hegemonies: Notes on the Contemporary Historiography of Modern China' in Arif Dirlik, Vinay Bahl & Peter Gran, (eds), *History after the Three Worlds: Post-Eurocentric Historiographies* (New York: Rowman and Littlefield., 2000), 125–156.
Douzinas, Costas & Gearey, Adam, *Critical Jurisprudence* (London: Hart, 2005).
Fang, Li-tian, *Chinese Buddhist Culture (trans., original: 中国佛教文化)* (Hong Kong: Joint Publication, 2008).
Faure, Bernard, *The Red Thread – Buddhist Approaches to Sexuality* (Princeton: Princeton University Press, 1998).
Foucault, Michel, *The History of Sexuality, Vol 1* (New York: Vintage, 1978).
Fu, Pei-rong, 'A Reflection on the Metaphyical Nature of Lao Zi's Dao: a Comparative Perspective' (trans., original: 從比較的角度反省老子『道』概念的形上性格) (1994) 7 *Journal of Philosophy* 24–37.
Gao, Quan-xi, *My Yoke: In between Politics and Law* (BeiJing: China Law Press, 2007).
Gong-Pi, Xiang (trans., original: 公丕祥), *The Legal Modernization in China (trans., original: 中国的法制现代化)* (BeiJing: China University of Political Science and Law, 2004).
Grosz, Elizabeth, 'Deleuze's Bergson: Duration, the Virtual and a Politics of Future' in Ian Buchanan & Claire Colebrook, (eds), *Deleuze and Feminist Theory* (Edinburgh: Edinburgh University Press, 2000), 214–234.
Grosz, Elizabeth, *Time Travels – Feminism, Nature, Power* (Durham: Duke University Press, 2005).
He, Qin-hua (trans., original: 何勤华), *Historical Discourse of Legal Culture (trans., original: 法律文化史论)* (BeiJing: Law Press, 1998).
He, Zhang-rong, *Gender Relationship Comes from YIN-YANG Dialectic (trans., original: 两性关系本乎阴阳)* (CheungDu: SiChuan People's Publishing House, 2006).
Hilsdon, Anne-Marie Hilsdon; Macintyre, Martha; Mackie, Vera & Stivens, Maila, (eds), *Human Rights and Gender Politics: Asia-Pacific Perspective* (New York: Routledge, 2000), at 20–21.
Hu, Xiao-guang (trans., original: 胡晓光), 'Alaya-vijñāna: an Opinion (trans, original: 阿赖耶识刍议)' (1999) 4 *FaYin* 法音 9.
Hu, Jian-ming, 'A Brief Introduction on the idea of Saṃvara in Chinese Buddhism' (2015) 2 *Vinaya* 135–156.
Huang, Li-li, *Interpersonal Harmony and Conflict (trans., original: 人际和谐与冲突)* (TaiPei: Laurel, 1999).
Ito, Takatoshi, *Critical Research on Chinese Buddhism (trans., original: 佛教中国化的批判性研究)* (Hong Kong: EconWorld, 2004).

Jiang, Jun (trans., original: 姜军) & Sun, Zhen-ping (trans., original: 孙镇平), *ZhongZuo LunLI Hua falu De SiKao 中国伦理化法律的思考* (BeiJing: HuaWen 华文, 1999).

Jiang, Shan (trans., original: 江山), *Concept of Chinese Law (trans., original: 中国法理念)* (BeiJing: China University of Political Science and Law, 2005).

Jin Yuan Yuan (trans., original: 金圆圆), (ed), (2011) *Rogue Squire (trans., original: 土豪劣绅)* (Hong Kong: Up Publication 上书房, 2011).

Joe Tom Sun, 'Psychology in Primitive Buddhism' in Anthony Molino, (ed), *The Couch and the Tree: Dialogues in Psychoanalysis and Buddhism* (New York: North Point Press, 1988), 3–11.

Koller, John, *Asian Philosophies* (*4th ed*, New Jersey: Prentice Hall, 2002).

Kuang, Zhi-ren, *The System of YIN-YANG and five elements (trans., original: 阴阳五行及其体系)* (TaiPei: WenJin 文津, 1998).

Kulatissa Nanda Jayatilleke, *Dhamma, Man, and Law* (Singapore: The Buddhist Research Society, undated).

Lau, Siu-kai, *Society and Politics in Hong Kong* (Hong Kong: Chinese University, 1982).

Lee, Eliza 'Introduction' in Eliza Lee, (ed), *Gender and Change in Hong Kong* (Hong Kong: Hong Kong University Press, 2003) 3–22.

Li, Long (trans., original: 李龙), (ed), *fa LI Xue 法理学* (WuHan: WuHan University Press, 2000).

Li, Xiang-ping, *The Conflict of Cultural Legitimacies (trans., original: 文化正当性的冲突)* (ShangHai: BaiJia 百家, 2006).

Li, Zhi-jiang (trans., original: 李志江), *Political Philosophy of a Well Ordered Society (trans., original: 良序社会的政治哲学——罗尔斯分配正义理论研究)* (BeiJing: People's Publishing House, 2009).

Lim, Chin-chown, *Huang Ye Zhong De Nü Ti 荒野中的女体: 张爱玲女性主义批评* (BeiJing: GuangXi Normal University, 2003).

Lin, Duan, *Confucian Ethic and Legal Culture–A Sociological Analysis* (TaiPei: JuLiu 巨流, 1994).

Lin, Wai-yi (trans., original: 林纬毅), *The Engagement of faism and Confucianism (trans., original: 法儒兼容)* (TaiPei: WenJin 文津, 2004).

Ling, D W, 'Confucianism and English Common Law: A Hong Kong Lawyer's Observations' (1995) 1(1) *Journal of Chinese and Comparative Law* 65–86.

Liu, Xiao-hong (trans., original: 刘筱红), *The Mysterious five elements (trans., original: 神祕的五行)* (BeiJing: GuangXi People's Publishing House, 2003).

Liu, Jen-pang et al, (eds), *Penumbrae Query Shadow: Queer Reading Tactics* (ChungLi: National Central University, 2007).

Lloyd, Moya, *Beyond Identity Politics: Feminism, Power and Politics* (London: Sage, 2005).

Lo, Kwai-cheung, *Gilles Deleuze* (TaiPei: Grand East, 1997).

Ma, Xiao-hong 马小红, (ed), *A Simple History of Chinese Legal Philosophy Development (trans., original: 中国法律思想发展简史)* (BeiJing: Law Press China, 1995).

Ma, Yong (trans., original: 马勇), *Dong Zhong-shu* (Hong Kong: ChungHwa 中华, 2001).

Ma, Zuo-wu (trans., original: 马作武), (ed), The *Study of Chinese Traditional Legal Culture (trans., original: 中国传统法律文化研究)* (GuangZhou: GuangZhou People's Publishing House, 2004).

Ma, Jian-xing (trans., original: 马建兴), *SangFu ZhiDu Yu ChuanTong falu WenHua 丧服制度与传统法律文化,* (BeiJing: China Intellectual Property, 2005).

Miao Yin (trans., original: 妙因), *Studies of Vinaya (trans., original: 律学)* (TaiPei: Heavenly Lotus, 1999).

Ng, Yu-kwan, *Contemporary Analysis of Lao-Chuang Philosophy (trans., original: 老庄哲学的现代析论)* (TaiPei: WenJin 文津, 1998).

Pan, Li-ping, *Concept of Harmony in Chinese Legal System (trans., original: 中华法系的和谐理念)* (BeiJing: Law Press, 2006).

Peerenboom, Randall, *Law and Morality in Ancient China: The Silk Manuscripts of Huang-Lao* (Albany: SUNY Press, 1993).

Rawls, John, *A Theory of Justice* (Cambridge, MA: Harvard University Press, 1971).

Rawls, John, 'Kantian Constructivism in Moral Theory' (1980) 77(9) *Journal of Philosophy* 515–572.

Samuels, Harriet, 'Hong Kong and Women, Asian Values, and the Law' (1997) 21 *Human Rights Quarterly* 707–734.

Sandland, Ralph, 'Between "Truth" and "Difference": Poststructuralism, Law and the Power of Feminism' (1995) 3 (1) *Feminist Legal Studies* 3–47.

Shih Chao Hwei 释昭慧, 'A Personal Explanation of a Humanistic Buddhism Practitioner' (trans., original: 人间佛教行者的「现身说法」– 从提倡动物权到提倡佛门女权) (2002) 173 *Contemporary Monthly* 62–71.

Smart, Carol, *Feminism and the Power of Law* (London: Routledge, 1989).

Sular, John, *Contemporary Psychoanalysis and Eastern Thought* (United States of America: State University of New York Press, 1993).

Taishō Tripiṭaka Editorial Committee (trans., original: 大藏经刊行委员会) *Taishō Tripiṭaka* (TaiPei: XinWenFeng 新文丰, 1986).

Tan, Lin & Jiang, Xiu-hua, (eds), *Gender Equality and Law: Research and Solutions* (BeiJing: Social Sciences Academic Press, 2007).

Tang, Kai-lin (trans., original: 唐凯麟) & Zhang, Huai-cheng (trans., original: 张怀承), *ChengREN Yu ChengSheng 成人與成聖* (ChangSha: HuNan University Press, 2003).

Teubner, Gunther, 'Legal Irritants, Good Faith in British Law or How Unifying Law Ends Up in New Divergences' (1998) 61(1) *Modern Law Review* 11–32.

Waldron, William, *The Buddhist Unconscious* (London: Routledge Curzon, 2003).

Wan, Guang-jun, S*tudy on Mengzi's theory of ren and yi (trans., original: 孟子仁义思想研究)* (JiNan: ShanDong University Press, 2009).

Wang, Ze-ying (trans., original: 王泽应), *ZiRan Yu DaoDe 自然与道德* (Changsha: HuNan University Press, 2003a).

Wang, Qing-jie, *Heidegger and a Hermeneutical Interpretation of Confucianism and Daoism* (BeiJing: RenMin University Press, 2004).

Williams, James, *Gilles Deleuze's Difference and Repetition: A Critical Introduction and Guide* (Edinburgh: Edinburgh University Press, 2003).

Xia, Xin-hua (trans., original: 夏新华), *Rule of Law: Realization and Transgression (trans., original: 法治: 实践与超越)* (BeiJing: China University of Political Science and Law, 2004).

Xia, Guang (trans., original: 夏光), *Modernity in East Asia and Modernity in the West (trans., original: 东亚现代性与西方现代性)* (GuiLin: GuangXi Normal University, 2005).

Xu, Dian-zheng (trans., original: 徐典正), *Themes of Vijñānamatra (trans., original: 唯识思想要义)* (TaiWan: FoGuang 佛光, 1993).

Xu, Zhong-ming & Ren, Qiang, *The Spirit of Chinese Law (trans., original: 中国法律精神)* (GuangZhou: GuangDong People's Publishing House, 2007).

Yang, Guo-rong, 'The Contemporary Meaning of Confucianism' '儒家的现代意义' in Zhu, Yi-ting (trans., original: 朱贻庭), *Yu KongZi Dui Hua 與孔子對話* (ShangHai: XueLin 学林, 2005), at 150.

Yao, Da-zhi, *John Rawls* (ChangChun: ChangChun Publishing House, 2011).

Ye, Jin-bao, *The Contemporary Value of Confucian Ideology of Harmony (trans., original: 儒家和谐思想的当代价值)* (GuangDong; GuangDong People's Publishing House, 2006).

Yin, Lin (trans., original: 尹立), *Comparative Study of Psychoanalysis and Buddhism (trans., original: 精神分析与佛学的比较研究)* (Chengdu: BaShu 巴蜀, 2003).

Yu, Rong-gen, *Dao Tong Yu fa Tong 道统与法统* (BeiJing: Law Press, 1999).

Yu, Ling-bo, *Vijñānamatra: An Outline (trans., original: 唯识学纲要)* (TaiPei: Grand East, 2019).

Yung Ming 永明, *Buddhist Perspective on Women (trans., original: 佛教的女性观)* (KaohSiung: Fo Guang Shan, 1997).

Zhang, Jin-fan, *The Tradition and Contemporary Transformation of Chinese Law (trans., original: 中国法律的传统与近代转型)* (BeiJing: Law Press, 1997).

Zhang, Ren-shan (trans., original: 张仁善), *li, fa, Society (trans., original: 礼・法・社会)* (TianJin: TianJin GuJi 天津古籍, 2001).
Zhao, Shi-lin (trans., original: 赵士林), *Xun Zi (trans., original: 荀子)* (TaiPei: Grand East, 1999).
Zhao, Ming, *Reflection and Transgression (trans., original: 反思与超越)* (BeiJing: China Legal Publishing House, 2007).
Zhou, Shu-jia, *Studies of vijñānamatra (trans., original: 唯识研究)* (TaiPei: Heavenly Lotus 天华, 1998).

Chapter 2
Beyond Colonialism (2): Deconstruction of Han-Chinese Traditional (Alternative) Socio-legal Culture

2.1 Introduction

In Chap. 1, the focus of my analysis was on destabilizing the mainstream interpretation of Han-Chinese 汉族华人 traditional socio-legal culture, by introducing the philosophy of Xun Zi 荀子, an 'alternative' Confucian and his follower, Han Fei Zi 韩非子, a renowned faist 法家学者. This chapter continues the path of analysis by elaborating in more detail the legal ideologies and formation of humanhood/subjectivity developed by both Xun Zi and Han Fei Zi. I will also, through critically discussing the theory of Zhu Zi 朱子, illustrate how hybrid Han-Chinese culture is and argue that an authenticity of culture is always absent, in the context of yi 义/justice. As an echo to my other book, *De/Sexing Law in Hong Kong*, Chap. 1 applies Vijñānamatra 唯识–Buddhist ontological psychology—in the discussion of transplantation of law; in this chapter, I will use Mādhyamika 中观 and Han-Chinese School of lu/Vinaya-Discipline 律宗 (also titled as Nan-shan School 南山宗) as the lens to study how justice can be produced in Buddhist discourse, a vital element in Han-Chinese culture. At the end of the chapter, I argue that transplantation of law and concept can start with locating matching points between cultures.

2.2 Indigenous Han-Chinese Socio-legal Culture in Contemporary Hong Kong

In Hong Kong, the Han-Chinese tradition is widely considered as a factor leading to the destabilization of marriage and the occurrence of domestic violence. As pointed out by Hong Kong Caritas, a major social service organization in Hong Kong, the main cause of adultery is the patriarchal Han-Chinese tradition, which advocates

This chapter is derived in part from an article published in *Hong Kong Law Journal* (2007) Sweet & Maxwell.

M.-C. Chiu, *Transforming the Hong Kong Legal Machine*,
https://doi.org/10.1007/978-981-19-1272-6_2

that women are male possessions and which has allowed male-centred polygamous marital practice (i.e. one husband one principal wife, multiple concubines and sex partners).[1] According to a survey conducted by the Chinese University of Hong Kong, the majority of Hong Kong women are still very conventional—they still consider having a son, who can continue the bloodline and name of their husbands' families, very important.[2] Academics agree that the enhancement of Hong Kong women's social and economic status is still hindered by traditional Han-Chinese beliefs.[3] As Harriet Samuels argues, Confucian-centric culture still has great influence in Greater China, and also on the development of customary law in colonial Hong Kong (which is still effective after the handover of Hong Kong in 1997).[4] Moreover, traditional marriage (any polygamous marriage formed before 1967) is still recognized by the Hong Kong common law system.[5]

It is not only Confucianism but faism 法家[6] that is also influential in Hong Kong. Both Donald Yam-kuen Tsang and Chee-hwa Tung, former Chief Executives of the Hong Kong SAR Government, always publicly appreciated the political-legal strategy of Kuan-yew Lee, the then Minister Mentor of Singapore, who is famous for using faism in his governance philosophy.[7] And, whenever the issue of anti sexual orientation discrimination is raised in the Legislative Council, lawmakers would also argue that Han-Chinese traditions should be considered and respected: Some Legislative Council members considered that as introducing legislation would have far-reaching implications for 'the prevailing *[Han-Chinese] traditions and moral standards* in the community, the social consequences of giving legal recognition to homosexual marriages should be studied seriously.' (emphasis added).[8]

The above facts demonstrate how substantial the Han-Chinese tradition influences and permeates different discourses in Hong Kong, including the law system and gender politics. Joseph Chan also writes that:

> Today, this Confucian vision of human life has not only fundamentally shaped the culture and the basic structure of Chinese societies such as mainland China, Taiwan and Hong Kong, but also penetrated deeply into their neighbouring countries, such as Korea, Japan and Singapore.[9]

---

[1] Kwok, Paulina 郭志英, (1998) 'Seek help when there is a family problem' (trans., original: 遇家庭问题应求助), *MingPao*, 14 Nov 1998.

[2] Law, Niki, 'HK women socially aware, but traditional at heart', *South China Morning Post*, 24 Jan 2003., p. 6.

[3] Singer (2000).

[4] Samuels (1997), at 712, 717, 724.

[5] For details, please see Chiu (2017).

[6] A pre-Qin 秦 Dynasty (221 BC to 206 BC) school of thought. For detailed discussion, please see below.

[7] Lee (2020).

[8] *Report of the Panel on Home Affairs for submission to the Legislative Council 2000–2001*, para 8.

[9] Chan (2005), at 56.

As Maria Jaschok indicates, even if a traditional Han-Chinese cultural practice (e.g. the Mei Zai 妹仔 institution[10]) disappears, 'its underlying social evaluations and attitude have survived, to be reckoned with today as much as yesterday.'[11] Nei-fei Ding, in her analysis of gender roles in the context of sex work, also writes:

> [A]ccording to recent work on the intersection of gender/sex and law in Qing [清] China, a historical formation of specific status-roles of female persons into embodiments of feminine (sexualized) immorality and evil. One such status-role is what I term the bondmaid-concubine trajectory. This particular trajectory continued in places like Hong Kong and Taiwan well into the mid-twentieth century…all the while exerting a compelling yet unspeakable force on gender, sexual and class politics in feminist theorizing and women's movement strategies to this day.[12]

No one can deny that Han-Chinese traditions have always been an element in the imbrication of Hong Kong contemporary culture, which represents and reproduces the local perspective on sexuality and law. When discussing indigenous Han-Chinese socio-legal culture, a number of academics have tended to essentialize/equate the Han-Chinese traditions with (Orthodox) Confucianism, which marginalizes law and is represented by Confucius 孔子 and Mencius 孟子.[13] Also, according to those scholars, Han-Chinese legal concepts promote patriarchal-harmonious-family-centred morality.[14] But a few questions then arise: Have the ideologies developed by Confucianism and faism influenced traditional Han-Chinese socio-legal culture? Is there a Confucian totalization in the development of Han-Chinese legal philosophy? Is there a monolithic notion of Confucian legal culture? If not, how do other schools of philosophy view law? And the most significant question is: How does the traditional Han-Chinese socio-legal culture articulate the dialogue between the constitution of human subjectivity and the discourse of law?

2.3 Differences and Challenges within Han-Chinese Socio-legal Culture: Xun Zi, Han Fei Zi, Zhu Zi and Mādhyamika

In this section, I am going to destabilize the mythologized authenticity of Confucianism in the traditional indigenous legal discourse of Han-Chinese traditional culture by exploring (further) how (1) Xun Zi, a renowned pre Qin Dynasty Confucian, viewed li 礼 (social moral order) and fa 法/law; and how his perspective differs from the so called 'Orthodox' Confucian jurisprudence; (2) Han Fei Zi,

[10] 'Mei Zai' system was a custom whereby the parents sold or gave away their underage daughters to the richer families. The minors would then work as unpaid domestic servants.

[11] Jaschok (1988), at 39.

[12] Ding (2002).

[13] He (1998), at 247, 258.

[14] Lee (1999).

one of Xun Zi's students and the most influential scholar of faism, analyzed fa; (3) Neo-Confucianism 理学 engaged Buddhism and Daoism in representing their particular jurisprudential paradigms; and (4) how subjectivity is re-constructed under the Buddhist philosophy of deconstruction and law. Not only would the differences in their views on fa/law be critically represented, but also the differences in how human subjectivity is articulated within different fa/legal discourses.

Let us start with the discussion of the definition of Han-Chinese socio-legal culture, which is composed of li, fa/law and lu 律/law (or regulations).

2.3.1 The Traditional Han-Chinese Legal Concept—The Dynamics Among li, fa and lu

li always plays a significant role in the 'Confucianism-centric' Han-Chinese culture. As illustrated in Chap. 1, li addresses the vitality of ren 仁 (not REN 人) and the related social class structure by specifying the duties related to each social category (sons, ministers, wives, brothers and friends).[15] li also despises and controls excessive desires, i.e. yin 淫 (over-obsessiveness, not YIN 阴), which according to Confucian teaching, would easily disturb harmonious interpersonal relationships.[16] In fact, (Orthodox) Confucians called fa 'ethical law', which means that the enactment and interpretation of fa must be grounded upon morality and li.[17] That is why, according to Tung-tsu Chu, fa was in fact part of li.[18] It is in this context that both Confucius and Mencius emphasize the importance of education, assuming that human nature can be modified.[19] Confucius says: 'In teaching there should be no distinction of classes.'[20] (trans., original: 有教无类。) In other words, as humans are essentially good and well—although some of them may misbehave and violate li and fa from time to time—education, which could be carried out by li and fa, can locate and enhance the hidden/subtle internal well-being of humans. Nonetheless, this (Orthodox) Confucian principle of li and fa, and assumption of human nature were challenged by Xun Zi, another influential 'Confucian' scholar.

[15] Zhang (1997), at 15.

[16] Zhang (2001), at 44.

[17] Sin & Chu (1998).

[18] Chu (1984), at 419.

[19] Ma (ed) (1995), at 58.

[20] Chapter 15 卫灵公, *The Analects of Confucius*, available at: https://ctext.org/analects/wei-ling-gong/ens (visited 16 Dec 2020).

2.3.2 Xun Zi: The Emphasis of fa in li

The conventional theory constructed by (Orthodox) Confucianism, as illustrated in Chap. 1 and above, is challenged by Xun Zi. While Xun Zi agreed that the principle of ren is very important, he said that it was impossible and impractical to assume that all humans are good beings. Xun Zi believed that there were always differences among humans and the inborn human desire could never be fulfilled.[21] In short, humans are 'evil' 恶 in nature. The evilness of human nature became acute and crucial as there was always a scarcity of resources—if every human only followed her/his desires, conflicts and chaos would be bound to follow.[22] Although Xun Zi has a very different view on human nature, he agreed that human nature could be controlled; and in order to control human desire, reduce the corrupted competition and maintain a harmonious hierarchical social order, rules and regulations—li, its function as social moral order, not education (and fa and lu within li)—were important and essential:[23]

> What is the origin of ritual [li]? I reply: Humans are born with desires. If their desires are not satisfied, they cannot but seek to satisfy them. If in seeking to satisfy their desires, humans observe no measure and apportion things without limits, then it would be impossible for them not to compete others to satisfy their desires. Such contention leads to disorder. Disorder leads to poverty.[24] (trans., original: 礼起于何也?曰: 人生而有欲, 欲而不得, 则不能无求, 求而无度量分界, 则不能不争。争则乱, 乱则穷)

Xun Zi believed that humans were willing to control desire if they understood clearly and followed strictly the underlying Confucian theory of li (and fa)[25] —the principle of ren.[26] So, in Xun Zi's philosophical aura, li (and fa) does not aim at changing the essential human nature, but at controlling it in accordance with ren. That explained why Xun Zi was still considered a Confucian, although he held a very different view on li and fa—he never questioned the inter-relationship between li (and fa) and ren, and the importance of education in controlling people's desire and maintaining harmony within society, as advocated by Confucius; he nonetheless highlighted the necessity and significance of fa coercion and punishment; not education.[27] He pointed out that for serious crime offenders, education was useless and the death penalty (fa) could be directly applied.[28] Xun Zi explicitly said that education was useful for the well-educated (upper class) officials and scholars but not for commoners. He wrote:

---

[21] Chapter 4 荣辱, *Xun Zi*. The translation is slightly modified from Knoblock (1994), at 55.

[22] Liu (2000), at 170, 178.

[23] Zhang (1997), at 16; Xia (2005), at 139.

[24] Chapter 19 礼论, *Xun Zi*.

[25] Liu (2000), at 172.

[26] Zhao (1999), at 5.

[27] Chapter 9 王制, *Xun Zi*.

[28] Tang & Zhang (2003), at 29.

> From the position of the knight up to the supreme position, all must be moderated through li and music. The common people must be controlled by law and norms of behavior.[29] (trans., original: 由士以上, 则必以礼乐节之; 众庶百姓, 则必以法数制之)

Xun Zi did not challenge the hierarchical societal structure which was appraised by Confucius and Mencius—hence, only the mass population, not the privileged officials and scholars, should be submitted to the monitor and control of li/fa; what Xun Zi advocated was the necessity of li and fa in the Han-Chinese societies, which were built on his assumption of human beings' evil nature.[30] But, Xun Zi did not answer the following questions: Why was there an essential ahistorical human nature? Why was it impossible for fa to change human nature/subjectivity?

Xun Zi's view on li and fa is claimed to be not typical 'Orthodox' Confucianism, as developed by Confucius and Mencius,[31] and is believed to have set the foundation for the further development of faist philosophy[32] via his student—Han Fei Zi.[33]

2.3.3 Han Fei Zi: Hegemony of fa

faism, like Confucianism and Daoism, was a school of thought developed during the pre-Qin period. Their aim, as with Confucianism, was to avoid human chaos. Han Fei Zi was always considered as the scholar who could thoroughly elaborate the faist ideology.[34] He adapted Xun Zi's assumption of human nature—all humans are selfish and hence evil. Also, since no one could change human nature and completely trust any kind of human relationships:

> The ruler keeps the minister in service with a calculating mind. So does the minister with a calculating mind serve the ruler. As both ruler and minister are equally calculating, each for himself, the minister never cares to injure his body and benefit the state, nor does the ruler want to injure the state and benefit the minister. By nature the minister would regard injury of himself as unprofitable. By nature the ruler would think the injury of the state as merciless. In short, ruler and minister work together, each with a calculating mind.[35] (trans., original: 君以计畜臣, 臣以计事君, 君臣之交, 计也。害身而利国, 臣弗为也; 富国而利臣, 君不行也。臣之情, 害身无利; 君之情, 害国无亲。君臣也者, 以计合者也。)

[29] Chapter 10 富国, *Xun Zi*. The translation is slightly modified from Knoblock (1994), at 122–123.

[30] Chang (1991), at 81, 83.

[31] Chang (1982), at 109.

[32] faism is usually referred as 'Legalism'. But in order to emphasize the cultural specificity of this legal concept, I choose to use the term 'faism'.

[33] Lin (2004), at 1.

[34] Lin (2004), at 75.

[35] Chapter 19 饰邪, *Han Fei Zi*, available at: http://www2.iath.virginia.edu/xwomen/texts/hanfei.xml (visited 17 Dec 2020).

Han Fei Zi hence did not totally believe in education, since human nature could not be changed.[36] Following this line of argument, Han Fei Zi firmly pointed out that conflict between people and the chaos caused could not be avoided, especially when there was a scarcity of resources.[37] So the only effectual way of governing a state and creating a strong nation is rule by fa.[38] Han Fei Zi advocated that through the usage of rewards and severe punishments, fa, not (only) li nor moral edification, could adequately and effectively indicate what kinds of behaviour were acceptable or not.

The faists always emphasized that fa must be uniformly (not equally) applied. Although li, which is hierarchal, could be maintained, it should not affect the uniform implementation of fa on everyone (besides the law maker, i.e. the ruler).[39] Everyone, including nobles and ministers, must submit to the rule of fa, formulated by the ruler. So, besides the ruler, all people were equal before fa. The social hierarchy, treasured by the Confucians, on one hand would be disturbed because the distinction between the aristocratic nobles and the commoners would disappear (in the discourse of fa);[40] however, on the other hand, the difference between the ruler and the others could be reinforced.

Han Fei Zi also pointed out how important context was in the development of fa. He argued that law had to be reformed, reviewed and changed in accordance with the transformations in times and contexts.[41] Only when the development of fa corresponded to the fluid shift in contexts, were fa and the government successful: 'If fa is adjusted to the times, there is good government. If government fits the age, there will be great accomplishment.'[42] (trans., original: 法与时转则治, 治与世宜则有功。).

Han Fei Zi, like Xun Zi, agreed that severe punishments are essential in deterring the violation of fa. He believed that people would be scared by the heavy penalties and so would not dare commit crimes. So, he suggested that even when a person commits minor offences, a very grave penalty has to be applied:[43] 'Han Fei Zi favored the ethically suspect doctrine of heavy punishments for minor infractions.'[44]

Han Fei Zi established a very sophisticated set of jurisprudential concepts which aimed at developing and making fa, the rules that govern the usage of fa and also

---

[36] Cheung (1989), at 99.

[37] Peerenboom (1993), at 155.

[38] Chang (1982), at 124; Ma (2001), at 151, 152. Han Fei Zi's notion of fa philosophy does not work alone, it has to work with political purchase (势, Shi) and the arts of rulership (术, Shu) in order to materialize the ruler's power. For details, please see Peerenboom, Randall (1993).

[39] Chu (1984), at 368.

[40] Chu (1984), at 369; Zhang (2001), at 33.

[41] Lin (2004), at 75.

[42] Chapter 54 心度, *Han Fei Zi*, available at: http://www2.iath.virginia.edu/xwomen/texts/hanfei.xml (visited 17 Dec 2020).

[43] Lin (2004), at 100.

[44] Peerenboom (1993), at 144.

the principle of fa modification. Han Fei Zi, nevertheless, like Mencius and Xun Zi, did not problematize the concept of essential human subjectivity; and failed to investigate the interaction among human (subjectivity), contexts and law.

2.3.4 Zhu Zi: Hybridity in the Name of Confucianism

From the above discussion, we can understand that there is an absence of any single definition of Han-Chinese socio-legal culture or Confucian domination in Han-Chinese legal tradition: While Xun Zi, unlike Confucius and Mencius, emphasized the importance of punishment; Han Fei Zi never denied the significance of Confucian ren. The dichotomy of li and fa diminished after Zhu Zi of Song 宋 Dynasty (960–1279) constructed his Neo-Confucian fa philosophy.

Neo-Confucianism, besides further fossilizing the hierarchical social structure by rigidifying the Orthodox Confucian principle of five constant virtues as a universal guiding philosophy, engaged a Confucian perspective with Daoism and Buddhism, which re-stressed (1) the harmony between universe and human (an influence coming from Daoism)[45] and (2) the existence of a mechanism by which human nature was constructed (an influence coming from both Daoism and Buddhism) —Neo-Confucianism thus explained how human nature was (pre-)determined.[46] Due to the influence of Daoist and Orthodox Confucian philosophy, Neo-Confucians reconfirmed and advocated that human nature was pre-given and encoded by the universe, i.e. Dao 道.[47] Human nature, in short, was an extension of the universe.[48] However, the formations of humans are not standardized and there are differences—which explains why there are differences among people and everyone is particular.[49] Hao Cheng 程颢 and Yi Cheng 程颐, further developed this perspective—they argued that human nature has two parts: One is TIAN LI 天理 (Universal Reasoning, NOT li 礼), which was actually the good human nature advocated by Mencius; and the other one is desire, which re-presented Xun Zi's concept of evil human nature.[50]

Zhu Zi, like Han Fei Zi in faism, was a well-recognized scholar of Neo-Confucianism who had constructed the most sophisticated philosophical perspective on fa/law. He started by devising his perspective by equating TIAN LI, good

[45] The harmonious relationship between nature and people was always vital to Han-Chinese since the agricultural industry was the foundation for the survival of the race. The perspective was further developed and elaborated by Daoism. For details, please see Chiu (2017).

[46] For the details on how Buddhism constructs the re-construction of subjectivity, please see Chap. 1 and see below.

[47] Tang & Zhang (2003), at 51.

[48] Jiang (2005), at 316.

[49] Chang (1978).

[50] Cheng (1981).

human nature, with the principle of ren and the five constant virtues, thus again re-constituting the socio-legal hegemony of (Orthodox) Confucian ideology of socio-familial interpersonal politics.[51] In order to substantiate TIAN LI, and permeate ren throughout the human world, the evil human nature/desire must be controlled. Please note that Zhu Zi was not saying that all desires must be neglected, but just yin/over-obsessiveness:[52] 'Never is there a case that heavenly principle will coexist with human desires.'[53] (trans., original: 未有天理人欲夹杂者。).

Since human nature and the universe had the same origin, good regulations (li and fa) within the human world was also an extension of the universe order[54]—fa must be a construction of li/ren and respect the five constant virtues. Zhu Zi pointed out that li always came before fa. He, like Confucius and Mencius, believed in the power of education; only if education failed, could the state then apply fa/law and punishment.[55] It therefore seems that Zhu Zi was a conventional Orthodox Confucian; however, in his discourse of fa; Zhu Zi agreed with Han Fei Zi, and advocates the significance of severe penalties:

> Today's judges are all deluded into following the practice of being soft on crime; they use the 'reverent' term to be more lenient and forgiving of crimes, even [to the point] of not supporting the death penalty. As a result, criminals that had committed crimes punishable by execution would be able to request and wait for leniency and amnesty decisions.[56] (trans., original: 今之法官惑于钦恤之说, 以为当宽人之罪而出其死; 故凡罪之当杀者, 必多为可出之涂, 以俟奏裁, 则率多减等。)

As with Han Fei Zi's theory, context also played an important role in Zhu Zi's philosophy. Although the reconstitution of Orthodox Confucian hegemony/the five constant virtues was the monolithic aim of fa, its formation and implementation had to be modified with the ever-changing social contexts.[57]

As a summary, Zhu Zi used ren—a universal philosophy—to unite the formation of human subjectivity and the derivation of fa. Although Zhu Zi developed an explanation of how human subjectivity was constructed and why there were differences among people, he did not elucidate how those differences were produced. Also, while

---

[51] Yang (ed) (1997), at 296.

[52] It is therefore not accurate to say that Neo-Confucianism restricted human sexuality and discriminated against women by praising chastity. For details, please see Chou (1997). Those confinements of desire were only the mainstream interpretation of Neo-Confucianism by the patriarchal mainstream society during the Song and Ming 明 (1368–1644) Dynasties.

[53] Chapter 13 学七, *Zhu Zi*, available at: https://www.academia.edu/30982161/Asian_Philosophy_Desire_The_unfolding_of_the_other (visited 17 Dec 2020).

[54] Jiang (2005), at 361.

[55] Yang (ed) (1997), at 301.

[56] Chapter 112 朱子七, *Zhu Zi*, cited from Ho (2011).

[57] Ho (2011).

he understood that fa had to be revised when different contexts emerged, he failed to challenge the transcendental philosophy of ren or articulate how context interactively constructed human subjectivity.

2.3.5 *Judicial Mechanism of Karmic Seeds: The Buddhist Jurisprudential Construction of Contextual Subjectivity*

As mentioned above, Neo-Confucianism was influenced by the Buddhist theory of the formation of humanhood, which can be exemplified by Mādhyamika—the Buddhist philosophy of deconstruction.[58] Mādhyamika, working together with Han-Chinese School of Vinaya-Discipline, the Buddhist jurisprudence, form a vital element of Han-Chinese socio-legal tradition.

2.3.5.1 Mādhyamika: Buddhist Challenges Against Universality

Besides Vijñānamatra,[59] there is another significant school of philosophy under Mahāyāna 大乘 Buddhism, called Mādhyamika, established by Nāgārjuna. According to *MūlaMādhyamika-kārikā* 中论, a sacred text of Mādhyamika, the theme of this school of thought is to problematize the existence of intrinsic existence 自性 (Svabhāva),[60] a perspective shared by Vijñānamatra.[61] While Vijñānamatra always emphasizes that consciousness (vijñāna) will operate if appropriate conditions 缘 arise; Mādhyamika puts the focus on how the concepts of emptiness (空, Śūnyatā) and condition challenge the belief of over-insistence, i.e. no intrinsic nature. Since there is no intrinsic nature, everything is subjected to change and is hence a becoming.

Hardline advocates of intrinsic nature stubbornly believe that everything has its own metaphysical essentiality, which can never be subverted.[62] Intrinsic nature, accordingly, has three distinctive features: (1) It is self-sufficient and independent—intrinsic nature can survive and grow all by itself, hence it has no connection with conditions; (2) It is unchangeable and absolute—intrinsic nature is regarded as the final and ultimate nature (e.g. the concept of law is static and universal, and thus can never be changed or challenged); and (3) it is natural and crucial—intrinsic nature cannot be

---

[58] Lau (2019), at 96.

[59] For more discussion on Vijñānamatra, please see Chap. 1.

[60] Ng (2018), at 7.

[61] There is, nonetheless, a discrepancy between Vijñānamatra and Mādhyamika: The latter critically points out that in Vijñānamatra, it seems that every sense and different vijñāna are independent from each other and thus there is a lack of synergy and harmony among themselves. Guo Yu (2016), at 192).

[62] Guo Yu (2016), at 22.

reproduced and is necessary for the definition of a theory (e.g. harmonious interpersonal relationships are essential for the construction of a fair fa/legal system).[63] In short, each object and each concept has its own fossilized, distinguishable and specific quality. Hence, change, reproduction, innovation or revolution become impossible in the eyes of intrinsic nature advocates.

In contrast, Nāgārjuna produces the theory of conditional dependence (缘起, Pratītya-samutpāda) so as to rebut the perspective of intrinsic nature. In short, every phenomenon in this universe relies on the politics of causal relationships: A cause can never be independent from a result, and vice versa. According to Nāgārjuna, when a (set of) condition(s) becomes sophisticated and appropriate, an action/a phenomenon will take place; this is what Nāgārjuna called conditional dependence.[64] Human subjectivity is, with reference to the theory, is constituted by different sets of conditions, and is therefore always discursive and a becoming.

Chapter 13 of *Sunyatasaptati* 七十空性论, a book also written by Nāgārjuna, states that there are two kinds of dependence (or causal relationship): Existential and notional, which are symmetrically dependent on each other. The former means a result cannot exist without a cause, while the latter is a descriptive relationship of dependence. The connection between local law and transplanted (overseas) law is a good example: When a piece of transplanted law exists, there must be/have been a piece of original law (existential dependence); and notionally speaking, without a source, i.e. a local law of another jurisdiction, there will be no transplanted law. Put simply, a cause cannot be a cause by itself, nor can the effect; each depends on the other both existentially and notionally—that is what Buddhism calls emptiness, meaning 'lack of intrinsic nature'.

Conditions do not work alone but have to connect with other conditions.[65] There are four kinds of condition: (1) Hetu-pratyaya 因缘 is the most vital condition, conducting the becoming of a phenomenon; Ng argues that it is equivalent to seeds (种子, Bīja); (2) Anantara-pratyaya 等无间缘 means the opportunity, created by the exercise of a consciousness, where another consciousness can start manufacturing the next effect; (3) Ālambana-pratyaya 所缘缘 is the condition where the object of an effect (i.e. exercise of a particular consciousness) can arise; and (4) Adhipati-pratyaya 增上缘 is the other condition which is not so closely linked with an effect or phenomenon.[66] Take visual perception as an example: What one can see is not decided by any intrinsic nature, but a result of different conditions (e.g. the biological function (can the eyes fully function?), physical environment (is it too dark? The objects that appear at that particular moment) and state of mind (is the person paying enough attention?); any changes in one of the above certainly has an impact on what images one perceives. The same machinic process applies to the other four senses/perceptions that constitute a biological body: Auditory perception 耳识, olfactory perception 鼻

[63] Westerhoff (2009), at 12.

[64] Chapters 4 & 15, *Mūlamadhyamaka-kārikā*, available at: https://aaari.info/notes/03-06-06Tam2.pdf (18 Dec 2020). For details, please see Ruegg (1981).

[65] Guo Yu (2016), at 316.

[66] Ng (2018), at 27–28.

识, gustatory perception 舌识 and tactile perception 身识. Hence, for the constitution of a male gay who is not allowed to get legally married to a person of the same sex in Hong Kong: The hierarchy between different sexual orientations and the lack of related anti-discrimination laws are the Hetu-pratyata; the sexual orientation of oneself is the Anantara-pratyaya; the refusal of getting legally married in Hong Kong is the Ālambana-pratyaya; and the news report of the case is the Adhipati-pratyaya.

Human subjectivity is the non-stop accumulation of 'karma', that decides at which point in time what conditions will be becoming mature and which vijñāna will work.[67] Karma is a record of action and thought, conducted in the past (including past lives). Karma cannot have any intrinsic nature as it is the consequence of human action and thought. Different actions and thought, in different contexts, will create different karmic results: An act which was supposed to be protective towards women, may be considered as gender discriminatory nowadays (e.g. different ages of consent for women and men). Also, as karma is being consumed and accumulated at the same time, karma cannot be unchanged and consistent:

> As (mind-)continuum is from the mind, and fruit-production is from the continuum, karmic fruit is preceded by action. Thus (action) is neither annihilated nor eternal. (trans., original: 从心有相续, 从相续有果, 先业后有果, 不断亦不常。)[68]

Karma created then have an impact on the seeds that are stored in storehouse-consciousness (阿赖耶识, Alaya-vijñāna), which then in turn decides the conditions. It is therefore a non-stop loop—karma, produced by an action, initiated by the seeds, decides the condition in which the next action takes place and the impacts on the seeds—in which the human subject is manufactured; as the loop never stops, the human subject is always a becoming; intrinsic nature hence becomes a myth. The question is: How can this line of thinking permeate and substantiate in the legal system. I argue that Vinaya-Discipline, as interpreted by the Nan-shan School is the functional channel.

[67] Chapters 8 and 17, *Mūlamadhyamaka-kārikā*, available at: https://aaari.info/notes/03-06-06Tam2.pdf (visited 18 Dec 2020).

[68] Chapter 17, *Mūlamadhyamaka-kārikā*, available at: https://aaari.info/notes/03-06-06Tam2.pdf (visited 18 Dec 2020).

Diagram 1 Interaction between Karma, Seeds and Contexts

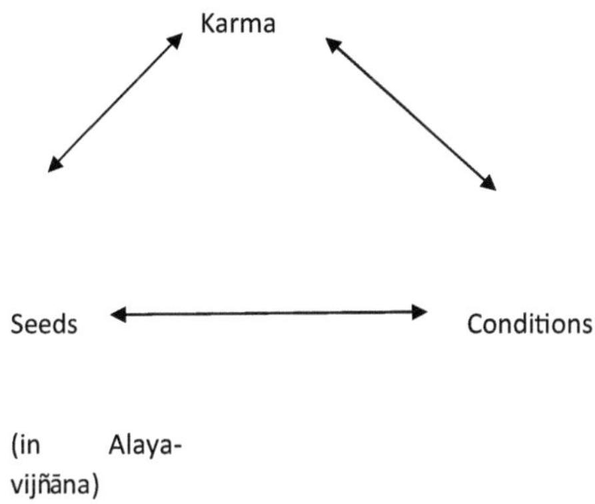

2.3.5.2 Buddhist Jurisprudence—The Han-Chinese School of lu (Precepts and Regulations)/Vinaya-Discipline

The (Han-Chinese) School of lu/Vinaya-Discipline[69] constructs a sophisticated jurisprudential perspective on lu/vinaya (i.e. precepts and regulations) not only in the context of Buddhist practice (修行, Caryā) but also in the commonsense world.[70] The vinaya, which was initially the oral record of Buddha Śākyamuni's teaching, later developed into a complete set of written rules and regulations which included detailed laws of procedures (e.g. Seven kinds of vinaya for ending disputes 七灭诤法 Saptādhikarana-śamathāh),[71] confessions and penalties (e.g. Expulsion from sangha 残僧法 Saṃghāvaśeṣa[72]). lu /vinaya, as Shih Sheng Yen argues, have developed into a complicated system of 'laws'.[73]

The hard-line fundamentalists of the (Han-Chinese) School of lu/Vinaya-discipline, following the advocates of intrinsic nature, argue that: 'What Buddha did not make should not be made nowadays, and what Buddha made cannot be altered'[74] (trans., original: 若佛先所不制, 今不应制; 佛先所制, 今不应却). They

[69] Although Indian Buddhism constitutes a view on vinaya, it does not have a particular school of philosophy on the issue. In contrast, Han-Chinese Buddhism constructs a much stronger and powerful view on lu / vinaya. For details, please see Voyce (2007).

[70] Shih Sheng Yen (1997), at 35; Lao (1999), at 10.

[71] The rules state the principles by which the disputes should be handled with, they include: face to face evidence, witness or proof; voluntary confession; decision by majority vote; condemnation of unconfessed sin.

[72] According to Samghādisesa 殘僧法, the lawful rights of a male monks (bhikṣu) or female monks (bhikṣuṇī) would be removed before being expelled.

[73] Shih Sheng Yen (1997), at 51.

[74] Vol 54, *Dharmagupta Vinaya*, available at: https://buddhism.lib.ntu.edu.tw/BDLM/sutra/chi_pdf/sutra11/T22n1429.pdf (visited 18 Dec 2020).

argue lu/vinaya is a set of ahistorical and acultural rules and regulations, and therefore it is 'unlawful' not to follow strictly all the rules.[75] One example is the lu/vinaya against gay men and man-with-man sexual activities. Hui-nan Yang, examining *Sarvastivada da Vinaya 十诵律 (The Recitable Vinaya in Ten Parts)* and *Abhidharmakosa 阿毗达磨俱舍论*, believes that the classic (Han-Chinese) Buddhist lu/vinaya did not allow gay men and transgender (including transsexuals) 黄门 (Paṇḍaka)[76] to join Buddhism and accept man-with-man sexual activities, as only opposite sex penile-vaginal penetration was and still is held to be legitimate.[77] This position has been severely criticized by contemporary Buddhist philosophers. As Shih Sheng Yen argued:

> The rules of (lu) vinaya are deadly rigid, while social evolution is lively and flexible.[78] Rigidly imposing dogmatic rules on different Buddhist followers during very different times, is both very difficult and unreasonable.[79] (trans., original: 戒律的条文是死的, 社会的演变是活的。要以死板板的条文, 硬生生地加社每一时代的每一个佛弟子头上, 实在是一件困难的事, 也是一件不合理的事。)

The status of context in the development of lu/vinaya is emphasized by Yin Shun 印顺[80] and Yang.[81] Dao Xuan 道宣, a renowned teacher of the Han-Chinese school of lu/Vinaya-discipline, also clearly pointed out that Buddhist system of lu/vinaya could be changed, updated, reviewed and revised with reference to differences, since every follower is different.[82] In fact, Buddha Śākyamuni had already pointed out that: '[M]inor vinaya can always be cancelled.'[83] (trans., original: 若欲除小小戒听除) What Buddha Śākyamuni meant is: Existing lu/vinaya must be reviewed and re-interpreted and new lu/vinaya could be enacted and formulated with regard to forever changing social contexts.[84] When Shih Chao Hwei discusses the definition of 'minor', she also points out that minor lu/vinaya is also a discursive definition; no rule is definitely and universally minor.[85] So 'abandonment of minor vinaya' means the reinterpretation of lu/vinaya. It is hence no surprise that when Yang suggests the establishment of a sangha which only contains gay followers, he argues that such a sangha will not disturb the harmony among the gay monks and will not cause any conflict between gay monks and straight monks. He thus advocates that

---

[75] Shih Sheng Yen (1997), at 45.

[76] Powers (2009), at 82.

[77] Yang (2006).

[78] Yin Shun (1992), at 3–5; Lao also agrees with his argument. For details, please see Lao (1999).

[79] Shih Sheng Yen (1997), at. 55.

[80] Yin Shun (1992), at 3–5.

[81] Yang, Hui-nan, '"Ten Unlawful Things Advocated by the Vaiśālī Monks": Discuss the Flexibility of lu/vinaya' (trans., original: 从「十事非法诤」论戒律的方便性), available at: http://ccbs.ntu.edu.tw/FULLTEXT/JR-NX012/nx00114.htm (1990) (visited 18 Apr 2007), at 27.

[82] Vol 40, Taishō Tripiṭaka Editorial Committee (1986).

[83] Vol 22, Taishō Tripiṭaka Editorial Committee (1986).

[84] Shih Chao Hwei (1999), at 113.

[85] Shih Chao Hwei (1999), at 122.

the lu/vinaya against male homosexuality should be changed, so as to justify and facilitate the establishment of gay assembly (saṅgha).[86]

Engaging Mādhyamika with the Han-Chinese School of lu/Vinaya-Discipline, the deficiency in the argument put forward by the advocates of intrinsic nature becomes obvious: lu/vinaya can only be represented and reproduced through language. Since consciousness) and language can only be interpreted with reference to conditions, which is an unstable concept, influenced by forever changing karmic activity, how can lu/vinaya be a fixed and monolithic conception? And if the interpretation of lu/vinaya relies on conditions, which is another product of karmic seeds, lu/vinaya can only be a conditional conception.

Another problem is: How is human subjectivity re-constituted by lu/vinaya? In *Sifenlu Xingshi Chao* 四分律行事钞, Dao Xuan points out that: Since making, studying, understanding, accepting, following and implementing lu /vinaya is a kind of activity (karma) occurring in the external world, activated by seeds, those activities themselves will also have their (positive) effect tattooed on the seeds which already exist—the impact is called the 'Substance' 戒体;[87] and the nature of the seeds affected therefore changes. This process also creates new seeds which will then be stored in storehouse-consciousness and will (re)format the subjectivities through the operations of the other consciousness. Since storehouse-consciousness can exist beyond current lives, it does not disappear or decompose after death, but continues to be effective in formatting and affecting every aspect of later/the next life (including sexual identity). In short, there are differences among people who are constituted by the seed mechanism, i.e. the outcome of the virtues and evils they commit. This is where the Buddhist concept of selfless-ness (Anātman) originates: In Buddhist philosophical discourse, because of the seed machine, there is a lack of acontextual human subjectivity, and any eternal definition of self/ (sexual) identity becomes meaningless.

As (part of) the seeds are influenced by the lu/vinaya, human subjectivity is a product of legal discourse. However, this condition, as argued above, is not a fixed conception either, but is also a reconstruction reproduced by the activities of humans/seeds. It is in fact a representation of the karma-seeds-condition loop. Due to the Buddhist philosophies of karma and selfless-ness, subjectivity/being and sexuality identity are not pregiven and preconditional concepts, and there is no eternal basis of hierarchical discrimination/inequality.[88]

[86] Yang (2006).

[87] Fo Hui (2015), at 126.

[88] Kulatissa Nanda, Jayatilleke (undated), at 74.

2.4 Problematization and Hybridization of Han-Chinese Socio-legal Culture

I do not intend to reconstruct an eternal truth of traditional Han-Chinese legal ideology or an authentic Han-Chinese traditional perspective on subjectivity/humanhood or fa/law—as argued above, culture is always changing and is always discursive—Zhu Zi's Neo-Confucianism is the best example—it demonstrates how Han-Chinese culture can change, accommodate and incorporate overseas philosophies (like Buddhism); and how Han-Chinese culture can be politicized and modified. Han-Chinese culture therefore is a hybridity and an authentic Han-Chinese culture does not exist. I also represent, under Han-Chinese cultural discourse, how fa/law changes and how human subjectivities can be constituted. Simply reducing the complicated Han-Chinese socio-legal culture into (Orthodox) Confucian jurisprudence omits the differences and multiplicities within the theory and context.

When examining the Han-Chinese socio-legal culture critically and meticulously, we will find that there is a lack of legal-philosophical perspective for the production of resistance/subversion. Changes are allowed under the theories of Zun Zi, Han Fei Zi and Zhu Zi; but they have to be conducted under a grand-narrative of ren/social harmony or the faist entrenchment of ruler's power, which are both highly hierarchical. In Buddhist discourse, changes and reforms are allowed and accepted; but, where is the motivation? Is there any appropriate and pragmatic linguistic paradigm which can be facilitated to conduct any resistance and subversion? Can the Buddhist penultimate theory—karmic machine—be challenged and subverted? That is why, in Chap. 1, I argue that Foucauldian politics is useful and functional to facilitate the development of an indigenous theory of (gender/sexual) justice. Engaging Foucauldian theory with the revision and examination of a Han-Chinese socio-legal tradition can therefore sensitize us to the unstable circulation of power and the possibilities/technology to locate, explore and expand the spaces of resistance.

The problem is: Even if Foucauldian theory (including Desexualization) is a valid and effective subversion strategy, can it, a Euro-American cultural product, incorporate with Hong Kong local socio-legal tradition smoothly without reconstituting elements of cultural colonialism?

Transplantation is not a problem; on the contrary, as Jacques Derrida rightly points out: There is a hymen between cultures, which makes them separate, but not isolated.[89] A vital factor which we have to consider in the Hong Kong context when examining the possibility of localizing the foreign theories and the related anti-discrimination socio-legal policy, as with a Foucauldian analysis of sexuality politics and Desexualization, is the socio-cultural factor: Can the framework—which is developed in a non-Han-Chinese context—work effectively in Hong Kong, a predominately Han-Chinese society?[90] If law and its underlying policy are the products of

[89] Chu (1994), at 213.

[90] Xia (2004), at 33.

cultural discourse, then they cannot be applied universally;[91] a successful engagement of a foreign legal model within a local socio-legal culture is usually an essential criterion for a smooth transplantation of law and legal policy.[92] As Xin-hua Xia rightly points out: In order to carry out a successful and smooth transplantation of law, we need to examine whether the indigenous culture can accommodate the changes brought about by such a project.[93] What we need to investigate is not whether there was/is any sexual justice in Hong Kong Han-Chinese civilization, but whether there are any cultural platforms or justification for an overseas socio-legal theory of sexual justice to engage with Hong Kong society and its legal system. A possible start is the search for matching point(s) between the cultures: The culture in which the legal reform was first introduced, and the indigenous culture into which the legal reform will be transplanted.[94]

Returning to the Han Chinese socio-legal philosophies above, we can see that the perspectives developed and devised by Han Fei Zi, Zhu Zi, Nāgārjuna and Shih Chao Hwei all stress the significance of context/condition, especially in the discourse of legal change/reform— both Han Fei Zi and Zhu Zi believed that legal development has to follow the transformation of social contexts; and Shih Chao Hwei points out that due to the changes in the social contexts, minor lu/vinaya and the meaning of 'minor' can be refined and reproduced. I therefore believe that the respect for context and the effects brought by its changes can be a valid stage on which Foucauldian (legal) philosophy, which emphasizes the significance of discourse, is able to engage with Han-Chinese Indigenous socio-legal culture.

One of the problems, when examining Han-Chinese socio-legal philosophy from a Foucauldian perspective, is the monolithic subjectivity devised by a number of jurists. While Mencius, Xun Zi, and Han Fei Zi always assumed the existence of an essential human subjectivity—Zhu Zi understood that there were differences among humans and Buddhist psychoanalysis has developed a mechanism by which human subjectivity can be reconstituted. According to the Buddhist theory of Mādhyamika, human subjectivity is always changing—seeds, which reproduce human nature, are also used and replaced with human action and thinking. Moreover, when and how seeds re-engineer the constitution of subjectivity also relates to the context and discourses seeds situate—it then provides another platform where a Foucauldian understanding of human subjectivity can be engaged with local Han-Chinese culture. As Yang argues: Anātman can effectively echo with the contemporary Euro-American theory of anti-essentialist subjectivity.[95]

The next question is: Can Foucauldian Desexualization engage with Han-Chinese socio-legal culture? Is there any platform for Desexualization to incorporate Han-Chinese philosophy? As argued in Chap. 1, although there are differences among different schools of Han-Chinese socio-legal theories, we can see that under them

[91] Su (1996), at 18.

[92] Yu (1999), at 302.

[93] Xia (2004), at 43.

[94] He (2001), at 117.

[95] Yang (2005), at 77.

(besides Buddhism), subjectivity/humanhood is not formatted by and hence can hardly be changed by fa/law. Also, sexuality did not play an important role in all their theorems of subjectivity formation and fa/law—the legal politics developed by Confucianism and faism actually do not put much emphasis on sexuality—sexuality is simply a kind of natural desire which people have to accept. They actually focus on harmony among people and harmony between the universe and humans—if one's (sexual) activity would not upset or disturb a harmonious social life, people will accept it. Another rule which is related to harmony is yin/over-obsessiveness (of sexual desire/activities) which disturbs social life, and thus has to be punished. Apart from these two rules, all kinds of sexual postures/positioning (e.g. anal sex) and the sexual identities involved in the activity are not problematic. The fact that Han-Chinese socio-legal culture does not have a strong sexual political perspective on one hand makes same-sex erotic activities acceptable, while on the other hand makes the culture insensitive towards contemporary problems/conflicts of sexuality discrimination. Desexualization can therefore fully facilitate non-discriminatory attitudes which already exist in Han-Chinese socio-legal culture, and sensitize the culture to sexuality politics.

Also, there is still a heterosexuality hegemony. That is why the Hong Kong SAR Government is still hesitant in discussing same sex marriage/partnership and enacting an anti sexual orientation discrimination bill. Problems, in short, still remain even if Desexualization is adopted as a legal policy, would desexualizing law without any regard to this political environment simply reduce the legal system to a value-free mechanism which in return further marginalizes the powerless (e.g. LesBiGayTransIntersexQueer/TongZhi)? Would Desexualization of law sustain sexual violence by totally neglecting the existing imbalance of power within the political discourse of sexuality?

References

Chan, Joseph 'Confucianism and Human Rights' in Rhona Smith & Christien Van Den Anker, (eds), *The Essentials of Human Rights* (Spain: Hodder Arnold, 2005), 55–74.

Chang, Tsai (trans., original: 张载), *Chang Tsai 's Reader (trans., original: 张载集)* (BeiJing: ChungHwa中华, 1978).

Chang, Kuo-hua (trans., original: 张国华) et al, (eds), *History of Chinese Legal Philosophy (trans, original: 中国法律思想史)* (BeiJing: Law Press, 1982).

Chang, Kuo-hua (trans., original: 张国华), *History of Chinese Legal Philosophy: A New Version (trans, original: 中国法律思想史新编)* (BeiJing: Peking University Press, 1991).

Cheng, Hao (trans., original: 程颢) & Cheng, Yi (trans., original: 程颐), *Two Chengs' Reader (trans., original: 二程集)* (BeiJing: ChungHwa中华, 1981).

Cheung, Tak-sing, *Confucian Ethics and the Order Complex (trans., original: 儒家伦理与秩序情结)* (TaiPei: JuLiu巨流, 1989).

Chiu, Man-Chung, *De/Sexing Hong Kong Law* (Hong Kong: Red Publish, 2017).

Chou, Wah-shan, *Post-Colonial TongZhi* (Hong Kong: Hong Kong Queer Forum, 1997).

Chu, Tung-tsu, *Law and Society in Traditional China (trans., original: 中国法律与中国社会)* (TaiPei: Liren 里仁, 1984).

Chu, Yiu-wai, *Post-Orientalism* (BanCiao: LuoTuo 骆驼, 1994).
Ding, Nei-fei, 'Feminist Knots: Shades of the Bondmaid-Concubine in Sex and Domestic Work' (2002) 3(3) *Inter-Asia Cultural Studies* 449–476.
Fo Hui 佛慧, 'Some Summaries on the Origin and Characteristics of Vinaya Master Dao Xuan's Idea on Saṃvara' (2015) 2 *Vinaya*, 124–134.
Guo Yu 果煜, (2016) *Mādhyamika paramartha-satya (trans., original: 中观胜义谛)* (TaiPei: Cite, 2016).
He, Qin-hua (trans., original: 何勤华), *Historical Discourse of Legal Culture (trans., original: 法律文化史论)* (BeiJing: Law Press, 1998).
He, Qin-hua (trans., 何勤华), (ed), *Transplantation of Law and Localization of Law (trans., original: 法的移植与法的本土化)* (BeiJing: Law Press, 2001).
Ho, Normal 'The Legal Philosophy of Zhu Xi (1130–1200) and Neo-Confucianism's Possible Contributions to Modern Chinese Legal Reform' (2011) *TsingHua Law Review* 167–214.
Jaschok, Maria, *Concubines and Bondservants: The Social History of a Chinese Custom* (London: Zed, 1988).
Jiang, Shan (trans., original: 江山), *Concept of Chinese Law (trans., original: 中国法理念)* (BeiJing: China University of Political Science and Law, 2005).
Knoblock, John, *Xunzi: A Translation and Study of the Complete Works. Vol 3* (Stanford: Stanford University Press, 1994).
Kulatissa Nanda Jayatilleke, *Dhamma, Man, and Law* (Singapore: The Buddhist Research Society, undated).
Lao, Zheng-wu (trans., original: 劳政武), *The Principle of the Monastic Code in Chinese Buddhism* (TaiPei: LaoKu老古, 1999).
Lau, Lawrence, (2019) *A Study of Buddhist Public Engagement in Thailand and Malaysia* (TaoYuan: Dharma Dhatu Publications, 2019).
Lee, Sang-wha, 'The Patriarchy in China: An Investigation of Public and Private Spheres' (1999) 5(1) *Asian Journal of Women Studies* 9–49.
Lee, Kuan-yew's view on Rule of Law (trans., original: 李光耀的法治观), available at: https://www.npf.org.tw/2/540 (visited 16 Dec 2020).
Lin, Wai-yi (trans., original: 林纬毅), *The Engagement of faism and Confucianism (trans., original: 法儒兼容)* (TaiPei: WenJin 文津, 2004).
Liu, Cheng-wei, 'The Theory of Transforming Human Nature' (2000) 33 *Philosophical Forum* 168–183.
Ma, Xiao-hong (trans., original: 马小红), (ed), *History of Chinese Legal Philosophy Development (trans. Original: 中国法律思想发展简史)* Beijing: China University of Political Science and Law, 1995).
Ma, Yong (trans., original: 马勇), *Dong Zhong-shu* (Hong Kong: ChungHwa中华, 2001).
Ng, Yu-kwan, Philosophical Interpretation of *Nagarjuna's Mūlamadhyamaka-kārikā (trans., original: 龙树中论的哲学解读)* (TaiPei: Student, 2018).
Peerenboom, Randall, *Law and Morality in Ancient China: The Silk Manuscripts of Huang-Lao* (Albany: SUNY Press, 1993).
Powers, John, *A Bull of a Man: Images of Masculinity, Sex and the Body in Indian Buddhism* (Cambridge, MA: Harvard University Press, 2009).
Ruegg, Seyfort, *The Literature of the Madhyamaka School of Philosophy in India* (Wiesbaden: Harrassowitz, 1981).
Samuels, Harriet, 'Hong Kong and Women, Asian Values, and the Law' (1997) 21 *Human Rights Quarterly* 707–734.
Shih Chao Hwei 释昭慧, *Contemporary Interpretation of Buddhist Jurisprudence (trans., original: 律学今诠)* (TaiPei: Dharma Dhatu Publications, 1999).
Shih Sheng Yen 释圣严, *School of Vinaya-Discipline – An Outline (trans., trans., original: 戒律学纲要)* TaiPei: Dharma Drum, 1997).
Sin, Wai-man & Chu, Yiu-wai, 'Whose Rule of Law?: Rethinking (Post-)colonial Legal Culture in Hong Kong' (1998) 7(2) *Journal of Social and Legal Studies* 147–169.

Singer, Allyson, 'Sex Discrimination in Hong Kong Special Administrative Region', (2000) 11(1) *Ind. Int'l & Comp. L. Rev.* 215–249.

Su, Li 苏力, *Rule of Law and Its Local Resources* (BeiJing: China University of Political Science and Law, 1996).

Taishō Tripiṭaka Editorial Committee (trans., original: 大藏经刊行委员会), *Taishō Tripiṭaka*, (TaiPei: XinWenFeng 新文丰, 1986).

Tang, Kai-lin (trans., original: 唐凯麟) & Zhang, Huai-cheng (trans., original: 张怀承), *ChengREN Yu ChengSheng 成人与成圣* (ChangSha: HuNan University Press, 2003).

Voyce, Malcolm 'The Vinaya and The Dharmaśāstra' (2007) 39(56) *The Journal of Legal Pluralism and Unofficial Law* 33–65.

Westerhoff, Jan, *Nagarjuna's Madhyamaka* (New York: Oxford University Press, 2009).

Xia, Xin-hua (trans., original: 夏新华) (2004) *Rule of Law: Realization and Transgression (trans., original: 法治: 实践与超越* (BeiJing: China University of Political Science and Law, 2004).

Xia, Guang (trans., original: 夏光), *Modernity in East Asia and Modernity in the West (trans., original:东亚现代性与西方现代性)* (GuiLin: Guangxi Normal University, 2005).

Yang, Hui-nan, '"Ten Unlawful Things Advocated by the Vais´a¯l¯ı Monks": Discuss the Flexibility of lu/vinaya' (trans., original: 从「十事非法诤」论戒律的方便性), available at: http://ccbs.ntu.edu.tw/FULLTEXT/JR-NX012/nx00114.htm (1990)

Yang, He-gao (trans., original: 杨鹤皋), (ed), *XinBioan ZhongGuo falu SiXiangShi 新版中国法律思想史*(HeFei: AnHui University Press, 1997).

Yang, Hui-nan, *Compassion and Belief (trans., original: 爱与信仰)* (TaiPei: Cite, 2005).

Yang, Hui-nan, 'Buddhism and TongZhi: A Study of paṇḍaka (Homosexuality) in Vinaya-piṭaka' (trans., original: 佛教与同志: 律典中的种种問題) (2006) 7 *Journal of the Center for Buddhist Studies 佛学研究中心学报*, 49–92.

Yin Shun印顺, *Study Buddhism from a Buddhist Perspective (trans., original: 以佛法研究佛法)* (TaiPei: ZhengWen正闻, 1992).

Yu, Rong-Gen, *Dao Tong Yu fa Tong道统与法统* (BeiJing: Law Press, 1999).

Zhang, Jin-fan, *The Tradition and Contemporary Transformation of Chinese Law (trans., original: 中国法律的传统与近代转型)* (Beijing: Law Press, 1997).

Zhang, Ren-shan (trans., original: 张仁善), *li, fa, Society (trans., original: 礼・法・社会)* TianJin: TianJin GuJi 天津古籍, 2001).

Zhao, Shi-lin (trans., original: 赵士林), *Xun Zi (trans., original: 荀子)* (TaiPei: Grand East, 1999).

Chapter 3
A Hybrid of Harmony and Resistance at the Margin: Articulating a Theory of Justice in Hong Kong Han-Chinese Culture

3.1 Introduction

In Chaps. 1 and 2, I suggest that Euro-American socio-legal concepts and related legal reform strategies (like Foucauldian Desexualization and Degenderization) are the policies by which sexual/gender justice can be re-constructed in the context of Hong Kong, a predominately Han-Chinese 汉族华人 society. If we can locate the matching points of cultures, the transplantation of Euro-American philosophical concepts can be conducted smoothly.[1] I also argue that in order to avoid a reinstatement of postcolonial violence and/or being insensitive towards the marginalized powerless—the possible consequences after engaging my suggestions with current legal discourse—we also need to develop an 'indigenous' theory of justice. However, I find that there are blind spots in the proposed theory: (1) Even though we can find the matching points between cultures, how the transplantation can be made smoothly and efficiently has not been clearly specified; and (2) Although I argue that there exists a theory of yi 义/ justice in Han-Chinese culture, the (un)conscious and (un)intentional use of Rawlsian theory, a Euro-American discursive product, as an ultimate reference to justify and reconstruct an indigenous theory of justice is still not ideal. In this chapter, besides trying to produce a perspective to analyze the existing transplantation model, I also aim to construct a paradigm to elaborate the re-articulation and mutual infiltration of a theory of justice, which is a cultural concept.

[1] Some academics, like Gunther Teubner, argue that 'transplantation' is a wrong term and should be replaced by 'irritant', which can avoid the dichotomy of original/copycat. For details, please see Teubner (1998). Other terms and theories are also proposed, like legal translation and legal transportation. For details, please see Gillespie (2008a, b), Pahuja (2007), and Harding (2002).

This chapter is derived in part from an article published in *Inter-Asia Cultural Studies* (2009) Routledge.

M.-C. Chiu, *Transforming the Hong Kong Legal Machine*,
https://doi.org/10.1007/978-981-19-1272-6_3

3.2 Transplantation: Mission Impossible?

3.2.1 Postcolonialization of Transplantation Models: The Mythologization of Cultural Conflict

There are many ways by which transplantation of conceptual perspectives and related legal reform proposals can be conducted.[2] The question is: Can the transplantation be done smoothly with the aims completely fulfilled? As Helena Kennedy and Roger Cotterell always stress, culture, especially tradition, is essential for the stable interpretation and development of law[3]—put simply, in order to make the concept transplantation successful, the concept in question (e.g. Foucauldian Desexualization) must be able to comply with the culture of the transplant jurisdiction (e.g. Hong Kong).[4]

However, if a philosophical concept and its related legal reform proposals are discursive products of a particular cultural context, then, as Pierre Legrand argues, any transplantation becomes impossible.[5] One of the best examples would be the huge scale of legal transplantation that occurred at the end of the Qing 清 Dynasty (1644–1911): The transplanted law failed to incorporate with the local culture and thus reproduced serious social conflicts.[6] De-ming Liu explains why a transplantation can fail: '[T]he norm is self-contradictory if suitable machinery for the implementation [of the object of transplantation] is lacking; or if non-compliance is widespread…'.[7]

Xing-zhong Yu, however, holds a different view. He argues that transplantation is still possible, even though the original jurisdiction of the concept experienced a very different cultural discourse when compared to the target of transplantation.[8] After analyzing the Turkish reception of the Swiss Civil Code in 1926, Cotterell summarizes the keys of successful transplantation:[9]

> [S]uccess or failure in transplantation may depend ultimately on organization, education and a flexible system of administration and judicial practice to adapt unfamiliar ideas to local conditions and perhaps to maximize incentives and remove disincentives to popular invocation of new legal ideas. (emphasis added)[10]

---

[2] Von Benda-Beckmann & Von Benda-Beckmann (2007), at 63.

[3] Kennedy (2005), at 6; Cotterell (2006), at 122.

[4] Jiang (2003), at 6; Liu (2006), at 738, Peerenboom (2006), at 840, But Jiang-yu Wang holds an holds an opposite view: He argues that culture does not play an important role in (legal) transplantation or transfer. For details, please see Wang (2004a), at 367.

[5] Legrand (2001).

[6] Jiang (2003), at 7.

[7] Liu (2006) at 738.

[8] Yu (2006), at 42.

[9] John Reitz also emphasizes that, for a successful transfer of 'rule of law', the legal culture of the transplant jurisdiction has to be changed. For details, please see Reitz (2003).

[10] Cotterell (2006), at 117.

However, is that exactly what pathologizes indigenous culture? Postcolonialists argue that the indigenous culture should not be misinterpreted, changed and/or peripheralized; and the reinstatement of postcolonialism in any format should not be accepted—i.e. indigenous cultures should not be misinterpreted, marginalized or even sacrificed for the sake of the transplantation of cultural norms and legal concepts.[11] That explains why Zheng-lai Deng always advocates that the Chinese should forget any adaptation of a Western legal model,[12] and Shi-gong Jiang strongly argues that Chinese legal philosophy should not be derived from Western theoretical paradigm but only from Chinese local experiences.[13]

In summary, the discourse of transplantation is always predicated on a dichotomy of local/foreign cultures, assuming a prediscursive incompatibility and inherent conflict of cultures and existence of uncontaminated and pure culture(s). Hence, it should be noted that whenever there is a proposed transplantation, struggle and conflict occur.

3.2.2 From Bhabha's Hybridization to Chang's Transcultural Articulation

Transplantation of law, however, seems inevitable, especially in the context of globalization—for example, the entry of PR China into the World Trade Organization—and the rapid development of internet technology has definitely impacted on the law in Hong Kong.[14] A problem then arises: Since the globalization of law started in Anglophone countries in the Northern Hemisphere,[15] can there be any globalization/transplantation of law which is not Euro-American-centric?[16] According to the transplantation models discussed earlier, if it is impossible to have a globalization/transplantation of law which is not Euro-American-centric, this merely means that we cannot have a modern legal project which is free from a Euro-American cultural hegemony; so in order to avoid post-colonial violence, we may need to develop an indigenous/a hybrid culture (e.g. customary law in Hong Kong) as a defence.[17] The problem is: Can we avoid this seemingly-inevitable struggle ?

[11] Please also see Merry (2003), at 571, 578; Carasik (2008), at 65; Baxi (2002).

[12] Deng (2006).

[13] Jiang (2003), at 77.

[14] Wang (2004a), at 349, 374–375.

[15] Gong-Pi (2006), at 443.

[16] Chen (2006), at 349.

[17] Chiu (2006).

Gayatri Spivak, when being criticized for using poststructuralism, a Euro-American cultural product, says: 'I cannot understand what indigenous theory there might be that can ignore the realities of nineteenth-century colonialism.'[18] What Spivak implies is: A pure notion of culture is only an illusion. As I argue in *De/Sexing Hong Kong Law*, (Han-Chinese) culture is always a hybrid—for example: Buddhism, which is a vital component of (contemporary) Han-Chinese culture, is not a locally developed philosophy.[19] Another example is the Small House policy in Hong Kong, which had to be translated into colonial legal jargon in order to persist and continue to be effective.[20] Hybridity, a strategic concept developed by Homi Bhabha,[21] can also reproduce resistance against mainstream colonial culture—the colonialized can facilitate the hybridized culture/linguistic perspective in translating the marginalized local culture into the language of the colonial system and hence subvert its (illusory) hegemony. The effect of hybridity as resistance is, however, ambiguous:

> On one hand, it [i.e. hybridity] works in the colonial system of representation, continuing to strengthen the existing relationship structure; on the other hand, it offers a very 'polite' resistance against the colonizers, although the colonizers do not notice it. (trans., original: 一方面它[混杂]在殖民再现体系内操作, 继续深化持续原有的关系架构, 另一方面它又对殖民者进行「有礼貌」的对抗, 继续这种对抗不被殖民者发所察觉。).[22]

In the context of globalization/transplantation, hybridity hence becomes a very effective method by which indigenous culture can be transformed (translated) and preserved (in name); it can also problematize the concept of a pure culture—however, a perspective of resistance still exists since the concept of hybridity assumes that any transplantation of culture is/starts with an imposition of the powerful culture on the powerless, i.e. struggle and conflict.

Hsiao-hung Chang in *Fake Globalization*, adopting the Deleuzian theory of 'simulacrum', politicizes the dichotomy of real/origin and fake/replica. Chang, in short, questions whether there exists any original culture (be it the colonial culture or indigenous culture, be it Euro-American culture or culture of Greater China), and puts the focus on the similarity between cultures, which are simulacra. Following this line of argument, an inherent contradiction or conflict between any two cultures, which assumes there is a genuine and stable notion of original culture, is only an illusion. Chang argues that the interaction of cultures goes beyond the postcolonial concept of hybridity, but with an osmosis/infiltration between cultures, not only is there similarity between cultures, cultures can sim*u*late each other.

---

[18] Quoted by Harasym (1990), at 69.

[19] Ito (2004). Please note: Inconsistencies between Confucianism, Daoism and Buddhism have always existed—Yiu-wai Chu points out that the conflict between Confucianism and Daoism represented the competition between the Northern and Southern Cultures during the Zhou 周 Dynasty (1029 BC-221 BC); During the Southern/Northern 南北 Dynasties (220–580), Daoism also resisted strongly the import of Buddhism; and Confucianism always holds that the Buddhist philosophy of equality violates hierarchical interpersonal politics. For details, please see Chu (1994).

[20] Chiu (2017).

[21] Bhabha (1994).

[22] Chen (2006), at 149.

Chang, in this context, proposes the concept of 'cultural sim*u*larity'.[23] According to Chang, the sim*u*larity is an imaginary, by which an ambiguous similarity and dissimilarity between cultures can be re-represented, re-engineered and re-articulated. In the matrix of the transcultural sim*u*larity, cultural concepts and related legal reform are articulated/represented through a mechanism of infiltration.[24] She uses the films, 'The Matrix' (1999) and 'Crouching Tiger, Hidden Dragon' (2000), as examples, to demonstrate how the former reproduces the context where audiences of United States of America could appreciate Chinese martial arts, and through this constructed sim*u*larity between the cultural techniques/practices shown in 'The Matrix' and 'Crouching Tiger, Hidden Dragon', the latter was popularly received in United States of America. It is not a question of whether authentic Chinese martial arts are represented in these films, or whether they are an expression of techniques performed by any American or an Americanized notion of Chinese martial arts in a film (i.e. translation) which allows the audience to understand (not accept) a cultural concept, but the existence of cultural sim*u*larity, and through the machine of 'transcultural articulation', a representation of particular cultural practices are re-articulated and embedded smoothly in another context (a simulacrum).

I would therefore argue that the articulation machine, which can be located by cultural sim*u*larity, does not only help in the understanding of cultural infiltration, but in achieving trans-jurisdictional/trans-legal osmosis. I also argue that, in the age of globalization (of law), philosophical concepts and related legal reforms, through the English common law system and international law mechanisms, are infiltrating Han-Chinese culture in the context of Hong Kong. The dialogue between different cultures (the colonial common law system and indigenous culture) is thus a simulacrum where the sim*u*larity between cultures (e.g. Desexualization and Degenderization) can be located where trans-articulation occurs.

3.3 Transcultural Articulation of Justice in Han-Chinese Culture

In this section, I will adopt Chang's machine of transcultural articulation to demonstrate how Rawlsian justice,[25] a Euro-American cultural product, can be transculturally articulated into Han-Chinese culture.

In his groundbreaking book, *A Theory of Justice*, John Rawls develops his philosophy on the foundation of a presumption: People have the following three attributes:

---

[23] Chang (2007), at 20, 68 and 73.

[24] Please see Chaps. 1 and 2.

[25] I choose Rawlsian theory because it is engaged with Desexualization, a strategy that I believe will bring gender/sexual justice in the works of Drucilla Cornell; so a discussion of Rawlsian notions of justice can effectively relate the thesis of this article with the themes of my other articles. Also, please note that, as Randall Peerenboom writes, justice can have different meanings and implications in the context of (Han-) Chinese culture. Please see Peerenboom (2006), at 843.

(1) Rationality; (2) A Sense of justice and (3) A capacity for good. Rawls held that 'justice' starts with 'fairness', which means equal distribution of primary goods (i.e. rights, freedom, power, income, resources and individual self-respect).[26] And, even though inequality is preordained, when it is accepted by the marginalized powerless in a society, it becomes positive and beneficial. In the words of Dun-hua Zhao (trans., original: 赵敦华): Rawls's proposal can prevent inequality from being gross and extreme, and can offer hope to the socially marginalized.[27]

Drucilla Cornell, in *The Imaginary Domain: Abortion, Pornography and Sexual Harassment*, further substantiates a Rawlsian Theory of Justice, and relates the theory with the significance of the 'imaginary domain': According to Lacanian psychoanalysis, the imaginary relates to self projection/introjection of erotic desire, which is vital in the construction of individual subjectivity. In the imaginary domain, one can fantasize oneself both having and being indefinite human identities.[28]

The imagination and fantasy machine is facilitated and its efficiency enhanced by the rapid development of internet technology.[29] Prohibiting people from imagining/representing their desires or imposing a particular political model on others is an eradication of others' self-respect, a kind of oppression and dehumanization which is simply unjust.[30] Among all primary goods, Cornell, like Rawls, especially stressed 'self-respect'.[31]

Engaging the concept of the imaginary domain with Rawlsian theory, we then ask: If a 'veil of ignorance'[32] can prevent everyone from understanding exactly the socio-political positions of themselves and others, how can people understand and feel the possible discrimination faced by others and then form a social contract? The answer, provided by Cornell, is the imaginary. In the imaginary domain, a person is able to fantasize herself/himself being others, and feel how others feel in the contexts where they are situated.[33]

---

[26] Rawls (1971), at 62, 95. This viewpoint is shared by many academics, including Jiang (2002), at 31.

[27] Zhao (1988), at 151.

[28] Grosz (2005), at 73.

[29] Lin (2008), at 82.

[30] Cornell (1995), at 7–8.

[31] Hu (2005), at 9.

[32] According to John Rawls, in 'Original Position', people are covered by a 'Veil of Ignorance'; hence they only have ordinary economic and political knowledge, they know nothing about 'real' social positions, resources under the control and life plans of themselves and the others. Rawls (1993), at 23.

[33] Cornell (2008), at 136.

3.3.1 *Locating Similarities: yi/Justice in the Contexts of Confucianism, Buddhism and Rawlsian Theory*

In contemporary Han-Chinese language, justice is translated as yi. However, yi does not start with equality but with harmonious hierarchical interpersonal relationships.[34] This is why Duan Lin says: In ancient China, there was no justice but yi.[35]

Daoism, an ancient school of philosophical thought, believes that yi, as a human project, violates Dao;[36] however, Guu-ying Chen points out that, Lao Zi 老子, a profound Daoist scholar, does not object to yi, provided that it is derived from Dao, the ultimate reference of everything.[37] In Orthodox Confucianism, yi always assumes a vital role: 'The superior man holds yi to be of the highest importance.'[38] (trans., original: 君子义以为上。) Both Confucius and Mencius provide an in-depth and influential analysis of yi—They started with the perspectives of ren 仁 (interpersonal harmony; not REN 人) and li 礼 (social moral orders), which mean harmonious hierarchical interpersonal dynamics.[39] In other words, yi is devised to maintain the smooth operation of the hierarchical social structure.[40]

The two most important elements of yi, in the discourse of ren and li, are Zhong 忠, i.e. faithfulness; and Shu 恕, i.e. forbearance. Zhong, according to Confucius, shows when a 'man of perfect virtue, wishing to be established himself, seeks also to

---

[34] Hu (2005), at 12; Jiang (2002), at 38.

[35] Lin (2007), at 437. For more discussion, please see Chap. 5.

[36] According to Lao Zi, the philosopher who is widely believed to be the founder of the school, Dao is the origin and reference of everything, including humans, society and culture. Thus, Dao consumes the status of the ultimate and transcendental metaphysics. For details, please see Wang (2003), at 23, 43, 98; Wang (2004b), at 149.

[37] Chen (2001).

[38] The translation is slightly modified from Chapter 17 阳货, *The Analects of Confucius*, available at: https://ctext.org/analects/yang-huo (visited 6 Jan 2021).

[39] Book 2, *Tso Commentary to Spring and Autumn Annals*, available at: http://www.chineseclassic.com/13jing/zoezuan/ch01_01.htm (visited 1 Jun 2009). For the definition and discussion of ren and li, please see Chiu (2006).

[40] Pan (2006), at 45.

establish others; wishing to be enlarged himself, he seeks also to enlarge others.'[41] (trans., original: 己欲立而立人, 己欲达而达人。) while Shu means '[w]hat you do not want done to yourself, do not do to others'.[42] (trans., original: 己所不欲, 勿施于人。) yi, hence, it is the idea of 'putting oneself in others' shoes'.[43] The mechanism of yi appreciates the existence of others, so there are others in one self, and one self in others. The interaction would/should not stop so as to re-constitute ren, li and the related harmony.[44] By putting oneself into others' shoes, we can go beyond the self vs others binarism and one's duties in the matrix of interpersonal politics:

> All humans have some things which they cannot bear; extend that feeling to what they can bear, and ren will be the result. All humans have some things which they will not do; extend that feeling to the things which they do, and yi will be the result.[45] (trans., original: 人皆有所不忍, 达之于其所忍, 仁也; 人皆有所不为, 达之于其所为, 义也。)

Mencius further relates yi to individual self-respect: 'There is heavenly nobility, and there is human nobility. ren, yi, self-consecration, and fidelity, with unwearied joy in these virtues: These constitute the nobility of Heaven. To be a gong, a qing, or a da fu; this constitutes the nobility of humans.'[46] (trans., original: 有天爵者, 有人爵者。仁义忠信, 乐善不倦, 此天爵也; 公卿大夫, 此人爵也。) What Mencius means is: Self-respect is the result of self discipline and must be protected and advocated by yi: 'I like life, and I also like yi. If I cannot keep the two together, I will let life go, and choose yi.'[47] (trans., original: 生, 亦我所欲也; 义, 亦我所欲也, 二者不可得兼, 舍生而取义者也。) Xun Zi 荀子, a Confucian and the teacher of the most influential faist 法家學者,[48] Han Fei Zi 韓非子, elaborates the interaction between rationality

[41] Chapter 6 雍也, *The Analects of Confucius*, available at: https://ctext.org/analects/yong-ye (visited 6 Jan 2021).

[42] Chapter 15 卫灵公, *The Analects of Confucius*, available at: https://ctext.org/analects/wei-ling-gong (visited 6 Jan 2021).

[43] *Zhu Zi's Explanation to Zhong Yong*. ECNU, available at: http://www.yjsy.ecnu.edu.cn/jszj/%E5%AD%90%E9%83%A8-%E9%AD%8F%E6%99%8B%E4%BB%A5%E4%B8%8B/%E6%9C%B1%E5%AD%90%E8%AA%9E%E9%A1%9E/gz00.htm (visited 1 Jun 2009). For more discussion on this process from perspectives of Rawlsian Justice and Daoism, please see Chaps. 4 and 8.

[44] Wang (2004b), at 246.

[45] The translation is slightly modified from Chap. 7 B 尽心下, *Mencius*, available at: https://ctext.org/mengzi/jin-xin-ii (visited 9 Jan 2021).

[46] The translation is slightly modified from Chap. 6 A 告子上, *Mencius*, available at: https://ctext.org/mengzi/gaozi-i (visited 9 Jan 2021).

[47] The translation is slightly modified from Chap. 6 A 告子上, *Mencius*, available at: https://ctext.org/mengzi/gaozi-i (visited 9 Jan 2021).

[48] In Han-Chinese culture, besides Daoism and Confucianism, faism also constructs a very influential paradigm of fa/law in the (ancient) China. Please see Chaps. 1 and 2.

and the concept of yi: Whether an action is just and appropriate is determined by rationality. He writes: 'yi follows the inherent order of things'.[49] (trans., original: 义者循理。).

Juxtaposing Rawlsian/Cornell's theory of justice and Han-Chinese concept of yi, we can locate transcultural sim*u*larities: Both are using yi/justice as the benchmark of human behaviour evaluation. Han-Chinese cultural accents on rationality (Xun Zi) (within a political discourse of interpersonal relationship) and Rawlsian respect of rationality can be an effective sim*u*larity of two theorems. Especially, both Rawlsian/Cornell's theory and Mencius's perspective put the stress on the nurture of individual self-respect. Cornell's respect for the personal representation of desire echoes the Orthodox Confucian concept of 'putting oneself into others' shoes': '[I]f you don't want others to impose their choice on you, should you not do the same to others?' Cornell's interpretation of the imaginary domain can also supplement Confucius's concept of Shu: Only if one can imagine what could happen to others, can one understand the importance of respect and acceptance; this technique can certainly help one to put oneself within the web of interpersonal politics and avoid imposing one's perspective on others.

The problem, however, is: yi is used to restrengthen and reconstruct the social hierarchy and hence inequality. In other words, equality is not an element in the formation of yi in Confucian socio-legal culture. This lack of equality, which is essential in Rawlsian/Cornell's theory is exemplified throughout the development of theories of fa 法 (law in Han-Chinese culture)—fa, which was developed to correspond with different assumptions of human nature/subjectivity, aimed at reinstating a hierarchical social structure.[50] But Buddhism, under meticulous analysis, is providing a platform for the construction of sim*u*larity. Buddhism is a vital element in the formation of Han-Chinese culture—where equality is its prime principle.[51]

According to Vasubandhu, a significant Buddhist philosopher, the interaction among the performances of the consciousness[52] engineer the representation of the objective world and reconstitutes the (fixed yet imaginary) human subjectivity. The interactive process between the consciousnesses and the external world also constitutes the karmic seeds (种子, Bīja), which are stored in storehouse-consciousness (阿赖耶识, alaya-vijñāna), determining the upcoming interaction between the consciousnesses (识, vijñāna) and the external world. Storehouse-consciousness 'collects and stores the effects or seeds of experience until they mature and give rise to new experiences'.[53] Seeds are the products of 'karma', which

---

[49] Chapter 15 议兵, *Xun Zi*. The translation is slightly modified from King, R A H, 'Along the Grain: yi (Justice) in the *Xun Zi*', available at: http://oriens-extremus.org/wp-content/uploads/2019/03/OE-55-3.pdf (visited 9 Jan 2021).

[50] Lin (2004).

[51] Fang (2006).

[52] For more discussion on Vijñānamatra 唯识 and classification of consciousness, please see Chaps. 1, 3 and 4.

[53] Koller (2002), at 222.

literally means 'action' and indicates the mechanism by which what a human did and/or thought in one point of time would determine her/his future action and/or status.[54] It is not a kind of absolute pre-determination of one's destiny, but a mechanism of choice and responsibility: One can choose her/his action and would be held responsible for that choice in the future. Although according to karma, the action a human has to take is pre-determined, the manner of the action can still be decided by her/him. Karma, put simply, is the 'power by virtue of which cause is followed by effect.'[55]

As karma is a non-stop accumulation, the production of seeds never ends. Seed is not a static concept either; it grows with the changes and evolution of context—the mechanism is called 'Perfume' (Vāsanā).[56] Every decision and action of a human subject will influence the ever-changing nature of seeds. Also, when a particular set of seeds becomes mature under a particular material environment, other seeds and other contexts are reproduced.[57] The external world is therefore a never-ending series of subjectivity constructions.

The interactive formation of body and world thus (re)produces the karma/seeds which would simultaneously re-constitute storehouse-consciousness. This mechanism is called 'Dependent-Arising thus Emptiness of Self Nature' 缘起性空, which means that (the mental constitutive reception of) every activity and phenomenon can never be a fixed essentiality, but is an illusion re-created and reproduced by the interaction of seeds under a particular discourse, which is also a product of the seeds mechanism. This line of argument leads to the development of an important Buddhist principle: 'Non-Insistence' or 'Selfless-ness' (无我, Anātman). 'Self' in this context does not only mean 'I', but over-insistence on a perspective.

Vijñānamatra hence constructs the theoretical foundation of another significant principle in Buddhism, i.e. 'Non-Permanence', which means there is no eternality in the material world. Since the composition of seeds keeps on changing, it is impossible to have any monolithic and universal subjectivity/self; and if the material world and its related activities and phenomena are only psychological products, initiated by a set of seeds and ending up with the production of another cluster of seeds, then the metanarrative or grand narrative is only an imaginary.

According to Hui Lu, the three principles, Dependent-Arising thus Emptiness of Self Nature, 'Non-Insistence' and 'Non-Permanence', in sum are called the 'Correct Law' (Prāvaccana), and are the most important principles in Buddhist philosophy.[58] It is in this context that Buddha Śākyamuni developed the theory of equality.

---

[54] Hu (1999).

[55] Joe Tom Sun (1998), at 3.

[56] For details, please see Chap. 1.

[57] Yang (2007), at 298–299.

[58] Hui Lu (trans., original: 慧律), (undated) 'Wish the Re-presentation of Correct Law' (trans., original: 祈願正法重現), available at: https://book.bfnn.org/books3/2076.htm#a07 (visited 23 May 2022).

Since the differences among people are formatted by different combinations of seeds, subjectivity/being and value judgments are not any pregiven, pre-discursive and fixed concepts, but are contextual (on-going) imaginary productions. In other words, while differences exist and should be accepted, differences do not and cannot reproduce any foundation of hierarchical discrimination/inequality, as differences and identities are only discursive and temporary. Li-tian Fang thus points out that, going beyond any insistences, accepting differences and reproducing equality is hence the ultimate goal of Buddhist practice.[59] Buddhism thus provides and reproduces a simulacrum of sim*u*larity and makes the osmosis of Rawlsian/Cornell's theory possible in the context of Han-Chinese culture.

'Correct Law', in the machine of Vijñānamatra, can be achieved by the 'transmutation of consciousness (vijñāna) to wisdom (jñāna)' (转识成智)'. According to *Vijnaptimatratasiddhi-sastra 成唯识论*,[60] the aim of Vijñānamatra is to transmute The Nature of Dependent on Other 依他起自性 (Paratantra-svabhāva) to The Perfect True Nature 圆成实性 (Parlinispanna-svabhāva) by excluding Reproduction of Fallacious Knowledge 遍计所执性 (Parikalpita-svabhāva). Through this transmutation, consciousness could be changed into wisdom, which is totally free from any insistent attachments.[61]

The rise of wisdom means the gradual disappearance of seeds which would bring insistent attachments. In other words, Vijñānamatra problematizes the establishment of an eternal hegemony of fixed principle and subjectivity where a particular set of universal and monolithic (moral) principles is insisted on and remains unchallenged and stable. From a Vijñānamatra perspective, the transformation of consciousness into wisdom means the acceptance of multiplicities and the elimination of fixed subjectivity and hegemony:

> [T]he contemporary psychoanalytic fascination with self-multiplicity appears to stem at least in part from a desire to challenge monolithic views of mental health that are implicitly conformist in nature. The emphasis in the Buddhist conception of no-self is on decreasing the sense of existential isolation, by emphasizing the constructed nature of the boundary between self and others and the interdependence of all living beings.[62]

3.4 Osmosis of Cultures: Modification Possible?

In the context of globalization, a possible osmosis between Buddhism and the Rawlsian/Cornell's Theory of Justice thus reproduces the cultural sim*u*larity through the common linguistic concept of equality. I further argue that, through this sim*u*larity,

---

[59] Fang (2008), at 138.

[60] Vol 31, Taishō Tripiṭaka Editorial Committee (1986).

[61] For details, please see Chaps. 1 and 4.

[62] Safran (2003), at 23.

the Rawlsian/Cornell's notion of justice, an object of globalization, can be transculturally articulated smoothly and efficiently in Han-Chinese culture. The transcultural articulation does not stop there; in the process, the interaction between cultures occurs and thus a modification of the object of transcultural articulation—Rawlsian justice in this context—can occur.

Transcultural articulation is not a one-way street, it also engineers an interactive reconstitution between cultural products. As Paul Brietzke argues, the culture of the transplanting culture will be changed by the object; but the object will also be influenced by the former. The purpose and the effects of the transplantation, which is invariably inconsistent with the original intention, will therefore be out of the control of the project architect.[63] Also, transcultural articulation and osmosis can always change the structure of the transplantation object. It is in this context that I argue that through transcultural articulation, a theory of justice can modify itself.

Rawlsian theory is not problem-free. Jürgen Habermas critically points out that Rawlsian theory, as a liberal modern project, is insensitive towards the possible multiplicities of justice(s), since there are differences in subjectivities, discourses and contexts.[64] Joseph Raz argues that only if a value pluralism which goes beyond toleration and anti-discrimination is reproduced, can there be a social justice that recognizes and accepts different cultural communities and individual subjectivities.[65] Cornell[66] also points out that constructing a rigid and pre-contextual definition of justice will only depoliticize the related discussion and debate. And from a Deleuzian perspective, justice is not a model (origin) that, as in the Rawlsian proposal, can be copied.[67]

When analyzing the dialectics between justice and law, the Rawlsian theory's limitations become more apparent. Derrida argues that it is impossible to offer any prediscursive and ahistorical definitions for both concepts as the meanings lie outside of the concepts themselves.[68] Put simply, not only are the universal and fixed definitions of both justice and law absent, there are also always differences within the concepts of justice and law. In fact, Derrida does not believe that law essentially contains justice or vice versa, because while the former is a product of precise and accurate calculation, the latter is infinite and rebellious to rule: Justice, in short, is always beyond law.[69] The argument is best summarized by Andrew Ross:

> The pursuit of justice cannot fully be accomplished through the formal work of legal process; it also involves social and cultural transformations that lie beyond the customary reach of legislation.[70]

---

[63] Brietzke (2004), at 24.

[64] Habermas (2005), at 9.

[65] Raz (1994); Cotterrell (2006).

[66] Cornell (1992), at 166.

[67] Deleuze (1994); Colebrook (2002), at 100.

[68] Cornell (1992), at 165.

[69] Milovanovic (2007), at 72.

[70] Ross (2005), at 203.

The problem, however, is: Law 'always claims to exercise itself in the name of justice and that justice is required to establish itself in the name of a law that must be 'enforced'.[71] In order to solve the problem, in 'Force of Law: The Mystical Foundation of Authority', Derrida advocates that justice should be fulfilled and reproduced in Symbolic Order, including law. What should be taken into consideration is the appropriateness of the behaviour.[72] Derrida further suggests a guideline through which justice can be done in the discourse of law:

> [F]or a decision to be just and responsible, it must, in its proper moment if there is one, be both regulated and without regulation: It must conserve the law and also destroy it or suspend it enough to reinvent it in each case, rejustify it, at least reinvent it in the reaffirmation and the new and free confirmation of its principle.[73]

In other words, a Derridean notion of justice goes beyond Rawlsian theory—although the former does not propose any formulae by which justice can be formatted and reproduced, it embeds the related discussion within contexts, thus arguing for the possibilities of reproducing multiple meanings of justice; it also keeps on destabilizing and problematizing the definition(s) of justice and its dialogue with law.

It is the dialogue between law and justice which on one hand differentiates Euro-American from Han-Chinese culture and on the other, creates another sim*u*larity and thus transcultural articulation between two cultural machines by which yi/justice is made possible. Han-Chinese philosophy discusses in detail the interaction between yi and fa/law. Xun Zi relates yi to fa; he writes: 'li and yi are abided by the proper li and law [i.e. fa].'[74] (trans., original: 仁义法正。) faism also takes yi into its construction of fa/legal theory. The anonymous author of *Guan Zi* 管子, a significant faist text, understands the important of yi, and argues that only fa/law can be used to promote yi:[75]

> [W]hen an enlightened prince occupies the throne, he is sparing in his punishments and exacts few penalties. Unless the punishments are necessary, he does not punish; unless the penalties are necessary he does not exact them. The enlightened prince shuts the door [on depravity and crime], blocks the way to them, and does not allow their manifestations to appear so there will be no place for people to come in contact with them. As a result, his people follow a proper path and their actions are good. If this becomes natural to them, punishment and penalties will be few, yet people will become orderly.[76](trans., original: 是故明君在上位, 刑省罚寡, 非可刑而不刑, 非可罪而不罪也。明君者, 闭其门, 塞其涂, 弇其迹, 使民毋由接于淫非之地。是以民之道正行善也若性然。故罪罚寡而民以治矣。)

[71] Derrida (1992), at 22.

[72] Derrida (1992).

[73] Derrida (1992), at 23. See also Douzinas & Warrington (1994).

[74] Chapter 23 性恶, *Xun Zi*. The translation is slightly modified from 'Xunzi and Mencius Meld', available at: https://warpweftandway.com/xunzi-and-mencius-meld/ (visited 9 Jan 2021).

[75] Yang (1997), at 141.

[76] Chapter 13 八观, *Guan Zi*, cited from Rickett (2001), at 228.

yi also played an important role in the theory developed by Han Fei Zi: He engaged yi with fa philosophy and, accepting Mencius's argument, he pointed out that yi—appropriateness, can only be realized with the enforcement of order—li and fa:[77]

> 'Propriety' refers to the mode in which one's feelings are expressed. It is concerned with the cultural embellishments of all righteous acts, such as the mutual relations of ruler and minister, father and son. It is the way whereby high and low, worthy and unworthy, are differentiated. For instance, when one pines after someone else but cannot make himself understood, he runs fast towards the person and bows low in front of him so as to express his attachment to that person. Similarly, when one loves someone from one's innermost heart and cannot make himself known, he uses pleasing words and beautiful phrases to convince the loved person. Thus, propriety is the outer embellishment whereby the inner heart is understood. Hence 'propriety' refers to the mode in which one's feelings are expressed. In general, when a man responds to external things, he does not know that the response reveals the propriety of his personality. The mass of the people practice propriety only to show respect for others, wherefore propriety is now cordial and again simple. The superior man practises propriety on purpose to cultivate his personality. Since propriety is practiced on purpose to cultivate his personality, it is intrinsic in mind and forms superior propriety. Since superior propriety is intrinsic in mind and popular propriety changes from time to time, they do not respond to each other. Since they do not respond to each other, hence the saying: 'Superior propriety acts and no one responds to it.' Though the mass of the people change propriety from time to time, yet the saintly man is always courteous and respectful, practising the rules of propriety which bind him hand and foot. In so doing he never slackens. Hence the saying: 'Superior virtue stretches its arm and enforces its rules.' Tao [Dao] accumulates; accumulation accomplishes an achievement; and Teh [Morality] is the achievement of Tao. Achievement solidifies; solidity shines; and Jên [ren] is the shining of Teh. Shine has gloss; gloss has function; and Ih [yi] is the function of Jen. Function has propriety; propriety has embellishment; and li is the embellishment of Ih.[78] (trans., original: 礼者, 所以貌情也, 群义之文章也, 君臣父子之交也, 贵贱贤不肖之所以别也。中心怀而不谕, 故疾趋卑拜而明之。实心爱而不知, 故好言繁辞以信之。礼者, 外节之所以谕内也。故曰: 「礼以貌情也。」凡人之为外物动也, 不知其为身之礼也。众人之为礼也, 以尊他人也, 故时劝时衰。君子之为礼, 以为其身, 以为其身, 故神之为上礼, 上礼神而众人贰, 故不能相应, 不能相应, 故曰: 「上礼为之而莫之应。」众人虽贰, 圣人之复恭敬尽手足之礼也不衰, 故曰: 「攘臂而仍之。」道有积而德有功, 德者道之功。功有实而实有光, 仁者德之光。光有泽而泽有事, 义者仁之事也。事有礼而礼有文, 礼者义之文也。)

As faists point out, fa can be used to reconstruct yi; there is already a theoretical discourse where it is acceptable to allow the legal system to construct and substantiate yi in Han-Chinese culture. This standpoint has influenced contemporary jurists, including Fu and Jiang, who have also argued that it is the goal of law to construct and entrench justice.[79] Besides faism, Buddhist jurisprudence also provides another platform or medium to construct a close partnership between law and justice.

---

[77] Lin (2004), at 40.

[78] Chapter 20 解老, *Han Fei Zi*, available at: http://www.xinfajia.net/7438.html (visited 27 Mar 2022).

[79] Fu (2008), at 295; Jiang (2002), at 310.

As one of the most important elements in constructing the Han-Chinese culture, a Buddhist perspective on law permeates Han-Chinese jurisprudence.[80] Like Confucianism and faism, Buddhist jurisprudence was developed by the Han-Chinese School of Vinaya-Discipline (Nan-shan School 南山宗), which also engineered the development of fa/law in Greater China[81]—starting from the period of the Southern-Northern 南北 Dynasties 420–589), Law in Greater China started engaging with the vinaya: According to Zhou, Buddhist philosophy had a great and positive impact on the development of traditional law, controlling pawnbrokers and commercial activities. The effect was even more obvious in the regulations governing amnesty.[82] Also, as Jiang points out: Buddhist philosophy and its emphasis on equality and non-discrimination also played a part in formatting the concept of yi/justice.[83]

The aim of setting and following the Buddhist vinaya is to realize the ultimate goals of Buddhist practice—equality and selfless-ness.[84] Buddha Śākyamuni stated that the most important principle of vinaya production and interpretation is the 'Persistence of Correct Law', which means the respect for 'Dependent-Arising thus Emptiness of Self Nature', 'Non-Insistence' and 'Non-Permanence'. Engaging Vijñānamatra with the (Han-Chinese) Nan-shan School of Vinaya-Discipline can facilitate the transmutation of consciousness to wisdom.

In *Sifenlu Xingshi Chao* 四分律行事钞, Dao Xuan 道宣 points out that: Making and implementing vinaya will also have their influences tattooed on the seeds which already exist i.e. the 'Substance' 戒体. This process changes the nature of the existing sees and creates new seeds—those seeds will then be stored in storehouse-consciousness and will (re)format the subjectivities. If the consciousness can have a substantial impact on the seeds, then they can certainly play a vital role in the transmutation—if the consciousness can facilitate critical investigation of material world and introduce the Buddhist ideology of equality, then by following and making the vinaya, transmutation can take off and proceed; and when the transmutation is completed, consciousness can in turn be enacted, interpreted and implemented by wisdom. And, from that perspective, by following and implementing such consciousness, people can fulfill the transmutation and, through the interaction between Buddhists and law, justice with equality as an essential perspective can further be realized.[85] Buddhist jurisprudence hence does not only reproduce a jurisprudential mechanism by which justice/equality can be constituted, it also

---

[80] Chiu (2017), at 161.

[81] Yan (2007), at 259–260. For more discussion on School of Vinaya-Discipline, please see Chap. 2.

[82] Zhou (2020).

[83] Jiang (2002), at 42.

[84] Yan (2007), at 2; Chiu (2017), at 159.

[85] Yan (2007), at 114.

sensitizes us to the multiplicities of justices—due to the karmic mechanism of the seeds, insistent attachment becomes impossible. Different and ever-changing concepts of justice can therefore be accommodated and accepted.

Han-Chinese jurisprudence (including faist jurisprudence and Buddhist jurisprudence) relates fa/law directly to the socio-cultural context, where appropriateness and multiplicities are emphasized. Through transcultural articulation and osmosis, these concepts (can) permeate the reconstruction of Rawlsian theory and thus answer sufficiently and fully the Derridean question of 'justice going beyond law': Law and justice become two sides of the same coin and each has to correspond to each other. Also, if everything is just an illusion, as argued by Vijñānamatra, then justice cannot be a fixed concept/object, but also an imaginary where there is no origin.

3.5 Conclusion

This chapter examines the discourse on cultural/legal transplantation and proposes that Chiang's model of cultural sim*u*larity and simulacra can be extended to the globalization of concepts and related legal reforms. Adopting that theoretical framework, examining how a Rawlsian theory of justice can be transcultural articulated in the Han-Chinese cultural context. This chapter, after scrutinizing meticulously the constructions of yi/justice under Confucianism and faism, and the notion of equality under Buddhist Vijñānamatra, argues that cultural sim*u*larities exist and that they facilitate the transcultural articulation of Rawlsian justice. Osmosis of cultures happens and can help modify a Rawlsian theory—the concepts of multiplicities and the interaction between justice and law that have been explored in Han-Chinese context can assist Rawlsians to respond to the criticisms effectively.

However, I have to emphasize that there are differences within Rawlsian/Confucian/faist/Buddhist notions of yi/justice theories. Thus, the articulation/transplantation/interaction/modification is always a matrix—different theories intermingle together and inter-influence each other under different cultures and new concepts will be generated, thus re-transforming the context in which they are produced. The process is not only multi-directional, but it also never ends and is accelerated by the rapid development of technology. Although it is becoming impossible to define yi/justice, however it also becomes necessary, as it is the totem, accepted universally, which can be used against the abuse of power and which can facilitate the acceptance and accommodation of differences.

References

Baxi, Upendra, *The Future of Human Rights* (Oxford & New York: Oxford University Press, 2002).

Bhabha, Homi, *The Location of Culture* (London & New York: Routledge, 1994).

Brietzke, Paul, 'The Politics of Legal Reform' (2004) 3 *Washington University Global Studies Law Review* 1–62.

Carasik, Lauren, '"Think Glocal, Act Glocal": The Praxis of Social Justice Lawyering in the Global Era' (2008) 15 *Clinical Law Review* 55–129.

Chan, Stephen, 'Buddhism and Human Rights' in Rhona Smith & Christien Van Den Anker, (eds), *The Essentials of Human Rights* (Spain: Hodder Arnold, 2005), 25–31.

Chang, Hsiao-hung, *Fake Globalization* (TaiWan: Unitas, 2007).

Chen, Guu-ying, 'The Perspective of li of Pre-*Qin* Daoism' (trans., original: 先秦道家之禮觀) in Chen Guu-ying & Da-wen Feng (trans., original: 冯达文), (ed), *Daoist Philosophy and Daoist Religion (trans., original: 道家与道教)* (GuangZhou: GuangZhou People's Publishing House, 2001), 39–61.

Chen, Kuan-hsing, *Towards De-Imperialization: Asian as Method* (TaiPei: Flaneur, 2006).

Chiu, Man-chung, *Ambiguity Desire Law 迷糊 情欲 法律* (Hong Kong: XinHua 新华, 2006).

Chiu, Man-chung, *De/Sexing Hong Kong Law* (Hong Kong: Red Publish, 2017).

Chu, Yiu-wai, *Post-Orientalism* (TaiPei: LuoTuo 骆驼, 1994).

Colebrook, Claire, *Gilles Deleuze* (London & New York: Routledge, 2002).

Cornell, Drucilla, *The Philosophy of the Limit* (New York: Routledge, 1992).

Cornell, Drucilla, *The Imaginary Domain* (London: Routledge, 1995).

Cornell, Drucilla, *Moral Images of Freedom: A Future for Critical Theory* (New York: Rowman and Littlefield, 2008).

Cotterrell, Roger, *Law, Culture and Society: Legal Ideas in the Mirror of Social Theory* (Britain: Ashgate, 2006).

Deleuze, Gilles, *Difference and Repetition* (New York: Columbia University Press, 1994).

Deng, Zheng-lai, *Where does Chinese Jurisprudence Go? (trans., original: 中国法学向何处去)* (BeiJing: Commercial Press, 2006).

Derrida, Jacques, 'Force of Law' in Drucilla Cornell, Michael Rosenfeld & David Gray Carlson, (eds), *Deconstruction and the Possibility of Justice* (New York: Routledge, 1992), 3–67.

Douzinas, Costas & Warrington, Ronnie, 'The Face of Justice: A Jurisprudence of Alterity' (1994) 3 *Social and Legal Studies* 405–425.

Fang, Li-tian & Xue Yu, (eds), *Buddhist Tradition and Contemporary Culture (trans., original: 佛教传统与当代文化)* (BeiJing: ZhongHua 中华, 2006).

Fang, Li-tian, *Chinese Buddhist Culture* (*trans., original:* 中国佛教文化) (Hong Kong: Joint Publication, 2008).

Fu, Zi-tang, (ed), *Lectures on Jurisprudence (trans., original: 法理学讲演录) Vol 3* (BeiJing: Law Press, 2008).

Gillespie, John, 'Towards a Discursive Analysis of Legal Transfers into Developing East Asia' (2008a) 41 *New York University Journal of International Law and Politics* 658–721.

Gillespie, John, 'Developing a Decentred Analysis of Legal Transfers' in Penelope Nicholson & Sarah Biddulph, (eds), *Examining Practice, Interrogating Theory: Comparative Legal Studies in Asia* (Boston: Martinus Nijhoff Publishers, 2008b), 25–69.

Gong-Pi, Xiang (trans., original: 公丕祥), *The Challenge of Modernization of Legal System (trans., original: 法制现代化的挑战)* (WuChang: WuHan University, 2006).

Grosz, Elizabeth, *Time Travels – Feminism, Nature, Power* (Durham: Duke University Press, 2005).

Habermas, Jürgen, *Truth and Justification* (Cambridge, MA: The MIT Press, 2005).

Harding, Andrew, 'Global Doctrine and Local Knowledge Law in South East Asia' (2002) 51(1) *ICLQ* 35–53.

Harasym, Sarah, *The Postcolonial Critic: Interviews, Strategies, Dialogues* (London: Routledge, 1990).

Hu, Xiao-guang (trans., original: 胡晓光) 'Alaya-Vijñāna: an Opinion (阿赖耶识刍议)' (1999) 4 *FaYin 法音* 9.

Hu, Shui-jun (trans., original: 胡水君), *Political Analysis of Law (trans., original: 法律的政治分析)* (BeiJing: Peking University Press, 2005).

Ito, Takatoshi, *Critical Research on Chinese Buddhism (trans., original: 佛教中国化的批判性研究)* (Hong Kong: EconWorld, 2004).

Jiang, Shan (trans., original: 江山), *Jurisprudence of Interpersonal Isomorphistic-structuralism (trans., original: 人际同构的法哲学)* (BeiJing: China University of Political Science and Law, 2002).

Jiang, Shi-gong, *Legal System and Administration (trans., original: 法制与治理)* (BeiJing: China University of Political Science and Law, 2003).

Joe Tom Sun, 'Psychology in Primitive Buddhism' in Anthony Molino, (ed), *The Couch and the Tree: Dialogues in Psychoanalysis and Buddhism* (New York: North Point Press, 1998), 3–11.

Kennedy, Helena, *Just Law* (Britain: Vintage, 2005).

Koller, John, *Asian Philosophies* (4th ed, New Jersey: Prentice Hall, 2002).

Legrand, Pierre, 'What "Legal Transplants"?' in Nelken David & Johannes Feest, (eds), *Adapting Legal Cultures* (Oxford: Hart, 2001), 55–70.

Lin, Dennis 'The Proscription of Online Male Queer Obscenity in Taiwan' in Yin-bin Ning & Josephine Ho, (eds), *Taking Pornography Seriously* (ZhongLi: National Central University of TaiWan, 2008), 77–95.

Lin, Duan, 'The Chinese Traditional Legal Culture: Kadi Justice or the Third Realm?' (2007) 6 *Sino-Western Legal Tradition (trans., original: 中西法律传统)* 425–453.

Lin, Wai-yi (trans., original: 林纬毅), *The Engagement of faism and Confucianism (trans., original: 法儒兼容)* (Taipei: WenJin 文津, 2004).

Liu, De-ming, 'The Transplant Effect of the Chinese Patent law' (2006) 5 *Chinese Journal of International Law* 733–751.

Merry, Sally Engle, 'From Law and Colonialism to Law and Globalization' (2003) 28 *Law & Soc. Inquiry* 569–589.

Milovanovic, Dragon, 'Diversity, Law and Justice: A Deleuzian Semiotic View of "Criminal Justice"' (2007) 20 *International Journal for the Semiotics of Law* 55–79.

Pahuja, Sundhya, 'Beheading the Hydra: Legal Positivism and Development' (2007) (1) *Law, Social Justice & Global Development Journal*, available at: http://go.warwick.ac.uk/lgd/2007_1/pahuja (visited 17 May 2009).

Pan, Li-ping, *Concept of Harmony in Chinese Legal System (trans., original: 中华法系的和谐理念)* (BeiJing: Law Press, 2006).

Peerenboom, Randall, 'Mixed Reception: Culture, International Norms, and Legal Change in East Asia' (2006) 27 *Michigan Journal of International Law* 823–871.

Rawls, John, *A Theory of Justice* (Cambridge, MA: Harvard University Press, 1971).

Rawls, John, *Political Liberalism* (New York: Columbia University Press, 1993).

Raz, Joseph, *Ethics in the Public Domain: Essays in the Morality of Law and Politics* (Oxford: Clarendon Press, 1994).

Reitz, John, 'Export of the Rule of Law' (2003) 13 *Transnational Law and Contemporary Problems* 464, 472.

Rickett, Allyn, (trans.), *Guan Zi* (Boston & Worcester: Cheng and Tsui, 2001).

Ross, Andrew, 'Components of Cultural Justice' in Austin Sarat & Thomas Kearns, (eds), *Law in the Domains of Culture* (United States of America: University of Michigan Press, 2005), 203–228.

Safran, Jeremy, 'Introduction' in Jeremy Safran, (ed), *Psychoanalysis and Buddhism: An Unfolding Dialogue* (Boston: Wisdom, 2003), 1–34.

Taishō Tripiṭaka Editorial Committee (trans., original: 大藏经刊行委员会) *Taishō Tripiṭaka* (TaiPei: XinWenFeng 新文丰, 1986).

Teubner, Gunther, 'Legal Irritants, Good Faith in British Law or How Unifying Law Ends UP in New Divergences' (1998) 61(1) *Modern Law Review* 11–32.

Von Benda-Beckmann, Franz, & Von Benda-Beckmann, Keebet, 'Transnationalisation of Law, Globalisation and Legal Pluralism: A Legal Anthropological Perspective' in Christoph Antons & Volkmar Gessner, (eds), *Globalization and Resistance: Law Reform in Asia since the Crisis* (Oxford: Hart, 2007), 53–81.

Wang, Ze-ying (trans., original: 王泽应), *ZiRan Yu DaoDe 自然与道德* (ChangSha: HuNan University Press, 2003).

Wang, Jiang-yu, 'The Rule of Law in China: A Realistic View of the Jurisprudence, the Impact of the WTO, and the Prospects for Future Development' (2004a) *Sing J. Legal Stud.* 347–389.

Wang, Qing-jie, *Heidegger and a Hermeneutical Interpretation of Confucianism and Daoism* (BeiJing, RenMin University Press, 2004b).

Yan, Yao-zhong, *Buddhist Vinaya and Chinese Society (trans., original 佛教戒律与中国社会)* (ShangHai: ShangHai GuJi上海古籍, 2007).

Yang, He-gao, *History of Chinese Legal Philosophy (trans., original: 新编中国法律思想史)* (HeFei: University of AnHui, 1997).

Yang, Wai-zhong, *A Research of the Nature of Mind of Chinese Buddhism (trans., original: 中国佛教心性论研究)* (BeiJing: Religious Culture, 2007).

Yu, Xing-zhong, *Rule of Law and Civil Orders* (BeiJing: Chinese University of Politics and Law Press, 2006).

Zhao, Dun-hua (trans., original: 赵敦华), *Rawls's Theory of Justice: A Comment (trans., original: 劳斯的正义论解说)* (Hong Kong: Joint Publication, 1988).

Zhou, Dong-ping, (2020) 'Impact of Buddhism on Chinese Legal Tradition' (trans, original: 论中国传统法律中的佛教影响 6 *Journal of Xiamen University (Arts and Social Sciences)* (2020) 131–140.

Part II
Becoming Justice, Desiring Transformation

Chapter 4
Un/Controlling Desire, Becoming Others: Negotiating Justice in the Hong Kong Milieu of the Mainland Pregnant Women Influx

4.1 Introduction

In 2011, the increasing number of Mainland pregnant women using Hong Kong's obstetrics services ignited/brought to the surface the continuing (yet implicit) conflict between Mainlanders and HongKongians.[1] The tension started with the competition for medical facilities, and extended to many other amenities including social welfare and housing; hence, a binarism of Mainlanders/Locust vs HongKongians/Dogs[2] developed fast and strong in the mass media and internet. In this chapter, I attempt to construct a philosophical perspective by which justice can be created and engineered in this context, by comparing and engaging three philosophical paradigms—Rawlsian justice, Buddhist equality and Deleuzian becoming. I argue that the three philosophical perspectives interact with different views on desire and identity; it is also through desire and identity that these three philosophical perspectives engage with each other and are sensitized towards each other's weak points. While John Rawls proposes a very well-structured set of principles for producing procedures to settle conflicts justly, caused by different life plans, which are the realization of different desires; both Buddhism and Deleuzian philosophy ask respectively if it is possible to manufacture an adiscursive identity and machine of justice creation. However, then can Buddhism and Deleuzian theory, which contradict each other with their respective views on desire, develop a positive step-by-step guideline, as Rawlsian formulae tend to do, to release the current tension? In this chapter, I discuss the possibility of developing a pathway through which the three paradigms can cooperate, in the context of the Mainlanders vs HongKongians conflict.

This chapter is derived in part from an article published in *Beijing Law Review* (2012) Scientific Research Publishing.

[1] The number of Mainland pregnant women giving birth in Hong Kong has risen from 27,000 in 2007 to 40,000 in 2010, *HK Liberal Studies*, available at: http://www.hkliberalstudies.com/modules/question/index.php?pa=viewads&lid=27 (visited 11 Mar 2012).

[2] For details of the related debate, please see the Sect. 4.6 Conclusion of this Chapter.

M.-C. Chiu, *Transforming the Hong Kong Legal Machine*,
https://doi.org/10.1007/978-981-19-1272-6_4

Let us start with an introduction to the conflict.

4.2 Production and Intensification of Mainlanders vs HongKongians Binarism

The conflict between Mainlanders and HongKongians started in March 2011, when the influx of Mainland pregnant women (whose husbands can be either residents or non-residents of Hong Kong) seemed to be depriving Hong Kong mothers-to-be of the opportunity to enjoy the medical services provided by Hong Kong's hospitals.[3] The Hong Kong SAR Government, in order to deal with the intensifying discontent among locals, formulated a few new policies: (1) Increasing the cost–raising the obstetrics package fee for non-local pregnant women on 4 March 2011;[4] (2) Setting a quota–starting in March 2011, Hong Kong public hospitals had stopped taking non-local pregnant women until the end of 2011. In April 2011, the Hong Kong SAR Government agreed to put a cap on the number of non-local pregnancy cases at 88,000 per year.[5] In May, 2011, the government set up a working group to determine the number of births that public hospitals could handle every year; (3) Issuing Booking Confirmation Certificates–after the government had urged the private hospitals to reject doctors if they were found issuing booking confirmation certificates[6] to non-local pregnant women before they came for assessment, the

---

[3] Wu, Kane, 'Great Expectations in Hong Kong', *China Daily*, 11 Mar 2011, H4. According to a report, 'A local man, whose mainland wife is due to give birth in November [2011], still cannot find an obstetric bed in Hong Kong [in July 2011]…The husband said that in the past few months he had contacted all 10 local private hospitals with maternity series and more than 30 doctors in a bid to secure a bed. '"All of them say they can't help us, some can only put us on a waiting list, but they say the chance is slim," he said.' (Tam, Fiona & Lee, Ella, 'Mainland wives rush to book hospital beds', *South China Morning Post*, 21 Jul 2011, CITY3).

[4] Wu, Kane, 'Great Expectations in Hong Kong', *China Daily* 11 Mar 2011, H4. The Hong Kong SAR Government in fact had already started a booking system for non-local pregnant women in February 2007: They are required to pay HK$ 39,000 when they make the appointment; the Hospital Authority would then issue them a booking confirmation certificate and only with that certificate, the non-local pregnant women (including Mainland pregnant women) can cross the border. For those using the facilities in Hong Kong hospital without prior booking—in theory, they could not cross the border—they would have to pay HK$ 48,000. The court, in *Fok Chun-wa* v *The Hospital Authority and The Secretary for Food and Health* FACV 10/2011, para 33, held that, although the policy is discriminatory against Mainlanders, since status of residence is not part of core human right values, such a policy is legitimate especially in the context where resources are limited. (para 77).

[5] Chong, Dennis, 'Border block urged to ease birth pains for hospitals', *Hong Kong Standard*, 6 Apr 2011, page 7. But the doctors working in public hospitals suggested a more rigourous measure: All pregnant Mainlanders whose husbands are not Hong Kong residents, should be banned from using Hong Kong obstetrics services. But, Chun-ying Leung, the then Chief Executive-elect on 16 April 2012 announced that there will be a '"zero quota" for pregnant mainland women whose husbands are non-residents,' starting in 2013. ('Doors shuts on moms' *Hong Kong Standard*, 17 Apr 2012).

[6] Ng, Yuk-hang, 'HK to tighten checks on mainland mums', *South China Morning Post*, 29 Apr 2011, EDT 3.

government then decided to centralize the issue of certification and new guidelines were issued—women whose pregnancies did not look normal would not be allowed to give birth in Hong Kong;[7] and (4) Tightening border controls–Mainland pregnant women without relevant documents (e.g. a Booking Confirmation Certificate) would not be permitted to enter into Hong Kong. Mainland authorities have also taken steps to discourage Mainland pregnant women from using Hong Kong medical facilities: (1) The Family Planning Committee of GuangDong Province stated that any second child of a first-marriage couple, no matter whether s/he was born on the Mainland, would be counted as 'additional', i.e. the parents, should they be civil servants, would be dismissed;[8] and (2) Xiao-dan Zhu, the then Governor of GuangDong Province, stated in March 2012 that any agency that arranged for Mainland pregnant women to travel to Hong Kong would be cracked down upon.[9] Since 2013, neither public nor private hospitals in Hong Kong have been allowed to accept non-local pregnant women (unless they are married to Hong Kong male residents).[10]

When no one knew if the policies could work effectively at the time, the influx of Mainland pregnant women had already given rise to the 'anti-locust' campaign—a campaign initiated by a group of Hong Kong netizens. They raised funds for a front page newspaper advert to criticize Mainlanders who visited Hong Kong, claiming that they, like locusts, were swamping Hong Kong's resources.[11] Also, according to Yung Jhon, one of the organizers of the campaign, Hong Kong residents were also unhappy with the usage of simplified Chinese characters in Hong Kong and the way Mainlanders were 'splashing' their cash on the local property market, leading to record high property prices and rental rates.[12] The 'anti-locust' advertisement, entitled 'HongKongians have had enough', appeared on 25 January 2012, in *Apple Daily*, one of the then best-selling newspapers in Hong Kong.

In response to these accusations, some Mainlanders protested: 'We are not consuming Hong Kong's welfare money. To the contrary, we boost local consumption in Hong Kong and our children might help solve the aging problem it's facing.'[13] This seemed very true as the private hospitals earned approximately HK$ 1 billion each year from treating Mainland pregnant women.[14] The editorial of the *South*

[7] See also *Fok Chun-wa* v *The Hospital Authority and The Secretary for Food and Health* FACV 10/2011, para 33.

[8] Wu, Kane, 'Great Expectations in Hong Kong', *China Daily*, 11 Mar 2011, H4.

[9] 'Hong Kong requests China to halt influx of pregnant women', available at: http://www.panarmenian.net/eng/news/91984/ (visited 11 Mar 2012).

[10] 'Arrangements on obstetric services provided by private hospitals to Mainland expectant mothers married to Hong Kong residents in 2013', available at: https://www.dh.gov.hk/english/press/2012/120806-2.html (visited 18 Nov 2020).

[11] Lee, Ada, 'Internet abuzz with "anti-locust" front-page ad drive', *South China Morning Post*, 26 Jan 2012, CITY1.

[12] Chow, Vivienne, 'Anger at mainlander visitors escalates with "locust" ad', *South China Morning Post*, 1 Feb 2012, CITY1.

[13] Wu, Kane, 'Great Expectations in Hong Kong', *China Daily*, 11 Mar 2011, H4.

[14] Chong, Dennis, 'Border block urged to ease birth pains for hospitals', *Hong Kong Standard*, 6 Apr 2011, p. 7. The debate with regard to resources becomes keen when a mock advertisement was uploaded on 26 January 2012 in the internet forum, saying: 'Because you [Hong Kong] are a son,

China Morning Post wrote: 'Given the birth rate here [Hong Kong] is among the world's lowest, there is a strong case for better accommodating Mainland mothers by expanding the capacity of our obstetric services in private hospitals in the longer term. It also reminded us that Hong Kong's medical service was identified by the Hong Kong SAR Government as one of the six pillars for the future economic prosperity'.[15] It is in this context that the following question is asked: 'How could Hong Kong, with such a low birth rate, supported by government policy to develop the medical industry including a reputable hospital system, not provide sufficient beds for local mothers or mainland mothers with local husbands?'.[16]

4.3 Rawlsian Justice: Rationalizing Desire, Devising Justice

Should we argue that the tension between Mainlanders and HongKongians originates from the competition between Mainland pregnant women and HongKongians with regard to the medical resources of Hong Kong is in fact a conflict of desires—the desire to have easier access to Hong Kong resources available? Assuming the resources are limited, Rawlsian theory, 'the strongest theory of political justice we have' in relation to resource distribution,[17] seems to be able to provide a quick fix to the question.[18]

Rarely does the discussion with regard to Rawlsian justice put the emphasis on desire, but when the concepts of good and life plan (which are devised to accommodate different choices and priorities of goods) are put in focus, we will find that how different individual desires can be regulated by the procedure is in fact what Rawlsian theory aims at achieving[19]—the key is not what one person chooses, according to her/his desire, but how s/he chooses.[20] From the Rawlsian point of view, if desire is not rationalized, this will create problems and intensify existing conflicts. Desire,

---

Father [Mainland China] gives you 210 billion yuan a year'; in response, another internet mock advertisement, titled 'Reply from your neighbour', said: 'If the father is giving 210 billion yuan to the son as pocket money, then the son is paying the father an allowance of 680 billion yuan'. For details, please see Chow, Vivienne, 'Anger at mainlander visitors escalates with "locust" ad', *South China Morning Post*, 1 Feb 2012, CITY1.

[15] 'Golden opportunity for medical sector', *South China Morning Post*, 18 Dec 2011, EDT12.

[16] Song, Sio-chong, 'Who causes the hospital beds shortage for local mothers?', *China Daily*, 19 Jan 2012, H3.

[17] Nussbaum (2006), at 24. Please note: According to Rawls, his theory cannot be applied in private zone of life. For details, please see Rawls (1993), at 225, 241.

[18] In the context of Mainland pregnant women's influx, it is commonly believed that there is a limitation of medical services/resources in Hong Kong; for example, Mr. Justice Ma (the then Chief Justice), in *Fok Chun-wa* v *The Hospital Authority and The Secretary for Food and Health* FACV 10/2011, writes: 'In the public sphere, financial resources are limited and decisions have to be made by the Government as to how Hong Kong's finite resources are to be utilized…Manpower resources are also finite: there is no limitless supply of professional or skilled people.' (para 10).

[19] Chow (2010), at 1.

[20] Yao (2011), at 10.

after rationalization, becomes and is termed 'good', as it can improve people's life quality.[21] That also explains why Rawls has to assume that the human subject's nature must be free (i.e. no one owns anyone),[22] equal (in terms of power and capacities; this notion of equality leads to the criticism of hierarchy), rational (i.e. everyone can seek to maximize one's self interest by forming social contracts and facilitating social cooperation),[23] and reasonable (only if a person is reasonable, can s/he respect other's interests, i.e. realizing the principles of reciprocity and mutuality);[24] because only with such human nature, desire will and can be put under control, and individual life plans could be regulated and accommodated by principles and related procedures. Put simply, desire would not then disturb social cooperations and intensify any existing and possible conflicts.

Rawls also assumes that everyone can put herself/himself into the position of others.[25] A Rawlsian human subject also has the capacity for a sense of justice; and a capacity for a conception of good;[26] in other words, everyone would (1) accept and understand that the others also accept Rawlsian justice; and (2) believe that social institutions can help realize justice.[27]

Rawlsian principles of justice start with fairness and are developed with Rawls's faith in social contract traditions,[28] 'with their emphasis on mutual advantage as the goal of social cooperation'.[29] Therefore, to Rawls, society is 'a cooperative venture for mutual advantage':[30] From this philosophical paradigm, Rawls develops a set of principles through which desire can be regulated and thus justice can be created: (1) '[E]ach person is to have an equal right to the most extensive basic liberty compatible with a similar liberty for others'; and (2) Social and economic inequalities are acceptable if they are arranged (a) to the greatest benefit to the least advantaged, and (b) attached to the 'offices and positions open to all under the conditions of equality of opportunity'.[31] Hence, according to Rawlsian principles and related procedures, even though inequality is preordained, when it is accepted by the marginalized powerless

---

[21] Lin (2008), at 32; Yao (2011), at 148.

[22] Nussbaum (2006), at 28.

[23] Lin (2008), at 6.

[24] Yao (2011), at 5, 6, 7. Rawlsian assumptions about the human subject is always under criticism—as Martha Nussbaum points out: the Rawlsian notion of the human subject excludes people who are mentally and physical challenged; and Rawlsian version of equality is blind towards the unequal distribution of authority and opportunity. Nussbaum (2006), at 29, 31.

[25] Chow (2010), at 193.

[26] Rawls (1993), at 302.

[27] Yao (2011), at 7.

[28] Nussbaum (2006), at 11.

[29] Nussbaum (2006), at 58.

[30] Rawls (1971), at 4, 126.

[31] Rawls (1971), at 60, 83.

in a society, it becomes positive and productive. In other words, Rawls's proposal can prevent inequality from being gross and extreme, and is able to construct hope for the socially marginalized.[32] It is important to note that, the above principles operate in a lexical order.

Therefore, according to Rawls, if social institutions (including law and medical services) can formulate sets of procedures, following his principles, then justice can be produced even when there are conflicts, created by different regulated individual desires and related rational plans of life.[33] Hence, an ideal social cooperation (law making institutions, law enforcement and hospitals), according to Rawls, devised to resolve the conflicts, should be conducted by rules and procedures, which are accepted by the public.[34]

4.3.1 Rawlsian Perspective on Law and Justice

In sum, what Rawls aims to construct ultimately by devising these principles is a set of 'correct' procedures; as he believes that only through these can a correct outcome—justice and fairness—be guaranteed in a society. If justice is the most important value for society and social structures, including law,[35] it is hence not surprising when Peter Feng said: It is the duty of law to guarantee the realization of justice.[36] Amartya Sen also points out:

> John Rawls's rightly celebrated approach of 'justice as fairness' yields a unique set of 'principles of justice' that are exclusively concerned with setting up 'just institutions…while requiring that people's behavior complies entirely with the demands of proper functioning of these institutions.[37]

Rawlsian theory is well accepted by the Hong Kong Judiciary—Mr. Justice Geoffrey Ma, the then Chief Justice of Hong Kong, offers a very clear definition of justice in the context of Hong Kong:

---

32 Zhao (1988), at 151.

33 Chow (2010), at 188.

34 Rawls (1971), at 62, 95.

35 Yao (2011), at 2, Barry (2005), at 16.

36 Feng (2007), at 40. This view is further elaborated by Brian Barry, who writes: 'Institutions [including law making organization, law enforcement agencies, law courts, law schools and prisons] are obviously key to the realization of social justice'. (Barry 2005, at 17).

37 Sen (2009), at xi. Whether there is any essential and natural relationship between law and justice always brings keen debate: Costas Douzinas and Ronnie Warrington argue that: Justice always lies in future and there is a distance between justice and law. Jacques Derrida also points out that it is impossible for justice to be present in law. For details, please see Douzinas & Warrington (1994); Derrida (1992).

> Justice requires that no one is above the law; in other words, equality. Justice also requires that an individual's rights and liberties must be protected even as against what may be the views of the majority of the public.[38]

Analysing the conflict between Mainlanders and HongKongians from a Rawlsian perspective, we can ask: Did the influx of Mainland pregnant women really deprive Hong Kong pregnant women of the opportunities to use the local medical services? Would the new law and regulation negatively affect the opportunity of Mainland pregnant women to use Hong Kong's medical facilities? Would the new law and regulation benefit the least advantaged groups? Would the new law and regulation guarantee that everyone can enjoy the opportunity in terms of medical services? However, there are a few questions that we need to tackle before we can answer the above questions: Are Mainlanders and HongKongians coming from the same society? If both groups cannot share the same view on justice and social institutions (including law and medical services), then is it possible for them to form a social contract with mutual advantages? If the answer is no, then another question arises: Can the Rawlsian formulae of justice work between societies, when there is a (power) difference?[39]

4.4 Mahāyāna Buddhist Schools of Vijñānamatra 唯识: Going Beyond Desire, Constructing Justice

Justice under Buddhism, as with Rawlsian theory, also starts with the control of desire and pursuit of equality.[40] When compared to Rawls, Buddhism provides a more detailed analysis of desire. There is more than one type of desire classification:[41] (a) Nature of desire: The desire for wholesome dharma[42] (good desire, 善法欲) and neutral desire; and (b) Number of desire.[43] In this chapter, I will use the classification used by Shih Chao Hwei in 'Emotional Connection and Desire: A Buddhist Perspective'. In that article, Shih Chao Hwei, relating Freudian theory to

---

[38] Ma, Geoffrey, 'CJ's speech at Ceremonial Opening of the Legal Year 2011', available at: http://www.info.gov.hk/gia/general/201101/10/P201101100201.htm (visited 4 Feb 2012).

[39] Nussbaum (2006), at 19.

[40] Engel & Engel (2010), at 128. I argue that both Buddhism (with equality as one of the highest principles) and Confucianism (with their emphasis on 'self-respect') offer two good matching points for Rawlsian theory to engage with Han-Chinese 汉族华人 socio-legal culture. For more discussion, please see Chap. 2.

[41] Chen (2007), at 926.

[42] 'Dharma' means the natural order which is discovered by enlightened beings: 'Dharma gets manifested in our moral actions of our present and future lives, that is, through karmic laws.' Mitra (2018), at 163.

[43] There are different views on the number of desires: Two (non sacred desire, like want for wife and asset; and sacred desire, like seeking Nirvāṇa 涅盘), three (eat, sleep and sex), four (asset, fame, health and longevity), etc. For details, please see Chen (2007), at 926–931.

Vijñānamatra 唯识,[44] proposes that there are five basic desires, which are developed from Avidyā 无明 (ignorance towards universe and life):[45] sight 色, sound 声, smell 香, taste 味 and touch 触. These desires correspond to the five consciousness 识 (vijñāna): Visual perception 眼识, auditory perception 耳识, olfactory perception 鼻识, gustatory perception 舌识, and tactile perception 身识 -- the five senses. Besides the five senses, there are three other senses: Mind-consciousness (sense-centred consciousness, 意识 , Mano-vijñāna), ego-consciousness (末那识, Mana-vijñāna) and storehouse-consciousness (阿赖耶识, Alaya-vijñāna).[46]

While the five senses can only respond to respective phenomena (e.g. visual perception can only be reactive towards sight); mind-consciousness responds to all five senses-related activities, and is sensitive towards the differences between perceived phenomena (e.g. huge vs. small, loud vs. silence); and the differences between past, present and future. Ego-consciousness is the source of insistent attachments and self-centredness, as it always takes the subjective images (见分, Dṛṣṭi) created by storehouse-consciousness as the objective and unchanged phenomenon. More unfortunately, the insistency created by ego-consciousness inevitably deeply affects the judgement made by mind-consciousness. Ego-consciousness therefore is called Klesa-vijñāna, the consciousess/vijñāna which contaminates others.[47] Storehouse-consciousness is the storehouse of seeds (种子, Bīja).

The universe manufactured by the consciousness machine is not objective—the so-called objective appearance (相分, Nimitta), perceived by a subject, is a projection of consciousness (e.g. visual perception) that is driven by the seeds in storehouse-consciousness. When and where that machine functions depends on the strength of different conditions 缘, both physical and mental, which can be felt, subjectively, by the subjective images of a consciousness. So, an objective identity (like a Mainlander) does not exist, and how a person perceives the identity of another person is a subjective exercise, although s/he may mis-take that for an objective phenomenon.[48]

From the perspective of Vijñānamatra, all phenomena are the products of three consciousness machines: The Nature of Dependent on Other (依他起自性. Paratantra-svabhāva), Reproduction of Fallacious Knowledge (遍计所执性, Parikalpita-vabhāva), and The Perfect True Nature (圆成实性; Parlinispanna-vabhāva):

(1) The Nature of Dependent on Other: The machine works closely with conditions, it itself does not have any intrinsic nature and has no particular insistent attachments.

(2) Reproduction of Fallacious Knowledge: As mind-consciousness always respond to five senses, this consciousness machine can cover every phenomenon

---

[44] Shih Chao Hwei (2011), at 71.

[45] Bagula Mukhi (2011), 'The circle of life revolved around avidya, desire & Karma', available at: http://www.free-news-release.com/The-circle-of-life-revolved-around-avidya-desire-amp-Karma-Detail_175778.html (visited 20 Mar 2012).

[46] For more discussion on Vijñānamatra, please see Chap. 1.

[47] Lau (2020), at 30.

[48] Yu (2019), at 73–74.

on the surface of the earth; however, as ego-consciousness is the reference of mind-consciousness, this machine is full of bias and extremely self-centred. This machine, following ego-consciousness, hence takes Dṛṣṭi as Nimitta. For example: A person with a Hong Kong birth certificate may think: 'Since you are an un-civilized Mainlander, you must not come and steal Hong Kong resources, created and contributed to by us', and thus reproducing an illusory Mainlander vs. Hong Kongian binarism.

(3) The Perfect True Nature aims to achieve two emptiness – self-emptiness and phenomenon-emptiness. Emptiness does not mean nothingness; it is an attempt to neutralize the influence of ego-consciousness and thus forgo over-insistencies.[49] Only through giving up all sorts of over-insistencies, can a person understand and implement the ultimate truth (真如, Bhūtatathatā), advocated by Buddhism. It is therefore the opposite of the Reproduction of Fallacious Knowledge. The Perfect True Nature will therefore abandon intrinsic nature and problematize the related hierarchal binarism (e.g. Mainlander vs Hong Kongian).

In other words, the Nature of Dependent on Other is describing how a consciousness machine works, while the Reproduction of Fallacious Knowledge insists that the machine has to be insistent; the Perfect True Nature, from a Buddhist perspective, advocates the theory of emptiness and attempts to neutralize the influence of the Reproduction of Fallacious Knowledge; arguing that being insistent will simply reproduce imaginary illusions.

With the rise of the Perfect True Nature, a person should start critically reflecting on the social rules developed and advocated by the majority and no longer judge the perceptions with reference to them solely. S/He also stops desiring and insisting on their worldview as the hegemonic standard (of law) and/or imposing it on others (Mainlanders). A person should be sensitized to the condition of unjust discrimination where there are less resourceful groups, including the pregnant women who cannot fully enjoy the medical services in Hong Kong (not essentially Mainland/Hong Kong pregnant women), and hence would start assisting and empowering the powerless (e.g. those pregnant women who cannot fully enjoy the medical facilities in Hong Kong), for instance, by drafting and enacting new laws and policies. In short, only when the Reproduction of Fallacious Knowledge is replaced by the Perfect True Nature, will the desire to be self-centred (gradually) disappear and can equality among lives be substantiated.

As Li-tian Fang points out, going beyond any insistences and related desires, accepting differences and producing equality are the ultimate goals of Buddhist practice.[50] Simon Duffy also writes about Buddhist equality:

---

[49] For details, please see Chap. 2.

[50] Fang (2008), at 138.

> Neither the self nor others, nor the relations of identity or difference among persons exist ultimately…It is therefore inappropriate to arbitrarily favour self over other, and not to take the suffering of others seriously.[51]

4.5 The Deleuzian Machine of Justice: Becoming the Least Advantaged Group

Gilles Deleuze has a very different understanding of desire: While Buddhists have multiple classifications and definitions of desires, Deleuze, like Friedrich Nietzsche, believes that desire, being instinctive, elementary, original and authentic, is the greatest power of life.[52] He argues that the object of desire is in fact a 'social formation' or 'infrastructure'—only when it injects desire into social formation, is Lacanian/Žižekian lack produced.[53] Deleuze hence always stresses the 'positivity' and 'productivity' of desire:[54] Deleuzian desire, with such power and energy, plays an important role in the creation of subjects and revolution.[55] A subject (including justice, law and identity) is always a product of connections, disconnections and reconnections, which are parts of a machine.[56] Félix Guattari, using the walkman as an example, gives a very good elaboration of how subject creation works:

> What it [walkman] is doing is inventing a musical universe, a different relation with musical objects: music that comes from within and not from somewhere outside. In other words, what it is doing is inventing a new perception.[57]

The creation is driven by different machinic assemblages and formulated by two lines of forces—desire and social force (including law courts, legislature, NGOs, hospitals and media).[58] Deleuze argues that social force always wants to capture and regulate desire, which provides the energy for the operation of assemblage,[59] and

---

[51] Duffy, Simon (2014) 'Deleuze, Spinoza and the question of reincarnation in the Mahāyāna tradition', paper presented in Deleuze's Cultural Encounters with the New Humanities, a conference organized by Hong Kong Shue Yan University, Hong Kong Baptist University and Chinese University of Hong Kong, on 9 Jun 2014.

[52] De Bolle (2010), at 8.

[53] Parr (2006); Smith (2012), at 188; Smith (2016), at 275.

[54] Goodley (2007), at 147. Desire, to Deleuze, means state of impulses and drives: 'Drives are simply the desiring-machines themselves.' (Deleuze & Guattari 1977, at 35). Please also see Smith (2012), at 182.

[55] Smith (2016), at 280.

[56] As Claire Colebrook illustrates: A machine is 'nothing more than its connections'. (Colebook 2002, at 56).

[57] Guattari & Rolnik (2008), at 45.

[58] According to Deleuze, while social forces are always sedimentary and rigid; desire flows freely and preexists humans. As Claire Colebrook writes: 'Life is a flow of desire' (Colebrook 2002, at 142). Please also see Deleuze & Guattari (1977); and Jun (2009). It seems desire is the key driver of machine: 'It is axiomatic for Deleuze and Guattari that no technical machine can exist without the prior investment of desire'. (Buchanan 2008, at 17).

[59] De Bolle (2010), at 17.

fixates a subject, through repetition and codification. As a result, certain procedures and qualities are read as universal marks[60] —a process of territorialization (e.g. Mainlanders are labeled as robbers of Hong Kong's limited resources).[61]

Territorialization does not nonetheless signify the end of subject creation—Deleuzian desires, which are always stronger and more powerful,[62] cannot be eternally controlled by molar lines of social force: Lines of desire are always multiple and contested—there are always simultaneously different/new types of desire (the desire to give birth to babies in Hong Kong may not have been very popular among Mainlanders before the 1970s) and social forces (e.g. new laws and new institutions);[63] so, (new) machines, driven by different forces, can connect, disconnect and reconnect with other machines; one machine can never be reduced to any singular connection, as machines are always fluid and dynamic.[64]

Deleuze argues that the molar lines of social forces are rhizomatic (not aberrant, as the social forces themselves assume) and thus lack an origin or a centre, and molecular lines of desire cannot be predicted, so subjects can only be multiple.[65] Hence, it is not surprising that deterritorialization (and revolution) initiated by desire (which then creates affect and thus action;[66] i.e. the lines of flight) are always created at the weaker edge of the rhizomatic matrix, where challenges coming from the desire that fuels the lines of flight, can easily take place.[67] Deterritorialization can be translated and fulfilled in the social force machine/assemblages, as argued by Jamie Murray.[68] Along with the deterritorialization (and thus revolution), the process of becoming starts and never ends.

Deleuze thus advocates that every concept/identity; especially the powerless, is always a 'becoming' and is thus nomadic, i.e. different in itself.[69] But, as Damian Sutton and David Martin-Jones point out, reterritorialization always happens, especially when the force of the deterritorialization and the desire that drives it is not strong enough. So becoming, as Levi Bryant said, would always contain contradictions and oppositions;[70] as lines of flight always take off after de/territorialization,

---

[60] Colebrook (2002), at 45.

[61] Rose (2000).

[62] Murray (2013), at 134.

[63] Winslade (2009), at 336, 337.

[64] Jun (2009), at 351.

[65] Linstead & Pullen (2006).

[66] As Michael Hardt writes: To the extent that our power to be affected is filled by active affections, it relates directly to our power to act, but to the extent it is filled by passive affections, it relates only to our power to feel or suffer. Passive affections really mark our lack of power. (Hardt 1993, at 92).

[67] Sutton & Martin-Jones (2008), at 6; Rizzo (2012).

[68] Murray (2013), at 48.

[69] Deleuze (1995), at 173, Lorraine (2011), at 76; Rizzo (2012), at 54. As Roland Faber elaborates: '[T]he event of becoming is the process by which nothing that happens is, in its subjective/objective moments, a predicate of an underlying substrate; rather, that which becomes repeats and alters patterns, structures, or modes of existence in order to become what it seems to be from the outset, but only is by re-instantiating such patterns in new events' (Faber 2011, at 13).

[70] Bryant (2008), at 58.

with the emergence and influx of different desires, challenging the hegemony of the powerful.[71] In other words, any effort to fixate a subject (like Hong Kong people as victim of the swamp of resources) or develop a universal and timeless formula for justice (as Rawls did), are doomed to be a failure; this echoes with Buddhism—deterritorialization always produces differences and resistance, which respect equality and challenge any fixed formula, although such resistance may not always be strong enough to subvert a rigid and territorialized social structure.[72]

Becoming does not mean identifying or imitating; but affecting.[73] Becoming is not a journey with a starting point and an end goal. It is a 'line-bloc' between two elements; and through becoming, both elements are transformed from their respective existing comfort zones.[74]

As elaborated by Ian Buchanan: Deleuzian desire therefore sows the seeds of revolution as it always tries to elude the coding imposed by lines of social force.[75] The Deleuzian notion of justice must be able to release desire (while the social force will not disappear suddenly and/or totally);[76] because only through this, would all 'attempts to ground any reasoning, rationale, or logic on some object measure' be destroyed and torn off.[77] In other words, according to Deleuze, justice would only be created when becoming and deterritorialization happen, where all layers and connections are broken by lines of flight initiated by the liberation of desire. This paradigm of justice, as Jami Weinstein puts it, will evoke better concepts to resolve the problems to which any attempt at developing a monolithic formula of justice was originally linked.[78] But Loretta Capeheart and Dragon Milovanovic also warn us: Moving away from any monolithic formula means moving away from an evaluative standard, which therefore may mean the development of unintentionally 'negative' consequences.[79]

4.5.1 The Deleuzian Perspective on Law and Justice

As justice is a kind of becoming, created by different lines of desire and social institutions (social control and law), it is impossible to develop and devise an ahistoric notion of the subject and an acontextual formula and procedure of justice construction (as per Rawlsian principles). Further, since Deleuzian desire has a very different definition, not only does it mean desires cannot be listed exhaustively, as a Rawlsian

---

71 Smith (1997), at xlv; Silberstein (2006), at 150. Bankston, in fact, titled 'line of flight' as 'radical deterritorialization'. (Bankston 2017, at 178).

72 Bell (2011), at 71.

73 Wilson (2019), 56–73.

74 Bankston (2017), at 96.

75 Buchanan (2008), at 45.

76 Bankston (2017), at 31, 64.

77 Capeheart & Milovanovic (2007), at 125.

78 Weinstein (2008), at 23.

79 Capeheart & Milovanovic (2007), at 135.

list of goods tries to do, but a Deleuzian would not aim at controlling or going beyond desire, as Buddhists and Rawlsians have advocated, but rather at activating desires so as to generate different lines of flight, that can activate deterritorizations, through which the existing layers and differences (and related discrimination) will be destabilized and challenged. In the words of Alexandre Lefebvre, desire makes law creative, which explains why and how new rights are invented.[80] In the case of the Mainlander vs HongKongian conflict, a Deleuzian will argue that existing desires (e.g. the request of more medical services, the desire of having better and more effective Mainland social institutions, and the mutual discrimination between HongKongians and Mainlanders) have successfully initiated the drive to revise and improve the existing social cooperations (between institutions and between Mainlanders and HongKongians), for example, better possible allocation of medical resources, revision of birth control policy and Race Discrimination Ordinance. (Cap 602, LHK)[81] In short, the conflict, generated by a clash of different desires, is in itself not negative, but productive. And the emergence of multiple desires will not bring society total chaos, as desire would still be influenced by the molar lines, however weak they might be. However, what Deleuzian theory fails to do is to provide a possible step by step formula to create positive and productive changes in the process of destabilization and constructing a positive strategy, and there may be negative consequences—of course, as Deleuzians argue, it is impossible to devise a once and for all solution, because justice is only a becoming, and any wrong will and can be corrected as desires will keep on arising and changes/revisions will be brought about.

4.6 Conclusion

It seems Buddhist philosophy and Deleuzian theory are not compatible with each other: Buddhism assumes that desires can bring negative effects and thus have to be put under control; Deleuze believes that it is good to have new and emerging desires. However, in fact, both share a number of commonalities: (1) Desires are multiple, thus it is impossible to have an exhausted list of desires (and Rawlsian goods)—for a Buddhist, whenever there are seeds, there can be desires; and for a Deleuzian, desires have always existed and keep on generating; (2) Not everyone is totally free (as Rawlsians claim)—for Buddhists, no one can escape from the karma machine (before 'transmutation of consciousness (vijñāna) to wisdom (jñāna)' (转识成智));[82] and for Deleuzians, human subjects are always the product of machines, driven by multiple and diversified lines of desire and social control; (3) There are

---

[80] Lefebvre (2008).

[81] People once argued that the Ordinance should be used to stop the publication of anti-locust advertisements as these obviously constituted racial vilification (Section 45), which is illegal. The Equal Opportunities Commission of Hong Kong clearly stated that as Mainlanders and HongKongians belong to the same Race (Han-Chinese), any conflict between two groups of people could not constitute racial discrimination. ('It is not Racial Discrimination, just tension between groups' (trans., original: 非种族歧视仅种群紧张), *MingPao*, 4 Feb 2012, A8).

[82] For details, please see Chap. 1.

no eternally fixed social layers and—with the development of Buddhist Perfect True Nature, inequality and hierarchal binarism can be eliminated; and with Deleuzian desires and related lines of flight, all existing social demarcations can be challenged—i.e. Deleuzians aim at 'thinking away from the influences of a "dogmatic image"', which creates discrimination, and Buddhists, as clearly argued, aspire to a universe of equality;[83] (4) Law is vital—Buddhism posits that law can help go beyond negative desire, Deleuzian theory claims that law is a product of re/territorialization; aiming to fixate desire; but, of course, this attempt is doomed to be a failure as new desire will groom deterritorialization and reterritorialization, which means existing laws can be repealed, and new laws can emerge; and (5) Equality has to be respected and sustained.

Even though Buddhism and Deleuzian philosophy have two very contradictory views on desire, their perspectives on desire, which leads to multiple understandings of the body, expose the major weak point of Rawlsian theory, i.e. it fails to provide a universally acceptable definition of the least advantaged group which is in turn essential to the construction of the theory. In the context of the Mainland pregnant women influx, the Hong Kong pregnant women who claimed that their opportunities to use Hong Kong's medical facilities are reduced are the least advantaged, but so are the Mainland pregnant women who desire to use the service in Hong Kong—as they have to spend more than HongKongians and their decision to come to Hong Kong is initiated by different desires, including escape from the Mainland birth control policy, a desire to see their offspring enjoy a more efficient medical, social, educational and legal system.[84] But then, when the consciousness, which composes the body, can be transmutated, according to Buddhist Vijñānamatra, is it possible to have a fixed identity? William Waldron summarizes the argument very well:

> In the Buddhist view, what keeps beings trapped in these cyclic patterns is both the deep-seated but mistaken apprehension that we are (or have) an unchanging, independent, self-subsistent entity or 'self' (Ātman) as well as the misguided activities motivated by attachment to such a self. These activities are misguided, the Buddhist assert, because no permanent and independent individuality can actually be found in our worldly existence.[85]

This view resonates with the Deleuzian concept of 'Body without Organs' (BwO hereafter). BwO, which is the medium by which becoming is initiated,[86] also signifying the resistance to any notion of a territorialized body that comes with a whole package of organized and hierarchized organs, is a metaphor for the shifting, interconnected, constantly moving and constructed body.[87] The body therefore keeps on

---

[83] See, Tony (2014) 'The Revolutionary Subject: On Deleuze's Idea of Subjectivity and the Notion of Self in Mahāyāna Buddhism', paper presented in Deleuze's Cultural Encounters with the New Humanities, a conference organized by Hong Kong Shue Yan University, Hong Kong Baptist University and Chinese University of Hong Kong, on 9 Jun 2014.

[84] As Johnny Mok SC indicates in 'Legal Measures to Address Mainland Births in Hong Kong' Symposium, held by University of Hong Kong on 9 Jun 2012, the Mainland pregnant women come to give birth in Hong Kong because of the better medical facilities in the social administrative region.

[85] Waldron (2003), at 1.

[86] Faber (2011), at 13.

[87] Rajchman (2000), at 267.

constructing itself.[88] Using BwO as the lens of scrutiny, we can then ask: Can we naturalize an identity? Why do we have to prioritize a certain dialect, language, or accent in defining an identity?

So the Rawlsian theory seems to be subverted by Buddhist and Deleuzian desire-based justice—people are not free, devising a list of primary goods is not practical and a definition of the least advantaged group is impossible. But this does not mean that the Rawlsian theory is completely useless—no one can deny that protection of the peripherally powerless is a good starting point and in order to fix a problem quickly, a clear set of step-by-step guidelines, as with Rawlsian theory, especially with its emphasis on equal opportunity, can be an efficient starting point. Yet we have to understand that a social contract, which assumes that human subjects are free and there must be mutual advantages, is not possible. So, we should not aim at reaching an agreement that is based on everyone's acceptance of justice; what we should seek is the acceptance and respect of different and changing desires and related changing life plans. This can be achieved by what the Rawlsians advocate: Everyone should step into the shoes of the others (especially the least advantaged);[89] but Buddhists and Deleuzians go further; the former advocate Wisdom of Equality (平等性智, Samata-jñāna), and the latter ask everyone to negotiate a way by which the conflict and tension can be settled and solved by becoming others, which should not only mean the 'powerless', since it is impossible to fixate any identity. 'Becoming others', Paul Patton argues, can create and spawn intra-subjective experiences, leading to production of new perspectives and hence new rights.[90] In short, justice is no longer simply a set of procedures, as argued by Rawls, but an attitude and perspective by which negotiation between parties can start and continue. What we need is to create a new reference, as Guattari said: the powerless 'must create their own modes of reference, their own cartographies, inventing their praxis in order to make breaches in the dominant system of subjectivity.'[91]

Going back to the influx of Mainland pregnant women, we should no longer question whether the desire to give birth in Hong Kong is right or not, but we should be becoming each other—becoming Mainland pregnant women and becoming Hong Kong pregnant women. This does not mean analyzing the situation from a different perspective, but creating an innovative viewpoint that goes beyond either or binarism. So what is needed is not Hong Kong people putting themselves in the shoes of Mainland pregnant women, or vice versa; and certainly not simply balancing different individual rights, but asking the following questions: Are the resources (in Hong Kong) really limited? Why can't the Hong Kong SAR Government spend more on developing medical services as it is one of the pillar industries and can the

[88] Smith (1997), at xxxxvii.

[89] For more discussion on this process from perspectives of Confucianism and Daoism, please see Chaps. 3 and 8.

[90] Patton (2012).

[91] Guattari & Rolnik (2008), at 67.

current medical resources available not even cater to all the needs (not only obstetrics services) of the locals?[92] If the Mainlanders spend so much in Hong Kong, are the resources growing? Is there any way that we can allocate the resources more effectively? In short, we should ask how we feel and what solutions we can propose, in every singular context, if we are becoming the party we challenge and if justice is also a becoming. And from that starting point, we should ask how equal opportunities can be guaranteed, not only by making laws and regulations, but by reflecting on and reviewing existing laws and regulations with regard to new situations (raised by new desires).

The dispute between Mainlanders and HongKongians has been further intensified by three incidents in 2012: (a) Dolce and Gabbana did not allow HongKongians to take photographs outside their Hong Kong flagship store in Harbour City, Tsim Shatsui, while allowing Mainlanders to do so; this incident provoked more than 1,000 people to gather in front of the shop for two consecutive Sundays (8 and 15 January 2012);[93] (b) Professor Qing-dong Kong labelled HongKongians 'running dogs of the British Government' in a Mainland television programme, 'Kong Monk Has Something to Say' 孔和尚有话说, on 19 January 2012, after footage showing a Hong Kong passenger and a Mainland family started quarrelling when the former said the latter should not allow their child to eat in the Mass Transit Railway, where eating and drinking were forbidden, was widely shown; (c) a new entry plan for Mainland cars, announced by the Hong Kong SAR Government on 13 February, 2012, also fuelled the conflict between Mainlanders and HongKongians. According to that scheme, 50 Hong Kong-registered vehicles will be allowed to travel directly into GuangDong per day. However, HongKongians fear that when Mainland-registered cars are allowed to come to Hong Kong, as a possible phase 2 of the programme, it will bring chaos on the roads of Hong Kong, as Mainland drivers are 'famous' for not obeying the rules:

> Our own drivers already have some really bad habits, such as changing lines without signaling, having no respect for pedestrians, and driving aggressively. Such bad behavior is even worse on the mainland. Can we expect these mainland drivers magically to improve once they hit local roads?[94]

When a protest started in February, 7,000 people had made an online pledge to join the demonstration. Also, one of the major political parties, the Democratic Party, also collected 1,400 signatures protesting against the scheme. Raymond Tam, the then Secretary for Constitutional and Mainland Affair responded by declaring that there was no timeline for phase 2.[95]

---

[92] Hong Kong: Public Hospital Nibbled by Privatization, Grassroot Mainland Immigrants being Blamed, (trans., original: 香港: 公营医院被私有化蚕食 迁怒内地移民基层), available at: http://chinaworker.info/zh/content/news/1431/ (visited 12 Mar 2012).

[93] 'One thousand protest at Dolce & Gabbana Hong Kong store over photo ban', *The Telegraph*, 8 Jan 2012; 'There Are Still Protesters Outside Dolce & Gabbana's Hong Kong Boutique' *New York Fashion*, 16 Jan 2012.

[94] Lo, Alex, 'Don't extend welcome to mainland cars', *South China Morning Post*, 13 Feb 2012, EDT2.

[95] Ip, Kelly, 'Hundreds push to block driving plan', *Hong Kong Standard*, 13 February 2012, P2.

Using the revised formulae of justice theory, when dealing with these situations, we should ask ourselves: (1) How will we feel if we are becoming labeled as 'Locusts'/'Dogs'? (2) Will we be happy if someone does not obey the law and regulations (like eating on trains) in our respective jurisdictions (Mainland or Hong Kong)? (3) If HongKongians are allowed to drive directly to the north of the border, why can't the same apply vice versa to Mainland drivers? (4) What can law do in order to solve the possible problems and conflicts (the desire to make sure everyone obeys the law and the desire not to follow the traffic laws of Hong Kong)? However, please note: As Buddhist and Deleuzian argue respectively: Nothing is permanent and there is always deterritorialization—transmutation of consciousness to wisdom and becoming are not once-for-all formulae of justice or acceptance of difference; the only eternal truth is the non-existence of fixation and permanence, and the meaning of justice keeps on evolving.

References

Bankston, Samantha, *Deleuze and Becoming* (London & New York: Bloomsbury, 2017).
Barry, Brian, *Why Social Justice Matters* (Cambridge: Polity, 2005).
Bell, Jeff, 'Nomad Thought: Deleuze, Whitehead, and the Adventure of Thinking' in Roland Faber & Andrea Stephenson, (eds), *Secrets of Becoming* (New York: Ford University Press, 2011), 70–81.
Bryant, Levi, *Difference and Givenness: Deleuze's Transcendental Empiricism and the Ontology of Immanence* (United States of America: Northwestern University Press, 2008).
Buchanan, Ian, *Deleuze and Guattari's Anti-Oedipus* (London & New York: Continuum, 2008).
Capcheart, Loretta & Milovanovic, Dragon, *Social Justice: Theories, Issues and Movements* (United States of America: Rutgers University Press, 2007).
Chen, Bing (trans., original: 陈兵), *Buddhist Psychology (trans., original: 佛教心理学)* (TaiPei: Buddha's Light, 2007).
Chow, Po-chung, *Politics of Liberal Equality* (BeiJing: Joint Publishing Company, 2010).
Colebrook, Claire, *Understanding Deleuze* (Australia: Allen and Unwin, 2002).
De Bolle, Leen, 'Desire and Schizophrenia' in Leen De Bolle, (ed), *Deleuze and Psychoanalysis* (Leuven, Belgium: Leuven University Press, 2010), 7–32.
Deleuze, Gilles, *Negotiations* (New York: Columbia University Press, 1995).
Deleuze, Gilles & Guattari, Félix, *Anti-Oedipus* (New York: Viking Penguin, 1977).
Derrida, Jacques, 'Force of Law' in Drucilla Cornell, Michael Rosenfeld & David Gray Carlson, (eds), *Deconstruction and the Possibility of Justice* (New York: Routledge, 1992), 3–67.
Douzinas, Costas & Warrington, Ronnie, 'The Face of Justice: A Jurisprudence of Alterity' (1994) 3(3) *Social and Legal Studies*, 405–425.
Engel, David M. & Engel, Jaruwan S., *Tort, Custom, and Karma: Globalization and Legal Consciousness in Thailand* (Stanford California: Stanford University Press, 2010).
Faber, Roland, 'Introduction: Negotiating Becoming' in Roland Faber & Andrea Stephenson, (eds), *Secrets of Becoming* (New York: Ford University Press, 2011), 1–52.
Fang, Li-tian, *Chinese Buddhist Culture (trans., original: 中国佛教文化)* (Hong Kong: Joint Publication, 2008).
Feng, Peter, *Wooden-Legged Justice* (BeiJing: Peking University Press, 2007).
Goodley, Dan, 'Becoming rhizomatic parents: Deleuze, Guattari and disabled babies' (2007) 22(2) *Disability and Society* 145–160.
Guattari, Félix & Rolnik, Suely (trans., Clapshow, Karel & Holmes, Brian), *Molecular Revolution in Brazil* (London: Semiotext(e), 2008).

Hardt, Michael, *Gilles Deleuze: An Apprenticeship in Philosophy* (Minneapolis: University of Minnesota Press, 1993).
Jun, Nathan, 'Deleuze and Normativity' (2009) 53(4) *Philosophy Today* 347–358.
Lau, Lawrence, *Kleśa and Vijñapti* (TaiPei: WenChin 文津, 2020).
Lefebvre, Alexandre, *The Image of Law: Deleuze, Bergson, Spinoza* (Stanford, Stanford University Press, 2008).
Lin, Huo-wang, *Justice and Citizenship* (ChangChun: JiLin Publishing Group, 2008).
Linstead, Stephen & Pullen, Alison, 'Gender as multiplicity: Desire, displacement, difference and dispersion' (2006) 59(9) *Human Relations* 1287–1311.
Lorraine, Tamsin, *Deleuze and Guattari's Immanent Ethics* (New York: State University of New York Press, 2011).
Mitra, Piyali 'Embryo experimentation in Buddhist Ethics' (2018) 1 *Journal of Dharma Studies* 163–178).
Murray, Jamie, *Deleuze & Guattari: Emergent Law* (New York: Routledge, 2013).
Nussbaum, Martha, *Frontiers of Justice: Disability, Nationality, Species Membership* (Cambridge, MA & London: The Belknap Press, 2006).
Parr, Adrian, 'Deterritorialising the Holocaust' in Ian Buchanan & Adrian Parr (eds), *Deleuze and the Contemporary World* (Edinburgh: Edinburgh University Press, 2006), 125–145.
Patton, Paul, 'Deleuze's Political Philosophy' in Daniel Smith & Henry Somers-Hall, (eds), *The Cambridge Companion to Deleuze* (Cambridge: Cambridge University Press, 2012), 198–219.
Rajchman, John, *The Deleuze Connections* (London: MIT Press, 2000).
Rawls, John, *A Theory of Justice* (Cambridge, MA: Harvard University Press, 1971).
Rawls, John, *Political Liberalism* (New York: Columbia University Press, 1993).
Rizzo, Teresa, *Deleuze and Film: A Feminist Introduction* (New York: Continuum, 2012).
Rose, Nikolas, 'Government and Control' (2000) 40 *Brit J. Criminal* 321–339.
Sen, Amartya, *The Idea of Justice* (Cambridge, MA: The Belknap Press, 2009).
Shih, Chao Hwei 释昭慧, 'Emotional Connection and Desire: A Buddhist Perspective' in Man-chung Chiu, (ed), *Chinese Sex(uality)/Gender-Age Machine* (Hong Kong: Red Publish, 2011), 69–107.
Silberstein, Laurence 'Becoming Israeli/Israeli Becomings' in Ian Buchanan & Adrian Parr (eds), *Deleuze and the Contemporary World* (Edinburgh: Edinburgh University Press, 2006), 146–160.
Smith, Daniel, 'Introduction' in Gilles Deleuze, *Essays Critical and Clinical* (Minneapolis, Minn: The University of Minnesota Press, 1997).
Smith, Daniel, *Essays on Deleuze* (Edinburgh: Edinburgh University Press, 2012).
Smith, Daniel, 'Two Concepts of Resistance' in Nicolae Morar, Thomas Nail & Daniel Smith, (eds), *Between Deleuze and Foucault* (Edinburgh: Edinburgh University Press, 2016), 264–284.
Sutton, Damian & Martin-Jones, David, *Deleuze Reframed* (London: I B Tauris, 2008).
Taishō Tripiṭaka Editorial Committee (trans., original: 大藏经刊行委员会), *Taishō Tripiṭaka*, (TaiPei: XinWenFeng 新文丰, 1986).
Waldron, William, *The Buddhist Unconscious* (London: Routledge Curzon, 2003).
Weinstein, Jami, 'Introduction Part II' in Claire Colebrook & Jami Weinstein, (eds), Deleuze and Gender (Edinburgh: Edinburgh University Press, 2008). 20–33.
Wilson, Scott, 'Gnomonology' in Boštjan Nedoh & Andreja Zevnik, (eds), *Lacan and Deleuze* (Edinburgh: Edinburgh University Press, 2019), 56–73.
Winslade, John, 'Tracing Lines of flight: Implications of the Work of Gilles Deleuze for Narrative Practice' (2009) 48(3) *Family Process* 332–346.
Yao, Da-zhi, *John Rawls* (ChangChun: ChangChun Publishing House, 2011).
Yu, Ling-po, *Outline of Vijñānamatra (trans., original: 唯识学纲要)* (TaiPei: Grand East, 2019).
Zhao, Dun-hua (trans., original: 赵敦华), *Rawls's Theory of Justice: A Comment (trans., original: 劳斯的正义论解说)* (Hong Kong: Joint Publication, 1988).

Chapter 5
Sim*u*larizing Vijñāna and Desire, Reproducing yi and Justice: Osmotic Production of Justice in the Condition of Hong Kong's Anti Domestic Violence Law

5.1 Introduction

Between 2007 and 2009, Hong Kong's Legislative Council passed a series of amendments in relation to the law controlling domestic violence. Two of the most controversial provisions were (1) the introduction of court-mandated counseling; and (2) the extension of protection to same sex couples. In *De/Sexing Hong Kong Law*, I have already argued that both court mandated counseling and legal recognition of same sex couples do not present any conflict with Han-Chinese 汉族华人 traditional culture and thus can work effectively in Hong Kong, a predominately Han-Chinese society. However, two questions remain unanswered: (1) Is Han-Chinese traditional culture still influential and relevant in twenty-first century Hong Kong society? (2) Can the legislative amendments enacted in 2008 and 2009 produce justice? This question has been briefly discussed in Chap. 1; in this chapter, I adopt a Deleuzian perspective on time/history and justice in responding to the questions in greater detail. Also, I will refer to the theory of 'transcultural sim*u*larity' when examining how the overseas theories I mention can engage smoothly with Hong Kong's legal culture. I also hope that the following discussion can shed light on the future development of legal devices in controlling domestic violence in Mainland China.

Let us start with a discussion of the details of the legislative amendments to the law controlling domestic violence.

This chapter is derived in part from a chapter published in *New Knowledge in a New Era of Globalization* (2011) Intech.

M.-C. Chiu, *Transforming the Hong Kong Legal Machine*,
https://doi.org/10.1007/978-981-19-1272-6_5

5.2 Hong Kong Anti Domestic Violence Law Reform in 2008 and 2009

Before 2008, a victim of domestic violence could apply for injunction orders under the original Domestic Violence Ordinance (CAP 189, LHK), and the court might, on the application of an abused party to the marriage, have granted an injunction. Such an injunction would have (1) restrained the other party from molesting the applicant and/or any child living with the applicant; and/or (2) would have excluded the other party from the matrimonial home, or from a specified part of the matrimonial home,[1] or from a specified area whether or not the matrimonial home is included in that area (like the applicant's place of work or her/his parent's apartment). In 2008, a series of amendments were introduced and one of the most important was the introduction of court-mandated counseling—in other words, after the amendment, the court could order the abuser to attend a counseling programme (e.g. anger management). And, in 2009, another significant amendment was passed, under which the same sex couples could also apply for injunctions.[2] Since same-sex couples do not enjoy the right

[1] Matrimonial home means 'a home in which the parties to a marriage ordinarily reside together whether or not it is occupied at the same time by other persons.' (section 2(1)) The order overrides any property rights. In other words, a cohabitant, who has no proprietary right, can also apply to exclude her/his partner, who is the owner of the property in question. Before the amendments introduced in 2008 and 2009, the orders which an abused party could apply for included: '(a) a provision restraining that other party from molesting the applicant; (b) a provision restraining that other party from molesting any child living with the applicant; (c) a provision excluding that other party from the matrimonial home, or from a specified part of the matrimonial home, or from a specified area whether or not the matrimonial home is included in that area; (d) a provision requiring that other party to permit the applicant to enter and remain in the matrimonial home or in a specified part of the matrimonial home, whether or not any other relief is being sought in the proceedings. Since the amendments, the orders available now include (a) a provision restraining the respondent from molesting the applicant; (b) a provision restraining the respondent from molesting any specified minor; (c) a provision prohibiting the respondent (i) (where the applicant has been molested by the respondent) from entering or remaining in—(A) the residence of the applicant; (B) a specified part of the residence of the applicant; or (C) a specified area whether or not the residence of the applicant is in that area, whether or not the residence is the common residence or matrimonial home of the applicant and the respondent; (ii) (where the specified minor has been molested by the respondent) from entering or remaining in—(A) the residence of the specified minor; (B) a specified part of the residence of the minor; or (C) a specified area whether or not the residence of the minor is in that area, whether or not the residence is the common residence of the minor and the respondent; (d) a provision requiring the respondent to permit—(i) (where the applicant resides with the respondent) the applicant to enter and remain in the common residence or matrimonial home of the applicant and the respondent or in a specified part of such common residence or matrimonial home; or (ii) (where the specified minor resides with the respondent) the minor to enter and remain in the common residence of the minor and the respondent or in a specified part of such common residence, whether or not any other relief is being sought in the proceedings. (1A) A court may in an injunction containing a provision mentioned in subsection (1)(a) or (b) include a provision requiring the respondent to participate in any programme, approved by the Director of Social Wel-f are, that is aimed at changing the attitude and behaviour that led to the granting of such injunction'.

[2] Before the amendment introduced in 2008 and 2009, only parties to marriage and their children could apply for an injunction order under the Ordinance. (Section 3) Under the amended

to marriage, and the Ordinance no longer only protects people within a familial relationship network, the Ordinance was retitled the 'Domestic and Cohabitation Relationship Violence Ordinance.'

5.3 Time is Always Out of Joint: Is the Past Always with Us?

I have always been in support of these amendments, not only because they can effectively prevent or deter wrongdoing, but because they positively engage with Han-Chinese traditional culture. When academics question the significance of Han-Chinese traditional culture in contemporary Hong Kong society, they tend to assume that heritage is a contextual product and since the discourse is no longer the same as in traditional society, Han-Chinese traditional culture is no longer applicable in current society. Underlying their argument is a linear model of time: Time as a join-up of numerous 'instants', linking or gluing together distinct moments of experience in a fixed uni-direction, i.e. the linear model of 'past → present → future'. Deleuzian philosophy challenges this way of thinking: As Todd May argues, if time is made up of 'instants', then it should be divisible into different units (years, months, days, hours…), otherwise the present cannot be grasped; but an instant in the end is always

---

Ordinance, the following persons can apply for an injunction: '(a) the applicant's father, mother, grandfather or grandmother (whether natural or adoptive); (b) the applicant's step-father, step-mother, step-grandfather or step-grandmother; (c) the applicant's father-in-law or mother-in-law who is the natural parent, adoptive parent or step-parent of the applicant's spouse; (d) the applicant's grandfather-in-law or grandmother-in-law who is the natural grandparent, adoptive grandparent or step-grandparent of the applicant's spouse; (e) the applicant's son, daughter, grandson or granddaughter (whether natural or adoptive); (f) the applicant's step-son, step-daughter, step-grandson or step-granddaughter; (g) the applicant's son-in-law or daughter-in-law who is the spouse of the applicant's natural child, adoptive child or step-child; (h) the applicant's grandson-in-law or granddaughter-in-law who is the spouse of the applicant's natural grandchild, adoptive grandchild or step-grandchild; (i) the applicant's brother or sister (whether of full or half blood or by virtue of adoption); (j) the brother or sister (whether of full or half blood or by virtue of adoption) of the applicant's spouse; (k) the applicant's step-brother or step-sister; (l) the step-brother or step-sister of the applicant's spouse; (m) the applicant's uncle, aunt, nephew, niece or cousin (whether of full or half blood or by virtue of adoption); (n) the uncle, aunt, nephew, niece or cousin (whether of full or half blood or by virtue of adoption) of the applicant's spouse; or (o) the spouse of any person mentioned in paragraph (i), (j), (k), (l), (m) or (n). Whether a couple who have not married are qualified to apply for an injunction is determined with regard to the following criteria: (a) whether the parties are living together in the same household; (b) whether the parties share the tasks and duties of their daily lives; (c) whether there is stability and permanence in the relationship; (d) the arrangement of sharing of expenses or financial support, and the degree of financial dependence or interdependence, between the parties; (e) whether there is a sexual relationship between the parties; (f) whether the parties share the care and support of a specified minor; (g) the parties' reasons for living together, and the degree of mutual commitment to a shared life; (h) whether the parties conduct themselves towards friends, relatives or other persons as parties to a cohabitation relationship, and whether the parties are so treated by their friends and relatives or other persons.' (section 3B).

indivisible, because 'however thinly we slice the instant of the Now [instants], we can always slice it thinner.'[3] In other words, the present can never be caught in the way some academics want it to, and assume it can, be caught.

The Deleuzian school argues that it is not the movement or moment which produces and derives time, but vice versa—time can create and invent movements, since time is a becoming and repetition which are made up of 'durations'. 'Duration' is different from 'instant': The former, as it is constituted by mental activities (perception and memory), can be divided. Whenever duration is divided, it changes, because how it is divided can be both a cause and effect of mental activities, which never stop and can never be forever consistent or totally predictable. If memory is part of the past, then how it is structured cannot be a pure objective outcome, but a product of consciousness. Gilles Deleuze writes:

> Duration divides up and does so constantly…but it does not divide up without changing in kind; it changes in kind in the process of dividing up: this is why it is a nonnumerical multiplicity.[4]

Duration, being a product of mental activities and repetition, contains both continuity and differences, as it is a product of repetition. Cliff Stagoll gives the best illustration: 'Mental states flow together as if parts of a melody, with previous notes lingering and future ones anticipated in the unity of a piece…To try and grasp this flow as a complete set of notes is pointless, because the music is always on the verge of ending and always altered by the addition of a new note.'[5] Deleuze also proposes that time/duration progresses, not in a linear direction, but by continuously fissioning into past and future,[6] where the living presence is the contraction of repetition. The Deleuzian first synthesis of time further explains this: Past is not the retention of what happened, but reflexive past of reproduced singularity.[7] This is, according to James Williams, a passive process.[8]

The Deleuzian second synthesis of time then states: Only if past presents, the present (past present) can pass into and fold with the past—only when that happens, can the new present replace the past present; simply put, past and present are becoming at the same dot:

> [I]f the present can pass away, it is because, in some sense, it is already past or has a past element to it. In other words, every present must have a past aspect in order for it to pass away.[9]

---

[3] May (2005), at 41.

[4] Deleuze (1991), at 42.

[5] Sagoll (2005), at 79.

[6] Bryant (2008), at 114.

[7] Somers-Hall (2013), at 63. Please note that the future is 'displaced by a topological transformation of lawyers of the past that co-exist even though their order is discontinuous and non-chronological'. (Rodowick 1997, at 82).

[8] Williams (2011), at 25, 28.

[9] Williams (2003), at 94. Please also see Berressem (2020), at 116.

That passing is always singular. When a past present, together with pure past, passes away, it becomes a past event for the forthcoming present (i.e. the new present/future). The difference between past and present however must exist, otherwise the passing cannot occur. What is the difference? Deleuze alleges that past is virtuality, and present actuality, as we are experiencing it. Please note: Creating/passing is not a dichotomy of past/virtuality vs present/actuality, because as argued above, past and present (durations) are repetitions, so there are multiple and different pasts and presents. In this machine, pasts always affect and influence presents affecting and influencing pasts.[10] In other words, even if the past is virtual, it does not mean it is fake or false; past/virtuality also needs the commonsense world as reference. Nathan Widder further argues: Past/virtuality is an open structure of differences, and the present/actuality constructs a perspective through which differences can be illustrated, and the past will then use this machine to show, not solve, these differences.[11]

When the present passes into the past, that past also engages (not mixes) with the present at the same duration—the past actualizes and becomes part of the present. Put simply, only the past can actualize the present, not vice versa.

> The present and former present are not, therefore, like two successive instants on the line of time; rather, the present one necessarily contains an extra dimension in which it represents the former and also represents itself.[12]

History, a concept of the past, as argued by Elizabeth Grosz, is thus still contemporaneously influential through 'its capacity to link to and thus to inform the present.'[13] Shui-jun Hu also proposes: The traditional legal system structures our current concept of justice.[14] When (part of) the past actualizes, it becomes the line of social force in a duration and 'conditions all the experience that we have, since actual experience is a composite of the virtual natural natures of perception and memory.'[15] This does not mean that the present is only a reconstitution of history/past; in fact, the entirety of past and history always coexists with the present. That is why Dean Tipps stresses that tradition is an integral part and product of modernity (present).[16] Nonetheless, the present, which is always together with past and history, can always be innovative and create novelty—a (forthcoming) present must be absolutely new, since once whenever a present passes into the past, a new present (the forthcoming present) is created.[17]

---

[10] Williams (2011), at 3; Žižek (2014), at 141.

[11] Widder (2012), at 40.

[12] Deleuze (1994), at 80.

[13] Grosz (2005), at 102.

[14] Quoted in Fu (2008), at 360. For more discussion in relation to yi/justice, please see Chap. 1 and below.

[15] Due (2007), at 31.

[16] Quoted in Fu (2008), at 297.

[17] Bryant (2008), at 118.

Time is, put simply, according to Deleuze, not only an objective and transcendental scale that exists outside human life,[18] but a circular and folding motion of duration (past ← (falling into) present 1—(forthcoming) present 2 (falling into) →past [+ present 1]). The Deleuzian concept of duration sensitizes us to multiple interpretations and constitutions of time, history, and memory.

Using this perspective, then Han-Chinese traditional culture (past) in fact has never left us, always existing with contemporary Hong Kong society (present), which is predominantly Han-Chinese. The traditional culture could become the force of social control in current society, but this also does not forbid current society from changing. In other words, the issue of whether the mechanism of court-mandated counseling and acceptance of same sex couples, originating from an overseas jurisdiction, can engage with Han-Chinese traditional culture and function in Hong Kong, a predominately Chinese society, must be considered in order to ensure or evaluate the effectiveness of the legislative amendments relating to domestic violence.

Another problem is: Although we have to take into account Han-Chinese traditional culture, another aim of reforming law is to maintain and produce justice. If harmony, as argued by some academics and lawmakers, is the core value of Han-Chinese traditional culture,[19] then we have to understand that legislating to protect harmony may also result in injustice—as disputes, especially familial conflicts, may be covered up and ignored so as to maintain a superficial peace of interpersonal relationships. In other words, the fact that the new provisions of Hong Kong anti domestic violence law can engage smoothly with traditional Han-Chinese culture and function well does not mean they will essentially bring just and fair consequences. So, are they just? And most importantly, what is justice?

5.4 Becoming Powerless: The Deleuzian Machine of Justice

In this section, I examine whether the newly introduced sections of law controlling domestic violence (i.e. court-mandated counseling and the inclusion of same sex couples) is just. A Deleuzian becoming of justice, motivated by different molecular desires (including, the desire to counsel abusers and for LesBiGayTransIntersexQueer/TongZhi to form families), aims to release a desire for reform in the present and for the future, while not abandoning the past completely; because otherwise all 'attempts to ground any reasoning, rationale, or logic on some object measure' would be destroyed and torn apart.[20] First, we have to define a Deleuzian machine of the future. According to David Rodowick, the present does not only fractures

[18] May (2005), at 41.

[19] Chiu (2017).

[20] Capeheart & Milovanovic (2007), at 125.

into present and past simultaneously, but present and future.[21] And it is in the future where (becoming) innovation, as advocated by Deleuze, is premised.[22]

As indicated in the last chapter, becoming is not a journey between two locations, but a line-bloc that can initiate transformation. Becoming, according to Deleuze, contains two inter-connected elements: Sensory becoming and absolute becoming. While sensory becoming serves to redefine memory, absolute becoming actively forgets:[23] In other words, on one hand, the former subverts the present by un/folding the past, and thus is closer to the material universe; on the other hand, the latter destabilizes 'the becomings that emerge in relation to varying durations.'[24] Both sensory becoming and absolute becoming work together in the creation of the future, though via different routes: Sensory becoming ungrounds (not disavows) the past; and absolute becoming manufactures a subject by cutting off the time flow.

In the case of legal reform in relation to the control of domestic violence, a Deleuzian will argue that existing desires (e.g. the introduction of court mandated counseling and recognition of same sex couples) have successfully initiated becoming, which revise and improve the existing social cooperations (between institutions). Sensory becoming supports the introduction of 'mandatory counselling', which can be related to a reconstruction of familial harmony, a traditional Han-Chinese concept. Also, the acceptance of same sex couples, a product that had no historical precedent in Hong Kong, in the legal control of domestic violence, could be referred to as an absolute becoming.

In Chap. 4, I have already elaborated why Deleuzian desire can be productive and positive, and is essential in the creation of subjects: While the molar/social force always wants to capture and regulate desire, and fixates the subject, by repetition and codification through territorialization (e.g. domestic violence perpetuators are essentially male and could not be converted; same sex couples are not able to form stable familial relationship),[25] lines of becoming, manufactured by Deleuzian desire, deterritorialize all the imagined fixations, and create innovative subjects (including justice, law and identity). The loops never end and are always fueled by multiple new desires. In other words, there is no universal or monolithic definition of justice, only if the reforms are allowed to accommodate different desires; while the past/tradition is not depreciated, justice can keep on redefining itself and being re-constituted.

---

[21] Rodowick (1997), at 82.

[22] Bankston (2017), at 50.

[23] Deleuze (2006).

[24] Bankston (2017), at 31.

[25] Rose (2000).

5.5 Engaging Foreign Concepts in Hong Kong Culture: Where are the Sim*u*larities?

As I argued in Part 1 of the book, in order to transplant into Hong Kong a Deleuzian perspective on time/history and justice, philosophical products reproduced in Euro-American socio-political-cultural matrix, we need to develop a machine by which the importation can be carried out smoothly.[26] The machine of transcultural sim*u*larity, developed by Hsiao-hung Chang, can offer us an efficient and functional paradigm to conduct an effective transplantation.

Chang argues an authentic original culture does not exist, so we need to strive to locate the zones of possible similarities between cultures, i.e. simulacra. Chang goes on to advocate that dialogue between cultures can be viewed as a sim*u*larity—there are similarities, and simulations can occur between cultures.[27] According to Chang, the sim*u*larity is a virtual zone, by which osmosis between cultures can be proactively conducted. In the milieu of transcultural sim*u*larity, cultural concepts and related legal reforms can be mutually infiltrated and replicated.[28] How is the infiltration carried out? The key word, as Xin-hua Xia argued, is 'matching point'—we need to locate and construct the points where the transcultural sim*u*larity machine can function as the starting points of infiltration.[29] We thus, in the context of anti domestic violence law, need to discover the matching points between Deleuzian concepts of time and justice and Han-Chinese traditional culture.

If we have to locate and construct such matching points, we have to understand how Han-Chinese traditional culture engineers its perspectives on time/history and justice. The Han-Chinese traditional concept of time is a hybridity of different schools of thought, and we are going to focus on (Orthodox) Confucianism, (Orthodox) Daoism and Buddhism—which are considered as the mainstream philosophies underpinning Han-Chinese traditional culture.[30]

---

[26] Any transplantation of law that lacks sensitivity towards possible conflicts between cultures can lead to failure and / or postcolonial violence. That is why I argue that a very in-depth investigation of the cultural contexts needs to be carried out before attempting any transplantation of law. For more details, please see Part 1.

[27] Chang (2007), at 20, 68, 73.

[28] For details, please see Part 1.

[29] Xia (2004), at 43.

[30] For details, please see Part 1.

5.5.1 Daoist and Confucian Perspectives on History: Medium of Promotion?

According to Lao Zi 老子, the philosopher who is believed to be the founder of (Orthodox) Daoism, Dao is the source and reference of everything, including nature and human society.[31] Thus, Dao assumes the status of a transcendental metaphysics.[32] So, Dao is not only a philosophical perspective; but a cosmic force. Since Dao determines everything, actionless-ness 无为, i.e. 'letting things work to their perfection naturally', becomes one of the thematic principles of Lao Zi's ideology.[33]

(Orthodox) Confucianism, produced and advocated by Confucius 孔子 and Mencius 孟子 during the Zhou 周 Dynasty (1029 BC–221 BC), advocates the importance of ren 仁 (not REN 人)—good being/benevolence, which is derived and considered as the most important guideline of Confucian interpersonal politics, since harmonious interpersonal relationships enjoy a very high status in Confucianism. Familial relationships are always at the centre of ren: ren always starts with filial piety and extends to other interhuman relationships. It is in this context where (Orthodox) Confucians formulated the famous five constant virtues (benevolence between father and son, righteousness between Emperor and ministers, differences between husband and wife, hierarchy between elder and the young, fidelity between friends), the core of li 礼 (social moral order), to engineer ren's smooth operation.[34] These principles influenced the development of a highly hierarchical society, which above all stressed harmony, in imperial China.

Analyzing tradition and history from the perspective of (Orthodox) Daoism and (Orthodox) Confucianism, philosophical historians have always used historical facts and issues as the tools or medium to promote and market their philosophical ideals—for instance, Daoists would praise Emperor Wen 汉文帝 of the West Han 汉 Dynasty (206 BC- 9) as he adopted the Daoist principle of actionless-ness[35] as his national policy, as *SiJi* 史記 says: 'Emperor Hsiao-wen [Emperor Wen] occupied the throne for twenty-three years. In his palaces and apartments, in his pastures and enclosures, in his carriages and saddle-horses, in his garments and daily needs, he made no addition or increase [over the requirements of his predecessors]… When he constructed the Pa Tomb, he only [used] objects of pottery and did not allow the use of gold,

[31] Wang (2003a); Wang (2004), at 149.

[32] Ng (1998), at 2.

[33] Koller (2002), at 288.

[34] Tang & Zhang (2003), at 76.

[35] For more discussion on actionless-ness, please see Chap. 8.

silver, copper, or tin as ornaments.'[36] (trans., original: 即位二十三年, 宫室, 苑囿, 车骑, 服御无所增益……治霸陵, 皆瓦器, 不得以金, 银, 铜, 锡为饰, 因其山, 不起坟。) Confucian academics appreciate those emperors who realized or recognized ren during their reigns; for instance, Confucius himself always praised Emperor Yao 尧—a legendary king—as he considered what Emperor Yao did established the highest standard of ren: 'Great indeed was Yao as a sovereign! How majestic was he! It is only Heaven that is grand, and only Yao corresponded to it. How vast was his virtue! The people could find no name for it. How majestic was he in the works which he accomplished! How glorious in the elegant regulations which he instituted!'[37] (trans., original: 大哉, 尧之为君也!巍巍乎!唯天为大, 唯尧则之。荡荡乎!民无能名焉。巍巍乎!其有成功也; 焕乎, 其有文章!) When carefully examining the Daoist and Confucian perspectives on history, we will find that they are in fact taking historic fact (past) as instructional examples for people in contemporary society (present). In other words, they are using the linear model of history, hence, it is impossible to have any simularity between a Deleuzian perspective on time/history and a Daoist/Confucian view on history—the latter cannot be the matching point for the transplantation of philosophy.

5.5.2 Buddhist Perspective on Time/History: Beyond Past/Present Dichotomy

One of the thematic principles of Buddhism is karma, which indicates the mechanism by which what a human did and/or thought would determine her/his future action and/or status.[38] This is not a kind of absolute pre-determination of one's destiny, but a mechanism of choice and responsibility: one can choose her/his act/thought and would be responsible for them. For example, Emperor Wu Zhong 武宗 of Tang 唐 Dynasty (618–907) decided to abolish Buddhism in 845, an incident titled 'Hui Chang Buddhism Abandonment' 会昌灭佛. In 846, someone saw two deities, dressed in official uniform, emerged from a tomb. The person asked why they came into the human world, and the deities said: Because Emperor Wu Zhong abandoned Buddhism, his life span has been cut short and he will pass away very soon. Three days later, Emperor Wu Zhong died suddenly.[39] The tale, which is extremely Buddhist -centric and aims at constructing the sacredness of Buddhism, indicates that bad

[36] 'Annals of Emperor Wen', 文帝纪 *Book of Han*, available at: http://www2.iath.virginia.edu/saxon/servlet/SaxonServlet?source=xwomen/texts/hanshu.xml&style=xwomen/xsl/dynaxml.xsl&chunk.id=d2.14&toc.depth=1&toc.id=d2.1&doc.lang=english (visited 28 Dec 2020).

[37] Chapter 8 泰伯, *The Analects of Confucius*, available at: http://www.yellowbridge.com/onlinelit/analects08.php (visited 22 Mar 2011).

[38] Hu (1999).

[39] Song (2009), at 20.

activities (leaving and abandoning Buddhism), will certainly bring bad consequences (even an early death) for a person; and even an emperor cannot escape their fate.

The interaction between humans and the commonsense world constitutes the seeds (种子, Bīja), which are stored in the storehouse consciousness (阿赖耶识, Alaya-vijñāna). The storehouse consciousness, which is a timeless concept, determines the forthcoming interaction between humans and the commonsense world.[40] As karma is a non-stop accumulation (and depletion), the production and reduction of seeds never ends. Every decision and action of human subjects influences the nature of seeds production. When a particular set of seeds becomes mature and is consumed under a certain singular condition 緣, other seeds and another conditions are manufactured.[41]

The Buddhist theory of karma offers a philosophical perspective which describes how past (action/thought) and present (forthcoming action/thought) intermingle in detail, although it mainly aims at elaborating and reconstructing the interaction between human action/thought and the constitution of one's subjectivity. Put simply, the concept goes beyond the binarism of past vs present. Karma also offers a perspective explaining how the past can be actualized in the present via seeds-conditional activities—Buddhism thus is able to create another machine in making past social control a force in Han-Chinese traditional culture. This Buddhist mechanism, in short, is very similar to and can simulate actively with Deleuzian concepts of time, i.e. the fission of time into the past and present and past folding with the present. Buddhist karma hence can be used as a matching platform for the successful and smooth transplantation of Deleuzian concept.

5.5.3 *yi and Equality = Justice in Han-Chinese Culture?*

In contemporary Han-Chinese language, justice is translated as yi 义. However, yi does not start with equality but with harmony.[42] This is why Duan Lin says: In ancient China, there was no justice (which starts with equality), but only yi 义 (that emphasizes harmony and appropriateness).[43] In this section, I will investigate if Lin's statement is valid.

[40] The mechanism will be further elaborated below.

[41] Yang (2007), at 298–299.

[42] Hu (2005), at 12; Jiang (2002), at 38.

[43] Lin (2007), at 437.

We start with (Orthodox) Daoism. (Orthodox) Daoists generally believe that yi, as a human product, violates the principle of actionless-ness and thus Dao.[44] Daoism also holds that the lesser the desire we have, the better the universe will be:

> In a little state with a small population, I would so order it, that, though there were individuals with the abilities of ten or a hundred men, there should be no employment of them; I would make the people, while looking on death as a grievous thing, yet not remove elsewhere (to avoid it). Though they had boats and carriages, they should have no occasion to ride in them; though they had buff coats and sharp weapons, they should have no occasion to don or use them. I would make the people return to the use of knotted cords (instead of the written characters). They should think their (coarse) food sweet; their (plain) clothes beautiful; their (poor) dwellings places of rest; and their common (simple) ways sources of enjoyment. There should be a neighbouring state within sight, and the voices of the fowls and dogs should be heard all the way from it to us, but I would make the people up to old age, even to death, not have any intercourse with it. (trans., original: 小国寡民, 使有什佰之器而不用, 使民重死而不远徙, 虽有舟舆, 无所乘之。虽有甲兵, 无所陈之。使民复结绳而用之。甘其食, 美其服, 安其居, 乐其俗, 邻国相望, 鸡, 狗之声相闻, 民至老死不相往来。)[45]

In fact, Daoists advocate that morality should aim at diminishing all kinds of desire:

> He who devotes himself to learning (seeks) from day to day to increase (his knowledge); he who devotes himself to the Tao [Dao] (seeks) from day to day to diminish (his doing). He diminishes it and again diminishes it, till he arrives at doing nothing (on purpose). Having arrived at this point of non-action, there is nothing which he does not do. (trans., original: 为学日益, 为道日损, 损之又损, 以至于无为, 无为而无不为。)[46]

In (Orthodox) Confucianism, desire does not have any negative meaning or connotation: 'Riches and honors are what men desire. If they cannot be obtained in the proper way, they should not be held.'[47] (trans., original: 富与贵, 是人之所欲也; 不以其道得之, 不处也。) Therefore, it is the governmental liability and responsibility to fulfill the desire of the population: 'It is simply to collect for them what they like, and not to impose on them what they dislike'[48] (trans., original: 所欲与之聚之, 所恶勿施尔也。) However, the process has to be conducted appropriately, i.e. in the way of yi. Both Confucius and Mencius advocate that yi, a natural product of ren and li, i.e. harmonious hierarchical interpersonal network,[49] aims at maintaining

[44] Wang (2003a), at 23, 43.; According to Lao Zi, the philosopher who is widely believed to be the founder of the school, Dao is the origin and reference of everything, including humans, society and culture. Thus, Dao assumes the status of ultimate and transcendental metaphysics. For details, please see Wang (2004), at 149. However, Guu-ying Chen has another interpretation, he points out that, Lao Zi does not object to yi, provided that it is derived from Dao. Please see Chen (2001).

[45] Verse 80, *Lao Zi*, available at: https://ctext.org/dao-de-jing (visited 29 Dec 2020).

[46] Verse 48, *Lao Zi*, available at: https://ctext.org/dao-de-jing (visited 29 Dec 2020).

[47] Chapter 4 里仁, *Analects of Confucius*, available at: https://ctext.org/analects/li-ren (visited 29 December 2020).

[48] Chapter 4A 离娄, *Mencius*, available at: http://ctext.org/mengzi/li-lou-i (visited 8 Apr 2013).

the operation of the hierarchical social structure.[50] Xun Zi 荀子, another Confucian (though not an Orthodox one),[51] also argued that desire cannot be suppressed or neglected, however he pointed out that li and law are the best machines to control any conflicts originating from desire.[52]

From the perspective of Madhyamakā 中觀, the interaction among the performances of the consciousness (vijñāna)[53] is a loop of production and constitutes (illusory and temporary) human subjecthood. The interactive production of the body and the conditions—the karma machine, the universal law of cause and effect—continuously produces/depletes seeds (i.e. the carrier of desire) when the conditions are becoming sophisticated, and maintains storehouse consciousness, as storehouse consciousness is 'a subliminal reservoir of memories, habits, tendencies and future possibilities'.[54] Please note: Karma cannot totally predetermine what is going to happen in a forthcoming duration, as karma always creates new seeds, thus new and unpredictable interaction between human; and unforeseeable interaction human and common sense world are allowed and encouraged. In other words, seeds activity can create a new condition for the forthcoming seed activities. According to this analysis, which would be agreed by Han-Chinese School of Vinaya-Discipline (Nan-shan school 南山宗), enactment of new law (e.g. the amendments to the anti domestic violence law and the introduction of court-mandated counseling), a kind of manifest activity, would positively 'Perfume' (Vāsanā),[55] or affect the nature of existing and forthcoming sets of seeds.[56] As law can certainly perfume seeds,[57] the seeds thus perfumed can create succeeding seeds of a similar kind; new seeds will then create new law, similar (perhaps not identical though) to the nature of the law of the preceding moment. In short, law can turn negative/good desire into positive/bad desire: 'Depending on the seeds of good or evil that been already been planted, various real and concrete good and evil activities occur'.[58]

Karma hence leads to one of the most significant Buddhist ideologies, Dependent-Arising of Alaya-vijñāna 赖耶缘起. This describes the mental constitutive reception of every activity and phenomenon that can never be a fixed or universal intrinsic nature (自性, Svabhāva), but a virtuality re-created and re-newed by the non-stop karma mechanism and seed exercise (e.g., consequences of perfume) under a proper condition—a forever changing set of connections between desire and social force (e.g. enactment of new law), which itself can be a (new) product of seed activity. The concept thus explains why Dependent-Arising thus Emptiness of Self Nature 缘起性空 appears.

---

[49] For the definition and discussion of ren and li, please see Chiu (2017).

[50] Pan (2006), at 45.

[51] For more discussion on Xun Zi, please see Chaps. 1 and 2.

[52] Chapter 19 礼论, *XunZi.*

[53] For more discussion on Vijñānamatra and classification of vijñāna, please see Chaps. 1 and 4.

[54] Jiang (2006), at 8.

[55] Fo Hui (2015), at 126. For details, please see Chap. 1.

[56] Jiang (2006), at 70.

[57] Chan (2017), at 49.

[58] Jiang (2006), at 37.

This line of argument devises and formulates another two important Buddhist principles: (1) 'Non-Insistence' 诸法无我 or 'Selfless-ness (Anātman)', 'self' in this context not only meaning 'I', but over-insistence of any philosophical perspective;[59] and (2) 'Non-Permanence' 诸行无常: Since the human body and subjectivity cannot be preset and can be changed, due to karma, changing conditions and seed exercise and perfume, there is no forever eternality and essentiality in the common sense world. In other words, since the composition of seeds goes on changing, it is impossible to have any monolithic or universal subjectivity/self; and if the commonsense world and its related activities and phenomena are only and partly psychological products, initiated by a set of seeds and ending up with the production of another cluster of seeds, any intrinsic nature/metanarrative is only a virtuality.

The two principles, 'Non-Insistence' and 'Non-Permanence', are part of Buddhist 'Correct Law' (正法, Prāvaccana), i.e. the most important beliefs in Buddhist philosophy.[60] It is therefore not surprising when Buddha Śākyamuni developed and advocated the Buddhist theory of justice, i.e. equality, since everything is not fixed, every identity/subjectivity and condition is not fixed and monolithic, thus any kind of hierarchy cannot exist forever and becomes meaningless.[61]

Juxtaposing Deleuzian desire-based justice and the Han-Chinese traditional cultural concept of yi, we can locate the transcultural sim*u*larities: Besides Daoism, both Confucianism and Buddhism can be effective platforms for transplantation. It seems (Orthodox) Confucianism, Buddhist philosophy and Deleuzian theory are not compatible with each other: Confucianism, though recognizing that desire is not negative in nature, argues that desire must be regulated, Buddhism assumes that desires could bring negative effects and thus have to be put under control; however, Deleuze argues that it is good to have new and emerging desires. In fact, all three theorems share two commonalities: (1) Desires exist, and we have to accept each other's desire—that is why (Orthodox) Confucianism indicates that desire is not essentially evil, Buddhists advocate equality and Deleuzians emphasize the importance of respect; and (2) Law is vital—Xun Zi of course agrees with this, Buddhism believes that law, a product of seeds/desire, can help control (or even eliminate) negative desire, Deleuzian theory holds that law is a product of re/territorialization; aiming to fixate desire; but, of course, this attempt is doomed to be a failure as new desire will groom deterritorialization and reterritorialization, which means existing laws can be repealed, and new laws can emerge. The respective perspectives of Confucianism, Buddhism and Deleuzian theory on law and desire therefore form an efficient platform by which transcultural similarity can happen.

---

[59] Chan (2005), at 25. According to Jiang, selfless-ness does not mean solely no self, but not self also. Buddhism, in short, opposes all kinds of metaphysicality. Jiang (2006).

[60] Quoted in Li (2009), at 440.

[61] Vol 22, Taishō Tripiṭaka Editorial Committee (1986).

I maintain that I would never try to propose that 'Hong Kong Culture = traditional Han-Chinese culture = Orthodox Confucianism + Orthodox Daoism + Buddhism': If a traditional cultural concept is a virtuality, and becoming, as argued by Deleuze, then an authentic original notion of culture simply does not exist. Please also note: Even if transcultural sim*u*larity is proactively created and/or located, and transplantation can be carried out, whether the new concept/law can reach its scheduled and planned effect cannot be predicted or guaranteed—transcultural similarity only promises the possibility of successful transplantation, and cannot guarantee its effects or outcomes.[62]

However, there is one remaining question: If Buddhism can be used as a philosophical paradigm for analyzing the effect and status of Han-Chinese traditions in contemporary Hong Kong and the production of justice, why do we still need to import foreign support? Why don't we simply utilize the materials we already have? The answer might be that in the case of interpreting and understanding tradition in the present, Buddhist theories of karma and seeds are mainly used to understand how human subjectivity is reconstructed—in the example I quote above, the incident was used to demonstrate how karma can work on a person: Even when the Emperor, who was usually called the 'Son of Heaven', had done something against Buddhism, he would be punished by his own decision and action—Buddhism has not frequently used the karma machine to investigate how culture and tradition work contemporarily. We therefore need a Deleuzian perspective to sensitize Buddhist theory towards how it can be used in deterritorializing the connections between time, instants and history. And, in relation to justice, as Guu-ying Chen sharply points out, there is a lack of critical perspective within Han-Chinese traditional culture.[63] In other words, there has traditionally been no philosophical perspective on developing a strategy that challenges injustice. Since (Orthodox) Confucianism is developed in the discourse of harmony, where conflicts are devalued, how can they develop an effective strategy of challenging injustice? This viewpoint has loomed especially large due to the hegemony of harmony in the cultural construction of a legal perspective—harmony is the prime principle and it would never encourage people to use litigation to resolve conflicts. While Daoism stresses actionless-ness and Buddhism emphasizes equality, have they said anything on the motivation/intention of challenging inequality and producing justice? Transplanting a Deleuzian theory of justice can certainly help connect Buddhist equality with the possible development of justice in Hong Kong.

---

[62] Chiu (2017).

[63] Chen (1988), at 1.

5.6 Conclusion

In this chapter, I have developed a line of argument, according to which, when making new policy and enacting new law, the stakeholders have to take into account of Han-Chinese traditional culture when considering whether the law controlling domestic violence in Hong Kong should adopt court-mandated counseling as a device to reform the behavior of the perpetrator and include same sex couples as part of the targets for protection: As I have argued in Part 1, since (Orthodox) Confucianism puts so much effort into maintaining and reproducing interpersonal harmony in the context of social hierarchy—as Confucius said: 'In hearing litigations, I am like any other body. What is necessary, however, is to cause the people to have no litigations.'[64] (trans., original: 听讼, 吾犹人也。必也使无讼乎!)—court-mandated counseling can certainly help in re-constructing familial harmony as it avoids directly sentencing the abuser to jail, and thus can be well accepted by, and engage with, Hong Kong Han-Chinese traditional culture. As (1) sexual orientation does not play any role in the Confucian philosophy of harmony; (2) when Daoism advocates actionless-ness and therefore would object to excessive and non-essential regulation of sexuality and sexual orientation; and (3) as one of the most important Buddhist principles is equality, Buddhism would certainly reject any proposition not embracing LesBiGayTransIntersexQueer/TongZhi in the orbit of its protection; the revision of Hong Kong's anti domestic violence law by which same sex couples are now protected, like the introduction of court-mandated counseling, will not be strongly challenged by a Han-Chinese traditional cultural perspective.[65]

Switching the focus to possible legal devices controlling domestic violence in Mainland China—like Hong Kong, Mainland China is dominated by Han peoples[66]—we can find that besides two provisions in the Mainland Chinese Criminal Law which prohibit people from abusing their marital partners, and one similar article under the Civil Code,[67] there has been an absence of law which particularly deals with domestic violence. The Anti Domestic Violence Law was enacted in 2015

---

[64] Chapter 12 颜渊, *The Analects of Confucius,* available at: https://ctext.org/analects/yan-yuan (visited 29 Dec 2020).

[65] Chiu (2017).

[66] According to the Consensus conducted in 2007, the population of Han race in Mainland China is 1,182,950,000, 90.56% of the total population.

[67] Article 260 of PRC Criminal Law 刑法; which writes that serious abuse of family members amounts to a criminal offence, the offender may be subjected to 2—7-year imprisonment. It is the so called 'Offence of (Domestic) Maltreatment' 虐待罪. Article 1042 of the PRC Civil Code 民法典 also includes the similar stipulation.

so as to fill that vacuum. According to this Law, habeas corpus could be issued in cases of domestic violence (Part 4); also, mediation, education and counseling, not court mandated though, can be implemented to prevent domestic violence or deal with cases with a lesser degree of violence (Articles 10, 16 and 22). The Law is not only concerned with the legal status of victim shelters (Article 15); it has also set up a compulsory reporting system and made educational institutions and medical service providers responsible (Article 14). While there have been recent studies related to the effectiveness of habeas corpus and the dialogue between the Law and the current criminal system, there is no research focusing on the interaction between the Law and familial culture. In order to fully utilize the Law and effectively control domestic violence, the following questions hence must be answered: In Mainland China, can criminalization and compulsory reporting of domestic violence work effectively and will it be welcomed by the society? In other words, will reporting domestic violence to the police, either by the victims or other professions (like medical practitioners), be taken as a further violation of interpersonal harmony (besides the damaged familial relationship), including neighbourhood and interpersonal relationship at work? Provided that Deleuzian justice is still new and is not yet fully engaged with Mainland (Han-)Chinese society, can implementation of the law, without the evaluation of a sophisticated perspective of justice, help to solve the problem of domestic violence and reveal the suppression of the powerless? It seems that the question as to whether law can be an effective means to control domestic violence in Mainland China still needs to be explored and discussed.

References

Bankston, Samantha, *Deleuze and Becoming* (London & New York: Bloomsbury, 2017).

Berressem, Hanjo, *Gilles Deleuzes Luminou's Philosophy* (Edinburgh: Edinburgh University Press, 2020).

Bryant, Levi, *Difference and Givenness: Deleuze's Transcendental Empiricism and the Ontology of Immanence* (United States of America: Northwestern University Press, 2008).

Capeheart, Loretta & Milovanovic, Dragon, *Social Justice: Theories, Issues and Movements* (United States of America: Rutgers University Press, 2007).

Chan, Stephen, (2005) 'Buddhism and Human Rights' in Rhona Smith & Van Den Anker, (eds), *Human Rights* (Spain: Hodder Arnold, 2005), 25–31.

Chan, Sum-tin, *Philosophical Interpretation of Buddhist Mādhyamika Theory (trans.,* original: *佛教中观学百论的哲学解读)* (TaiPei: Student, 2017).

Chang, Hsiao-hung, *Fake Globalization* (TaiWan: Unitas, 2007).

Chen, Guu-ying, (1988) *Nietzsche: A New Perspective (trans., original: 尼采新论)* (Hong Kong: Commercial Press, 1988).

Chen, Guu-ying, 'The Renewal of the Taoist Tradition in Contemporary World' (2001) 37 *Philosophical Forum* 136–143.

Chiu, Man-chung, *De/Sexing Hong Kong Law* (Hong Kong: Red Publish, 2017).

Deleuze, Gilles, *Bergsonism* (New York: Zone Books, 1991).

Deleuze, Gilles, *Differences and Repetition* (New York: Columbia University Press, 1994).

Deleuze, Gilles, *Two Regimes of Madness* (New York: Semiotext(e), 2006).
Due, Reidar, *Deleuze* (Cambridge: Polity, 2007).
Fo Hui 佛慧, 'Some Summaries on the Origin and Characteristics of Vinaya Master Dao Xuan's Idea on Saṃvara' (2015) 2 *Vinaya* 124–134.
Fu, Zi-tang, (ed), *Lectures on Jurisprudence (trans., original: 法理学讲演录) Vol 3* (BeiJing: Law Press, 2008).
Grosz, Elizabeth, *Time Travels—Feminism, Nature, Power* (Durham: Duke University Press, 2005).
Hu, Xiao-guang (trans., original: 胡晓光), *'Alaya-vijñāna: An Opinion (trans., original: 阿赖耶识刍议)'*, (1999) 4 *FaYin 法音* 9.
Hu, Shui-jun (trans., original: 胡水君), *Political Analysis of Law (trans., original: 法律的政治分析)* (BeiJing: Peking University Press, 2005).
Jiang, Shan (trans., original: 江山), *Jurisprudence of Interpersonal Isomorphistic-structuralism (trans., original: 人际同构的法哲学)* (BeiJing: China University of Political Science and Law, 2002).
Jiang, Tao, *Contexts and Dialogue: Yogacara Buddhism and Modern Psychology on the Subliminal Mind* (Honolulu: University of Hawai'i Press, 2006).
Joe Tom Sun, 'Psychology in Primitive Buddhism' in Anthony Molino, (ed), *The Couch and the Tree: Dialogues in Psychoanalysis and Buddhism* (New York: North Point Press, 1988), 3–11.
Koller, John, *Asian Philosophies* (New Jersey: Prentice Hall, 2002).
Li, Cun-shan, *Study of Qi and Theory of ren (trans., original: 气论与仁学)* (ZhengZhou: ZhongZhou GuJi 中州古籍, 2009).
Lin, Duan, 'The Chinese traditional legal culture: Kadi justice or the Third Realm?' (2007) 6 *Sino-western legal tradition (trans., original: 中西法律传统)* 425–453.
May, Todd, *Gilles Deleuze: An Introduction* (Cambridge: Cambridge University Press, 2005).
Ng, Yu-kwan, *Contemporary Analysis of Lao-Chuang Philosophy (trans., original: 老庄哲学的现代析论)* (TaiPei: WenJin 文津, 1998).
Pan, Li-ping, *Concept of Harmony in Chinese Legal System (trans., original: 中华法系的和谐理念)* (BeiJing: Law Press, 2006).
Rodowick, David, *Gilles Deleuze's Time Machine* (Durham & London: Duke University Press, 1997).
Rose, Nikolas, Government and Control, (2000) 40 *Brit J. Criminol*, 321–339.
Sagoll, Cliff, 'Duration (Duree)' in Adrian Parr, (ed), *The Deleuze Dictionary* (United Kingdom: Columbia University Press, 2005), 78–80.
Somers-Hall, Henry, *Deleuze's Difference and Repetition* (Edinburgh: Edinburgh University Press, 2013).
Song, Dao-fa, *Study of Buddhist View on Buddhism (trans., original: 佛教史观研究)* (BeiJing: Religious Culture, 2009).
Taishō Tripiṭaka Editorial Committee (trans., original: 大藏经刊行委员会), *Taishō Tripiṭaka* (TaiPei: XinWenFeng 新文丰, 1986).
Tang, Kai-lin (trans., original: 唐凯麟) & Zhang, Huai-cheng (trans., original: 张怀承), *ChengREN Yu ChengSheng 成人與成聖* (ChangSha: HuNan University Press, 2003).
Wang, Ze-ying (trans., original: 王泽应), *ZiRan Yu DaoDe 自然与道德* (ChangSha: HuNan University Press, 2003a).
Wang, Qing-jie, *Heidegger and a Hermeneutical Interpretation of Confucianism and Daoism* (BeiJing: RenMin University Press, 2004).
Widder, Nathan, *Political Theory after Deleuze* (London & New York: Continuum, 2012).
Williams, James, *Gilles Deleuze's Difference and Repetition: A Critical Introduction and Guide* (Edinburgh: Edinburgh UP, 2003).
Williams, John, *Gilles Deleuze's Philosophy of Time* (Edinburgh: Edinburgh University Press, 2011).
Xia, Xin-hua (trans., original: 夏新华), *Rule of Law: Realization and Transgression (trans., original: 法治: 实践与超越)* (BeiJing: China University of Political Science and Law, 2004).

Xu, Ke-qian, *'Pre-Qin Confucian theory of Desire ' (trans., original: 先秦儒家关于「欲」的理论)* (2006) 5 *Academic Journal of ZhongZhou (trans., original: 中州学刊)* 166–170.
Yang, Wai-zhong, *A Research of the Nature of Mind of Chinese Buddhism (trans., original: 中国佛教心性论研究)* (BeiJing: Religious Culture, 2007).
Žižek, Slavoj, *Event* (London: Penguin, 2014).

Chapter 6
Desiring Justice, Acting Anātman: Transforming the Legal Transsexual Fantasy from the Perspectives of Žižekian and Mahāyāna Buddhist Philosophies

6.1 Introduction: Transsexual Marriage and Rawlsian Justice

On 13 May 2013, a ground-breaking judgement was delivered by the Hong Kong Court of Final Appeal. According to the decision of *W* v *The Registrar of Marriages,*[1] although the current Marriage Reform Ordinance (Cap 178, LHK)[2] in Hong Kong only allows opposite sex (not essentially heterosexual) marriage, a person's newly acquired gender identity, which is different from her/his original gender identity (e.g. from a man to a woman), is now recognized and s/he can legitimately marry a person of the opposite sex (a man). With one judge dissenting (Mr. Justice Patrick Chan), the majority of the Bench (Mr. Justice Geoffrey Ma, Mr. Justice Roberto Ribeiro, Mr. Justice Kemal Bokhary and Lord Leonard Hoffman) laid down their reasoning:

(1) Consummation, which is essential in making a valid marital contract,[3] can happen with a transsexual;[4]
(2) With the change in social conditions, purely biological factors should not be the only conclusive criteria when deciding the gender identity of a person,[5] so, *Corbett*[6] is no longer good law;[7]
(3) Although it is stated in the Marriage Ordinance (Cap 181, LHK) that only Christian Marriage or equivalent are legal, religious factors should be ignored;[8]

This chapter is derived in part from a chapter published in *Globalized Religion and Sexual Identity: Contexts, Contestations, Voices* (2014) Brill.

[1] FACV 4/2012.

[2] Section 4.

[3] Section 20(2), Matrimonial CausesOrdinance (Cap 179, LHK).

[4] FACV 4/2012, para 55.

[5] FACV 4/2012, para 77 (b).

[6] [1971] P 83.

[7] FACV 4/2012, para 94.

[8] FACV 4/2012, para 205.

M.-C. Chiu, *Transforming the Hong Kong Legal Machine*,
https://doi.org/10.1007/978-981-19-1272-6_6

(4) To deny transsexuals marital rights amounts to a denial of their humanity.[9]

The majority of the bench also took the opportunity to lay down the most important principle when handling cases in relation to the protection of human rights, human dignity and freedom: It is unjust to reject minority rights if there is an 'absence of a majority consensus',[10] and the court should not leave the manufacture of new protections to the legislature.[11] This judgment resonates with the statement made by Mr. Justice Ma, who was also the then Chief Justice, during the 2010 Legal Year Opening Ceremony:

> Justice requires that no one is above the law; in other words, equality. Justice also requires that an individual's rights and liberties must be protected even against what may be the views of the majority of the public.[12]

Both the judgment in *W*'s case and the statement made by Mr. Justice Ma can be seen as applying Rawlsian justice in the context of Hong Kong, and not just to marriage law. For John Rawls, all kinds of desire have to be regulated and rationalized.[13] He assumes that all humans are free, equal and rational and reasonable,[14] so, everyone can accept justice and should be able to trust that social institutions, including law, can achieve and maintain justice.[15] From this paradigm, Rawls derives a set of principles (and procedures), by which justice can be created: (1) '[E]ach person is to have an equal right to the most extensive basic liberty compatible with a similar liberty for others'; and (2) Social and economic inequalities are acceptable if they are arranged (a) to the greatest benefit to the least advantaged, and (b) attached to the 'offices and positions open to all under the conditions of equality of opportunity'.[16]

The problem is: Can Rawlsian theory be transplanted that smoothly, simply by a judgment and a public statement? As argued in Chap. 1, successful transplantation of a foreign concept (e.g. the Rawlsian concept of justice) needs a cultural platform

---

[9] FACV 4/2012, para 224. The request made by W had earlier been rejected respectively in the Court of First Instance and at the Court of Appeal, where the reasons given were: (1) Recognizing the marital rights of transsexuals will open the debate in relation to same sex marriage (HCA 120/2009, para 9; CACV 266/2010, para 142); (2) *Corbett* v *Corbett* ([1971] P 83), where transsexual marital rights were rejected, was still good law in Hong Kong (HCAL 120/2009, para 121; CACV 266/2009, para 55, 57); (3) Although marital rights are projected by the International Human Rights Law (including *Goodwin* v *UK* (2002) 35 EHRR 18, where transsexual marital rights are recognized), they only apply to natural born females and males (HCAL 120/2009, para 186; CACV 266/2010, para 138); and (4) Any amendments to the relevant law should only be made by the legislature, when there is a social consensus (HCA 120/2009, para 194; CACV 266/2010, paras 111, 142).

[10] FACV 4/2012, para 115.

[11] FACV 4/2012, para 122.

[12] Ma, Geoffrey, 'CJ's speech at Ceremonial Opening of the Legal Year 2011.' Speech presented at the Ceremonial Opening of the Legal Year 2011, available at: http://www.info.gov.hk/gia/general/201101/10/P201101100201.htm (visited 4 Feb 2012).

[13] Lin (2008); Yao (2011).

[14] Rawls (1971).

[15] Yao (2011).

[16] Rawls (1971).

whereby 'transcultural sim*u*larity' can work efficiently and effectively and postcolonial violence can then be avoided. Mahāyāna大众 Buddhism, which like Rawlsian philosophy, also emphasizes equality, can therefore be that platform.[17] Rawlsian justice, though highly respected by the Hong Kong judiciary, from Slavoj Žižek's perspective, does not create equality, but justifies discrimination:

> Rawls thus proposes a terrifying model of a society in which hierarchy is directly legitimized in natural properties.[18]

Even though the opportunities and rights of transsexuals in Hong Kong, one of the many powerless diversities, are now protected, and justice, from a Rawlsian perspective, has been achieved by the judiciary at the highest level, several questions remain unanswered: Mr. Justice Ma and Mr. Justice Ribeiro, when suggesting that the Hong Kong legislature should consider setting up a system to vet gender recognition claims and referring to the Gender Recognition Act of the United Kingdom as a model, ask: 'What impact would that have on marriages and on the existing wife's [or husband's] rights (and, if there are children, on the children's rights)? Does the transsexual woman [or man] retain the rights and duties of a husband and father [or a wife and mother]? If the couple wish to end the marriage, does the gender change provide a ground for doing so?'[19] The Court of Final Appeal also suggested that the Hong Kong legislature establish procedures by which transsexual gender identity can be recognized and confirmed.[20]

In order to answer the above questions, we have to pose two further questions: (1) Why, according to Rawls, does desire (e.g. the desire to get married, to maintain a family and to nurture children or the desire to stop others getting married, maintaining a family, and nurturing children) have to be controlled and regulated? (2) Is it possible to define gender identity (including transsexuals)? One of the arguments put forward by local Christian fundamentalists is: LesBiGayTransIntersexQueer/Tongzhi,[21] including transsexuals, are in fact advantaged, not the least advantaged, as stated in Rawlsian theory, and any anti-discrimination measures would only reproduce and become reverse discrimination. But what is the definition of the (least) advantaged? In short, is it possible to have a fixed meaning of identity? If Žižek's view on the Rawlsian concept is valid, then would the judgment only re-create injustice? Can Žižek's view still be relevant in the context of Hong Kong?

In this chapter, I attempt to create a triangular interactive framework of justice, desire and identity based on the philosophical perspectives of Žižek and Mahāyāna Buddhism, offering some responses and possibilities regarding the above questions.

---

[17] For details, please see Part 1.

[18] Žižek (2009), at 75.

[19] FACV 4/2012, para 141.

[20] FACV 4/2012, para 136.

[21] In the vocabulary of Hong Kong Chinese, 'TongZhi' means connotes all people who fight against the hegemony of heterosexism. For details, please see Chap. 1.

6.2 Žižekian Jouissance on Fantasy and Superego: Justice Acts

Desire, according to Žižek, is the desire for the desire for object a,[22] which is the lack that exists in the Real,[23] a zone that is invariably anti-symbolic.[24] According to Jacques Lacan, the human subject is constituted by the gaze of others, and the problem is who the others are.[25] Since a human subject can never locate object a (as no one knows exactly what it is), the gaze always comes from an object of desire (at one particular moment), which is a temporary displacement of the mysterious object a. That explains why a human may know what s/he wants, but not exactly why s/he desires that particular object.[26] The search and the related displacement are the life goals and a (compulsive) repetitive process of all human subjects; i.e. jouissance.[27] When the human subject is hit by the gaze of an object of desire, s/he does not ask what s/he wants from the object, since s/he knows that is only a replacement of object a, but 'what the object wants from her/him' (a question that the object also asks). According to Žižek, the answer is simple: It is decided by the Big Other of the Symbolic Order, i.e. endless social expectations and customs (e.g. the gender roles of woman and man in a patriarchal society).[28] The next question is: 'What are the criteria that decide what the replacement objects desire?'—a question that leads to the manufacture of Lacanian fantasy (i.e. the desire constructed by the castrated human subject towards object a).

Fantasy (e.g. an ideology) does not aim at providing a correct answer, only at preventing a human subject from getting too close to the Real—a zone where residual pleasure is located.[29] Fantasy, hence, on the one hand shows desire a direction; and on the other hand, it also shields and defends human subjects against the irritating yet

---

[22] Object a is an objectification of a void, which is opened in the reality of a signifier. Object a thus has no positive consistency. As Žižek describes it, object a is 'the objective supplement which sustains subjectivity in its contrast to the subjectless objective order'. (Butler, Laclau & Žižek 2000, at 239).

[23] As the Symbolic Order is itself full of conflicts, it cannot eliminate all sorts of pleasure during the castration of human subjects. The Real is the leftover/surplus of the Symbolic Order: 'It [the Real] is the measure of our failure to fully symbolize the world'. (Vighi & Feldner 2010, at 39). As Žižek describes it: 'It [the Real] is not an external thing that resists being caught in the symbolic network, but the fissure within the symbolic network itself'. (Žižek 2006a, at 72). It is thus a 'distorted perspective on reality' (Žižek 2004a, at xxvii). According to Kelsey Wood, the Real therefore can prove the absence of universality in all perspectives as it is always paradoxical. (Wood 2012, at 17)

[24] Han (2014), at 49, 129; Zhao (2018), at 4.

[25] Žižek (1991).

[26] Matthew Sharpe and Geoff Boucher further explain the principle: Desire of the Other means the 'fatal attraction' humans have 'towards what is prohibited, transgressive, transcendent, off limits…its satisfaction always points the subject "beyond Law" towards what we fantasize has been lost to us as civilized, "castrated" subjects.' (Sharpe & Boucher 2010, at 51).

[27] Liu (2011), at 129.

[28] Sharpe & Boucher (2010), at 53, Zhao (2018), at 102.

[29] Han (2014), at 53.

energetic Real.[30] Fantasy then acts as the gluing buffer factor that links the subject and common sense reality—making sure that every human subject firmly believes that s/he lives without any possible inconsistencies by harmonizing all the conflicts s/he experiences in common sense reality. In order to reach these goals, fantasy has to make sure the residual pleasures stay within the Real and cover up object a.[31]

While fantasy helps humans to comport with the common sense world, it also at the same time constructs a context where jouissance is enjoyed by the human subjects, otherwise the comportment would not be smoothly conducted.[32] Fantasy, like symbolic language, is not omnipotent and is invariably full of cracks and leakages, so it needs jouissance to recognize its authority. Jouissance, which is closely related to the Freudian death drive, is a transcendental transgression in the form of nonstop repetitive visits to the Real in order to collect the residual pleasure and render the human subject complete (again).[33] So, while satisfaction comes from following symbolic regulations and fantasy, jouissance also creates enjoyment; the two pleasures supplement each other and make the common sense world function smoothly (temporarily).[34] Jouissance, a (side)product of following and obeying a (dominant) ideology, hence makes us happy with the current situation, but less happy with any (possible) changes;[35] the natural consequence is that humans will indulge more and more in jouissance. Žižek gives a very good example of jouissance—a self-destructive drug addict who understands the harmful effect of an overdose and accepts the negativity of the death drive.[36] In the contemporary gender-sexuality politics of Hong Kong, jouissance means the compulsive drive to challenge the powerful patriarchal heterosexist script of daily life—no matter whether a person really desires to subvert that script or whether their action is conducted without critical thinking; such actions can of course bring pleasure initially (like the excitement of watching an online porn website before becoming an adult), but they can also transform into pain in the end: Watching online porn behind the back of one's parents can be burdensome, but the teens are still 'instructed' to enjoy watching.

Desire hence has multiple and different layers of meanings and definitions: It is the Big Other/Symbolic Order (un/written social constitution)[37] and simultaneously, the prohibition, fantasy and jouissance accumulated in the Real. Circulation of desire cannot be separated by circulation of fantasy, since the Symbolic Order operates around a void, which is filled up by the fantasy and object a. A symbolic self does

---

30 Rickert (2007), at 59.

31 Zhao (2018), at 78.

32 Rickert (2007), at 62.

33 Sharpe & Boucher (2010), at 51. Žižek argues that the death drive, the 'blind, indestructible insistence of libido' that makes humans enjoy nonstop repetition of painful experience, forbids them from fully immersing themselves into the common sense world: '[Death drive] designates a blind persistence which follows its path with utter disregard for the requirements of our concrete life-world'. (Žižek 2008, at xvi).

34 Chen (2019), at 83.

35 Rickert (2007), at 20.

36 Žižek (2012).

37 Sharpe & Boucher (2010), at 51.

not know exactly what the Big Other desires of her/him (that is why people can never exhaust what a society expects from wo/men), and fantasy (e.g. patriarchal heterosexism) seems to be able to provide a definite answer for the self, however false it may be. Applying this perspective to the analysis of gender-sexuality politics, a person, even after submitting herself/himself to current law in Hong Kong, would still not completely understand the legal definition of wo/man; s/he may seek powerful references from court cases and judgments, which were made under, and in turn reproduce, the heterosexist discourse, though they could be appealed and overruled in future. This constitution of desire thus never stops as humans are invariably indecisive and not clear vis-à-vis others' desires (social expectations—e.g. the expectations of gender roles are always changing and debatable),[38] and humans are invariably obsessed with the outlaw (all social expectations are questioned and challenged—e.g. Tongzhi, cross dressers and transsexuals).[39] Subjectivity and identity are, like desire, always decentred and unstable:

> What I desire is predetermined by the big Other…Even when my desires are transgressive, even when they violate social norms, this very transgression relies on what it transgresses…
>
> Not only does the other address me with enigmatic desire, it also confronts me with the fact I myself do not know what I really desire, with the enigma of my own desire.[40]

Engaging a Žižekian perspective on destabilized identity with the impact brought about by *W*'s case in the context of Hong Kong's legal-gender-sexuality politics, we can then understand why it is impossible to define any essential nature of the transsexual—which also explains why there is an absence of a definition of transsexual in the UK Gender Recognition Act.

6.2.1 The Žižekian Perspective on Law and Justice

The superego is the law in daily life (Symbolic Order)—when law needs support and confirmation, the power of the superego underneath would exert its influence.[41] As Chen argues, the superego represents the desire and the will of the Big Other, so human subjects can only learn the law by understanding the Big Other (if they can):[42]

> The superego functions not only as a custodian of the symbolic order regarding meaning at the level of what can and cannot be said, but also it acts as a guardian of society's laws, morals and codes of good behavior and proper conduct.[43]

---

[38] Vighi & Feldner (2010), at 39.

[39] For details, please see Part 1.

[40] Žižek (2006a), at 42.

[41] Žižek (1994), at 54. For a detailed discussion on how lifestyle interacts with law and create effective governance of 'deviance', please see Valverde (2003).

[42] Chen (2019), at 129.

[43] Kul-Want & Piero (2011), at 71.

Simply put, the superego embodies the law by ordering us not to satisfy our desire but to enjoy and sustain jouissance.[44] Hence, under current gender-sexuality politics, whether a person wants to lead the life of a good lady or gentleman does not matter, but law and custom would instruct her/him to enjoy being a straight, even if s/he may be becoming tired of becoming so. As discussed above, it is also not surprising that jouissance goes against and fails to address the law[45]—for example: It may consider the law is too open or not strict enough. This does not essentially imply or mean complete criminality or breach of law—creating new law and repealing old law principles are also challenges to the existing regime which are brought forward by jouissance and the superego.[46] While law needs the outlaw (i.e. jouissance) to justify itself on one hand, on the other hand, it also needs a justification (superego) for its reliance on violence.[47] Jodi Dean explains: Only when humans believe there is something more than violence (law), will they have faith in law; in other words, law needs and thus creates its own ideological justification (e.g. justice).[48] As Žižek puts it:

> At the beginning of the law, there is a certain 'outlaw', a certain Real of violence which coincides with the act itself of the establishment of the reign of law.[49]

In *How to Read Lacan*, Žižek argues that although Lacan agreed that justice starts with equality (as Rawls declared) and only via shared prohibition can justice be achieved, the perspective and means should be modified and changed today, as human are instructed to enjoy jouissance (though they may not be happy at the end of the day).[50] Though the instruction to make us follow the law does not come directly from law but superego, law has to endorse this instruction.[51]

To Žižek, injustice derives from the problem that everyone has to submit herself/himself to the Big Other, and cannot return to herself/himself; as a result, everyone submits to jouissance and is instructed to enjoy. So, Žižek advocates that the only way to achieve justice is through a 'total awakening'.[52] In order to achieve justice, humans have to repeal the instruction to enjoy—we cannot totally rely on the repeal of old law and the making of new law, as that would not challenge the superego and thus could only mark a further entrenchment of the existing Symbolic Order. Following the same logic, the recognition of transsexual marriage only confirms the opposite sex monogamous marital format, because transsexual is not a singular gender identity, the law after *W*'s case only eliminated the differences between the

---

[44] Myers goes on and advocates: [T]he authority of the law stems not from some concept of justice, but because it is the law…If the law is to function properly, however, we must experience it as just'. (Myers 2003, at 53, 54).

[45] Dean (2006), at 35.

[46] Scuillo (2011), at 308.

[47] Dean (2006), at 143.

[48] Dean (2006), at 142–143.

[49] Žižek (2004a), at 204.

[50] Žižek (2006a), at 37.

[51] Scuillo (2011), at 310.

[52] Žižek (2006a), at 60.

post transsexual operation gender identity and natural born gender identity, the legal requirement of one woman—one man for marital purposes is not yet challenged. Justice, in the context of marriage law, would be possible only if humans are prepared to give up the concepts of ideal and fixed identity.[53] Žižek argues that the giving up of these concepts could be achieved by an act initiated by jouissance (the Real)—it is through the Real that a human understands that the patronizing power of Symbolic Order does not always work; s/he then starts the act, not willingly but naturally. The Real has two roles here: The fantasy blinds us and the jouissance enlightens us.

The act, though not belonging to Symbolic Order and being excluded by the Big Other, usually starts at the margin of the symbolic; the act also at the same time attacks/traverses the fantasy.[54] The best example is that of transsexuality. A Žižekian act is a voluntary, 'groundless', violent, excessive and 'trans-strategic' intervention towards Symbolic Order,[55] which redefines what is possible and creates the context where the possible can be possible.[56] A Žižekian act does not mean the total destruction of a Symbolic Order, it only 'does the impossible within the *existing* order.' (emphasis original)[57] Seeking marital rights for transsexuals is a good starting point—in the case of *W*, W is a transsexual who has led her life as a woman for more than a decade and was seeking recognition of her right to marry the opposite sex, as Hong Kong marriage law only allows marriage of opposite sexes. However, as I argue above, recognition cannot challenge the superego; a more powerful act would be the abandonment of gender identity restriction, but that does not only mean recognition of same sex marriage. An act rejects or suspends the Symbolic Order by breaking all the conventions, thus the symbolic instructions and superego orders become ineffective. An example of such an act, in the context of *W*, is, but does not only stop at, the filing of the case and going through the court session. It starts with an expansion of rights and subverting of legal tradition, which is predicated upon a heterosexist script of life. This act therefore constructs an opportunity for her/his re-birth and reform:[58]

> [I]t is only through an act that I effectively assume the Big Other's inexistence, that is, I enact the impossible, namely what appears as impossible within the coordinates of the existing sociosymbolic order.[59]

An act, in short, creates an opportunity by which a new common sense world and a new Master Signifier[60] can be produced (though an act never proposes any new Master Signifier). In the case of *W*, it is thus understood why the court does

---

[53] Kul-Want & Piero (2011), at 118.

[54] Butler, Laclau & Žižek (2000), at 123–124.

[55] Sharpe & Boucher (2010), at 185; Žižek (2004b), at 511.

[56] Žižek (2004c), at 121.

[57] Devenney (2007), at 55.

[58] Myers (2003), at 59.

[59] Žižek (2004b), at 510.

[60] The Master Signifier 'is an empty signifier which has no signified content, and which unifies a field of meaning precisely through this very lack or inconsistency'. (Wood 2012, at 8) Žižek writes: 'Lacan's "Master Signifier" is the "subjective" signifying feature which sustains the very "objective" symbolic order: If we abstract this subjective excess from the objective symbolic order, the very objectivity of this order disintegrates'. (Butler, Laclau & Žižek 2000, at 239)

not propose anything innovative (e.g. same sex marriage or civil partnership) but the recognition of rights within an opposite sex marital format.[61] In other words, an act expands the possibility to create a new Symbolic Order and can also recreate history, so that when the new order is created, it looks as if it was already there.[62]

Hence, the recognition of the transsexual's marital rights is the starting point of the Žižekian act within the machine of Hong Kong marriage law and gender politics—the fight for the right to marry is automatically initiated by and started at the margin of heterosexist patriarchal fantasy. However, it is important to note that, while an act is not a conscious activity of a subject, a subject, nonetheless, can prepare herself/himself to accept the act and the consequences.[63] In the case of *W*, that will mean people in Hong Kong should open themselves to accept the changes brought about by the decision.

It is thus not surprising that Žižek disagrees with the Rawlsian perspective on justice. According to Žižek, Rawls failed to understand that a society can construct a ressentiment, through which people would accept their fate and would not criticize the existing social injustice.[64] The second criticism posed by Žižek of Rawlsian justice is its reliance on a social contract; Žižek argues that the social contract is only a fantasy that creates violence, as those who do not consent would be taken as enemies and finally be eliminated.[65] Žižek believes that justice can be temporarily achieved through suspending the Big Other, so everyone can be her/his own self. However, as with Deleuzean deterrorialization and lines of flight, the Žižekian act, which does not expect any particular impact, cannot guarantee any success.[66]

Žižekian philosophy, in summary, constructs a very strong challenge against Rawlsian theory on one hand, while on the other, it proposes a reflective and constitutive paradigm of justice. If Rawlsian procedure sets the foundation for creating justice, then the Žižekian framework creates a constant initiative which repetitively challenges the discrimination created by nonstop re/territorialization of identity. The problem again is: How can Žižekian philosophy, a product of European legal-socio-cultural matrix, be transplanted into Hong Kong, a predominantly Chinese society? Again, I argue that Mahāyāna Buddhism can provide an effective platform for this transplantation to occur, since there are enough commonalities between Žižekian theory and Mahāyāna Buddhism for transcultural sim*u*larity to take place.

---

61 Kay (2003), at 5; Wood (2012), at 30.

62 Wood (2012), at 15.

63 Ramey (2013), at 86, 89.

64 Žižek (2006a), at 36.

65 Žižek (2001), at 81–82.

66 Devenney (2007), at 56, 64–81.

6.3 Mahāyāna Buddhist Jurisprudence: Constructing Justice Beyond Desire

Desire is also seriously studied and investigated by Buddhism, especially Vijñānamatra[67] 唯识 (the Buddhist ontological psychology), as discussed in Chap. 1. According to Vijñānamatra, desires are driven by different consciousness (vijñāna),[68] which in turn are motivated by different sets of seeds (种子, Bīja) under different appropriate conditions. Hence all phenomena (including identities) are simply subjective projections, i.e. Dṛṣṭi 见分. Put simply, intrinsic nature and essentiality do not exist. That is why, as Žižek rightly puts it in *Sex and the Failed Absolute*, what Buddhism, both Mahāyāna and Hīnayāna 小乘, with the understanding of the exercise of desire, aims to achieve is enlightenment; i.e. selfless-ness (无我, Anātman),[69] 'Self' in this context means '(self-centred) insistent attachment' or intrinsic nature (自性, Svabhāva), that are the symptoms of ignorance (无明, Avidyā). Due to the Buddhist philosophies of Anātman, subjectivity/being and gender/sexuality identity are not any pregiven or prediscursive concepts, so there is no eternal basis of hierarchical discrimination/inequality.[70] Buddhism does not only advocate equality among humans, but all lives—if that is the case, then how can Buddhism tolerate discrimination between women and men, between people with different sexualities/sexual orientations?[71]

Selfless-ness, which constitutes a strong foundation for the Buddhist notion of justice—equality among all kinds of lives—is the natural result of the analysis and deduction, put forward by Vijñānamatra and Mādhyamika 中观 (Buddhist post-structuralism).[72] Selfless-ness, in the machine of Vijñānamatra, can be achieved by 'transmutation of consciousness (vijñāna) to wisdom (jñāna)' 转识成智;[73] and when a person reaches the state of selfless-ness, s/he would understand the Perfect True Nature (圆成实性, Parlinispanna-svabhāva); which also means emptiness (空, Śūnyatā). A person, through completely understanding emptiness, can reach the state of Nirvāṇa 涅盘. Nirvāṇa is a psychological state where a person is no longer driven

[67] For more discussion on Vijñānamatra, please see Chap. 1.

[68] For more discussion on Vijñānamatra and classification of consciousness, please see Chaps. 1 and 4.

[69] Žižek (2020), at 90.

[70] Kulatissa Nanda Jayatilleke (undated), at 74.

[71] Yung Ming (1997), at 1.

[72] Lau (2019), at 96. For more discussion on Mādhyamika, please see Chap. 2.

[73] For details, please see Chap. 1

by consciousness, which is in turn motivated by desire, and is no longer bound by the (conventional) rules and regulations which are supposed to have essentialities and intrinsic nature (according to Mādhyamika).[74] Nirvāṇa is not the ultimate state of Buddhist practice, but a state of mind that needs constant maintenance and nurture.

Law, that is enacted or created according to emptiness, can assist in achieving selfless-ness and maintaining Nirvāṇa, as it can (1) overcome the chaos produced by different desires; and (2) focus on manufacturing quality lives for multitude[75]—and, certainly, justice (which also means equality) is one of the qualities that every Buddhist should assist in constructing. Hence, it is not surprising that *W*'s case in Hong Kong can be taken as the realization of Buddhist justice/equality by which equal access to marital institutions is promised and accommodated, regardless of different gender identities. Also, only with the success in controlling consciousness and producing the desire to constitute justice, can more people transmute consciousness to wisdom, achieve selfless-ness and stay in Nirvāṇa.[76] The loop never ends. If law in Hong Kong adopts a Buddhist philosophical perspective, we can expect more court cases substantiating and adopting the spirit created by *W*'s case.

There are, nevertheless, two problems. If Buddhist jurisprudence is a product of emptiness and is anti-discriminatory, how could there be (classic) Buddhist lu/vinaya (precepts or regulations) which oppresses transgender? Hui-nan Yang, after examining *Sarvastivada davinaya* 十诵律 *(The Recitable Vinaya in Ten Parts)* and *Abhidharma-kosa* **阿毘达磨俱舍论** believes that the classic Buddhist lu vinaya did not allow gay men and transgender (including transsexual) (黄门, Paṇḍaka) to join Buddhism.[77] As I argue in Chap. 2, this view, which is supported by the ideology of intrinsic nature, is severely criticized by contemporary Buddhist philosophers. Another problem is, however, what can we do to translate the idea of equality and anātman into the language and technique of Vinaya-Discipline, the Han-Chinese 汉族华人 Buddhist jurisprudence, that was developed by the Nan-shan school 南山宗? This is exactly why we have to investigate meticulously how the transplantation of legal concepts and technique can take place.[78]

Because there is no essential and universal definition of identity (e.g. the least advantaged group; including transsexuals) and equality, as identity (e.g. gender identities) is always changing; and because identity cannot be fixed, there is no justification for any kind of discriminatory hierarchy. In the context of *W*'s case, not allowing transsexuals to enjoy the right to marry in the same way as straight couples therefore relegates them to a secondary category—in the words of Mr. Justice Bokhary, that

---

[74] Ng (2018), at 233, 267.

[75] Lau (2019), at 76.

[76] Lau (2019), at 78.

[77] Yang (2006).

[78] Please see Chap. 2.

policy is denying their humanity,[79] and thus producing hierarchical discrimination.[80] (Mahāyāna) Buddhism, advocating and creating the concepts of justice and equality, would definitely not accept any denial of humanity; and by making new law, i.e. the Court of Final Appeal's decision in the *W*'s case, unfairness and inequality (negative desire) can be controlled, and will be gradually eliminated.[81]

6.4 Conclusion

Žižek argues that an act is very similar to Buddhist Enlightenment by which Nirvāṇa can be attained.[82] Žižek also points out that Buddhist desire is not Freudian drive. Žižek also thinks that the ultimate goal of Buddhist practice is to 'enable a person to achieve Enlightenment by "traversing" the illusion of the Self and rejoining the Void'.[83] It therefore seems Žižekian theory and Buddhist philosophy are not compatible with each other. However, both share a number of commonalities:

(1) Desire is multiple and floating, thus it is impossible to have an exhausted list of desires (or Rawlsian goods)—for Žižek, desire always keeps on manufacturing; and for Buddhists, whenever there are seeds, there can be desires;
(2) Not everyone is totally free (a Rawlsian claim)—for Žižekians, human subjects are always the product of desire, fantasy and jouissance; and for Buddhists, no one can escape from the Vijñānamatra machine (before transmutation); and subject formation always depends—for Žižek (and Lacan), it depends on the Big Other, while for Vijñānamatra, it depends on the external world;
(3) There are no eternally fixed social layers—in a Buddhist universe, inequality and discrimination can be eliminated with the final disappearance of seeds/desire; while with the Žižekian jouissance and acts, all existing structures can be problematized and challenged;
(4) Law is vital—Buddhism believes that law can help humans go beyond negative desire, while Žižekian theory believes that new law, reproduced by jouissance,

[79] FACV 4/2012, para 224.

[80] Please also see Cossman (2007).

[81] In Hong Kong, the mainstream Buddhist organizations did not express any views publicly on transsexual marriage; however, it is not surprising that they lend their support to the concept of same sex marriage, which is another challenge to the heterosexist marital format: As Raymond Lam writes in the Editorial of *New Lotus*, a Buddhist magazine: 'It matters not if you're in the US, the UK, Hong Kong or anywhere else. This is no longer an issue of being "conservative" or "progressive." I support gay rights and gay marriage not in spite of being a Buddhist, but because I am a Buddhist.' (Available at: http://newlotus.buddhistdoor.com/en/news/d/23704, visited 8 Jul 2013).

[82] Žižek (2004a), at xli.

[83] Žižek (2012), at 108.

> can be used to subvert the existing Symbolic Order and law. We can thus understand and propose that both Žižekians and (Mahāyāna) Buddhists will support the decision in the *W*'s case as the judgment sensitizes us to the impossibility of maintaining existing social layers (built upon different gender identities, where transsexuality is peripherized), and to a respect for different desires, the desire to marry and the desire to pass to another sex.

So, there are commonalities for transcultural sim*u*larity to take place and so a transplantation of Žižekian theory into Hong Kong should not be a problem. A question however remains: If Mahāyāna Buddhism can create justice, why do we still need to transplant Žižekian theory? The answer is: As Guu-ying Chen points out, Chinese culture and Buddhism lack a critical and subversive perspective.[84] This is echoed by Rita Gross who argues that 'what Buddhism has lacked, as I have said previously, is the will to direct significant amounts of communal energy into social concerns and reconstructions.'[85] Mahāyāna Buddhist schools of Vijñānamatra, Madhyamakā, Han-Chinese School of Vinaya-Discipline, construct a machine by which law and regulation can be modified and can manufacture justice, but where is the motivation to start the engine of the machine? That is why we need Žižekian perspective, which can repetitively produce challenges towards discrimination.[86]

Going back to the questions posed by the Hong Kong Court of Final Appeal, if we analyze them again from the perspectives of Žižek and Mahāyāna Buddhism, then given the impossibility of defining (gender) identity, which is always unstable and illusory, is it still meaningful and productive to define transsexual, wo/man, husband, wife and children? If so, then perhaps we do not have to look into the questions posed, but should instead start to investigate whether the gender identity requirement under the current marriage law should still be entrenched, and whether the Degenderization of (marriage) law is possible and appropriate: So, everyone can marry one another with mutual consent (when they have the capacity to give consent). Hopefully, such a legal strategy and policy, adopted and started by the UK Gender Recognition Act, can help create a justice system in which discrimination produced by the current Master Signifier (patriarchal heterosexism) and insistent attachment, can be subverted.

---

[84] Chen (1988).

[85] Gross (1993), at 183.

[86] Ho (2002), at 208–228.

References

Butler, Judith; Laclau, Ernesto & Žižek, Slavoj, *Contingency, Hegemony, Universality: Contemporary Dialogues on the Left* (London & New York: Verso, 2000).

Chan, Stephen, 'Buddhism and Human Rights' in Rhona Smith & Christien Van Den Anker, (eds), *Human Rights* (Spain: Hodder Arnold, 2005), 25–31.

Chen, Guu-ying, *Nietzsche: A New Perspective (trans., original: 尼采新论)* (Hong Kong: Commercial Press, 1988).

Chen, Jian, *From Ideology to Moral Law* (GuangZhou: JiNan University, 2019).

Chiu, Man-chung, *De/Sexing Hong Kong Law* (Hong Kong: Red Publish, 2017).

Cossman, Brenda, *Sexual Citizen* (Stanford: Stanford University Press, 2007).

Dean, Jodi, *Žižek's Politics* (London & New York: Routledge, 2006).

Devenney, Mark, 'Žižek's Passion for the Real' in Paul Bowman & Richard Stamp, (eds), *The Truth of Žižek* (London & New York: Continuum, 2007), 45–60.

Gross, Rita, *Buddhism after Patriarchy: A Feminist History, Analysis and Reconstruction of Buddhism* (Delhi, India: Sri Satguru, 1993).

Han, Zhen-jiang, *Slavoj Žižek: Neo-Marxism Critical Philosophy* (BeiJing: People's Publishing House, 2014).

Ho, Hsin-chuan, 'The Future of Confucian Political Philosophy (trans., original: 儒家政治哲学的前景)' in Huang Chun-Chieh, (ed), *The Conflict and Synergy between Traditional Chinese Culture and Contemporary Value (trans., original: 传统中华文化与现代价值的激荡与调融)* (TaiPei: Himalaya Foundation, 2002), 208–228.

Kay, Sarah, *Žižek: A Critical Introduction* (Oxford & Cambridge: Polity, 2003).

Kulatissa Nanda Jayatilleke, *Dhamma, Man, and Law* (Singapore: The Buddhist Research Society, undated).

Kul-Want, Christopher & Piero, *Introducing Slavoj Žižek* (Malta: Gutenberg Press, 2011).

Lau, Lawrence, *A Study of Buddhist Public Engagement in Thailand and Malaysia (trans., original: 左翼佛教和公民社会: 泰国和马来西亚的佛教公共介入之研究)* (TaoYuan: Dharma-Dhatu Publications, 2019).

Lin, Huo-wang, *Justice and Citizenship* (ChangChun: JiLin Publishing Group Limited, 2008).

Liu, Shi-heng, *Unbreakable Phantasm: Research on Slavoj Žižek's Ideological Theory (trans., original: 难以摆脱的幻象缠绕 - 齐泽克意识形态理论研究)* (BeiJing: Intellectual Property Publishing House, 2011).

Myers, Tony, *Slavoj Žižek* (London & New York: Routledge, 2003).

Ng, Yu-kwan, *Philosophical Interpretation of Nagarjuna's Mūlamadhyamaka-kārikā (trans., original: 龙树中论的哲学解读)* (TaiPei: Student, 2018).

Ramey, Joshua, 'Ceremonial contingencies and the ambiguous rites' in Jamil Khader & Molly Rothenberg, (eds), *Žižek Now: Current Perspectives in Žižek Studies* (Cambridge: Polity, 2013), 84–102.

Rawls, John, *A Theory of Justice* (Cambridge, MA: Harvard University Press, 1971).

Rickert, Thomas, *Acts of Enjoyment: Rhetoric, Žižek, and the Return of the Subject* (Pittsburgh, PA: University of Pittsburgh Press, 2007).

Scuillo, Nick, 'Žižek/Questions/Failing' (2011) 47 *Willamette Law Review* 286–325.

Sharpe, Matthew & Boucher, Geoff, *Žižek and Politics: A Critical Introduction* (Edinburgh: Edinburgh University Press, 2010).

Valverde, Marianna, *Law's Dream of Common Knowledge* (Princeton: Princeton University Press, 2003.

Vighi, Fabio & Feldner, Heiko, 'From Subject to Politics: The Žižekian Field Today' (2010) 3(1) *Subjectivity* 31–52.

Wood, Kelsey, *Žižek: A Reader's Guide* (West Sussex: Wiley-Blackwell, 2012).

Yang, Hui-nan, 'Buddhism and TongZhi: A Study of paṇḍaka (Homosexuality) in Vinaya-piṭaka' (trans., original: 佛教与同志: 律典中的种种问题) (2006), 7 *Journal of the Center for Buddhist Studies* 49–92.

Yao, Da-zhi, *John Rawls* (ChangChun: ChangChun Publishing House, 2011).
Yung Ming 永明, *Buddhist Perspective on Women (trans., original: 佛教的女性观)* (KaohSiung: FoGuang, 1997).
Zhao, Chun, *Discussion on Žižekian Psychoanalysis (trans., original: 齐泽克精神分析学文论)* (BeiJing: China Social Sciences Press, 2018).
Žižek, Slavoj, *Looking Awry* (London: MIT Press, 1991).
Žižek, Slavoj, *Metastases of Enjoyment* (London: Verso, 1994).
Žižek, Slavoj, *Enjoy Your Symptom* (London & New York: Routledge, 2001).
Žižek, Slavoj, *For They Know Not What They Do* (London: Verso, 2004a).
Žižek, Slavoj, 'From Politics to Biopolitics… and Back' (2004b) 103 (2/3) *The South Atlantic Quarterly* 501–521.
Žižek, Slavoj, *Iraq: The Borrowed Kettle* (London: Verso, 2004c).
Žižek, Slavoj, *How to Read Lacan* (London & New York: W. W. Norton & Co, 2006a).
Žižek, Slavoj, *Parallax View* (Cambridge, MA: The MIT Press, 2006b).
Žižek, Slavoj, *For They Know Not What They Do: Enjoyment as a Political Factor* (London: Verso, 2008).
Žižek, Slavoj, *Violence* (London: Profile, 2009).
Žižek, Slavoj, *Less than Nothing* (London: Verso, 2012).
Žižek, Slavoj, *Sex and the Failed Absolute* (London: Bloomsbury, 2020).

References

Chapter 7
'Confession of Law?': A Critical Perspective on the Production of the Child Subject in Hong Kong Law Controlling Child Sexual Abuse

7.1 Introduction

Since the year 2000, the 'child' has been a primary focus of legal development in Hong Kong. Besides the two proposals made by the Hong Kong Law Reform Commission in relation to child abuse, the Government has also made other suggestions or efforts to protect children: In 2000, it tried to set up a new criminal offence titled 'Persistent Sexual Abuse of a Child'. In 2003, the age of criminal responsibility was raised to 10 from seven and the Prevention of Child Pornography Ordinance (Cap 579, LHK) was enacted; and the report on *Child Custody and Access* was published by the Law Reform Commission in 2005. In 2008, a consultation paper concerning the possible reform of the Control of Obscene and Indecent Articles Ordinance (Cap 390, LHK) and a proposal on mandatory drug testing were issued.[1] And, in 2019, the Law Reform Commission issued its *Final Report on the Review of Substantive Sexual Offences*.[2] However, there has been a lack of critical and in-depth discussion on the child subject underlying all the discussions and legal proposals: Are children all essentially innocent (and comparatively powerless) and thus in need of protection and to be controlled? What is the definition of a child and who can define a child?

This chapter puts the focus on Hong Kong criminal law in relation to child sexual abuse, and investigates how it formats and produces the concept of the child from a poststructuralist perspective. I will also examine a possible shift in perspective and whether related changes can be successfully implemented in Hong Kong.

This chapter is derived in part from an article published in *Liverpool Law Review* (2012) Springer.

[1] The suggestions have been shelved. In 2015, the Government proposed to abolish the administrative function of Obscene Articles Tribunal; this proposal is also shelved. (available at: https://www.legco.gov.hk/yr18-19/english/panels/itb/papers/itb20190510cb1-1020-7-e.pdf visited 26 Feb 2020).

[2] For further discussion of the document, please see Chap. 8.

M.-C. Chiu, *Transforming the Hong Kong Legal Machine*,
https://doi.org/10.1007/978-981-19-1272-6_7

7.2 Criminal Law Relating to Child Sexual Abuse in Hong Kong

The law relating to 'child sexual abuse' mainly comes from the Crimes Ordinance (Cap 200, LHK). I will put the focus on criminal offences related to opposite sex physical assault,[3] where consent to body contact and age (definition of child) are the major themes; thus, offences related to child pornography,[4] same sex sexual conduct, sex work,[5] abduction[6] and procurement[7] will not be discussed.

Incest: Section 47 states that any man who has sexual intercourse with his granddaughter, daughter, sister or mother, shall be guilty of an offence. Also, according to Section 48, any woman of or above the age of 16 who has sexual intercourse with her grandfather, father, brother or son shall also be guilty of offence. Consent is not an issue.

Rape: Section 118 stipulates: '[A] man commits rape if (a) he has unlawful sexual intercourse with a woman who at the time of the intercourse does not consent to it;' and (b) 'at that time he knows that she does not consent to the intercourse' or he is

---

[3] A child, suffering from domestic abuse, can also apply for an injunction under civil law, through her/his next friend, under Section 3A, Domestic and Cohabitation Relationships Violence Ordinance (Cap 189, LHK). It is important to note that: (1) A victim of child abuse can seek damages by using negligence (and vicarious liability) as cause of action; (2) The claim will not be handicapped by limitation if the incident happened during the claimant's infancy. Please see Section 22, Limitation Ordinance (Cap 347, LHK) and *H* v *Lau Ka-yee Michael and Another* [2006] HKEC 1944. Since the article concentrates on the discussion of criminal law, details of civil remedy will not be discussed.

[4] Prevention of Child Pornography Ordinance (Cap 579, LHK).

[5] A person who owns, occupies, manages, assists to manage or control a premises or vessel, induces or knowingly suffers a woman or a man under 13 to resort there for the purpose of doing an unlawful sexual act or sex work shall be guilty of an offence. (Section 140, Crimes Ordinance) If such person induces or knowingly suffers a woman under 16, for the purpose of doing an unlawful sexual act or sex work; or a man under 21, for the purpose of having buggery or committing gross indecency with another man, to resort on the premises or vessel, s/he shall be guilty of an offence (Section 141, Crimes Ordinance).

[6] The law forbids anyone from taking an unmarried woman under age 16 out of the possession of her parent or guardian and against their will. (Section 126, Crimes Ordinance) A person who takes an unmarried woman under age of 18 out of the possession of her parent or guardian, against their will, with the intention that she shall have unlawful sexual intercourse with a male shall also be guilty of an offence (Section 127, Crimes Ordinance).

[7] Section 132, Crimes Ordinance states that a person who procures a woman under age 21 to have unlawful sexual intercourse in Hong Kong or elsewhere with a third person shall be guilty of an offence. Section 135(1), Crimes Ordinance also says: A person who causes or encourages sex work of or an unlawful sexual act with a girl or boy under the age of 16 for whom that person is responsible shall be guilty of an offence. Persons to be treated as responsible include: Parents, guardians, people who have actual possession or control of the child and people who have the custody, charge or care of the child. (Section 135(3), Crimes Ordinance) A person who uses, procures or offers another person under age 18 for making pornography, or for performing a live pornographic show, where the under age 18 person is or is to be pornographically depicted shall be guilty of an offence. (Section 138A, Crimes Ordinance).

'reckless' as to whether she consents to it. Please note: The age of consent, which applies only to females, is 16; in other words, females under 16 are not able to give consent with regard to vaginal intercourse.

Intercourse with Underage Women: A man who has unlawful sexual intercourse with a woman under the age of either 13[8] or 16[9] shall be guilty of an offense. These two offences are the ones where the prosecution does not need to prove that the defendant knew or had no genuine belief that the woman was under either 13 or 16 (i.e. the defendant has absolute liability) when the incident occurred.[10]

Indecent Assault: Section 122 reads: 'A person who indecently assaults another person shall be guilty of an offence and shall be liable on conviction on indictment to imprisonment for 10 years'. Please also note: A person under the age of 16 cannot, in law, give any consent which would make the act in question lawful.

Indecent Conduct towards Child under 16: Section 146 reads: A person who commits gross indecency with or towards a child (female or male) under the age of 16, or who incites a child under the age of 16 to commit such an act with or towards her/him or another, shall be guilty of an offence. Consent of the child involved cannot be a defence.

Buggery: A person who commits buggery with another person who at the time of the buggery does not consent to it shall be guilty of an offence.[11] Section 118C states: A man who commits buggery with a man under age 21 shall be guilty; so is a man being under the age of 21 commits buggery with another man. Section 118D states: A man who commits buggery with a woman who is under age 21 shall be guilty of an offence. However, the court in *Leung William Roy* v *Secretary for Justice*[12] decided that the said provisions violate the Hong Kong Basic Law[13] and the Bill of Rights Ordinance,[14] of which section 118C is thus ruled unconstitutional, one of the reasons being: The age of consent in buggery is different with the age of consent in opposite sex vaginal intercourse. What is interesting is: The statutory provisions related to (male with male) anal intercourse are not yet repealed and are now under revision

---

[8] Section 123.

[9] Section 124.

[10] *HKSAR* v *So Wai-lun* [2005] 1 HKLRD 443, per Mr. Justice Ma.

[11] Section 118A.

[12] [2005] 1 HKLRD 657.

[13] The provisions violated include Article 2, which reads: 'All Hong Kong residents shall be equal before the law', and Article 39 which reads: 'The provisions of the International Covenant on Civil and Political Rights, the International Covenant on Economic, Social and Cultural Rights, and international labour conventions as applied to Hong Kong shall remain in force and shall be implemented through the laws of the Hong Kong Special Administrative Region. The rights and freedoms enjoyed by Hong Kong residents shall not be restricted unless as prescribed by law. Such restrictions shall not contravene the provisions of the preceding paragraph of this Article.'

[14] Cap 383, LHK. The articles that the present provision violates include Article 1 (Entitlement to rights without distinction), Article 14 (Protection of privacy, family, home, correspondence, honour and reputation) and Article 22 (Equality before and equal protection of law).

by the Sub-committee on the Review of Sexual Offences, Law Reform Commission of Hong Kong ('the Sub-committee' hereafter).[15] The de facto age, according to the Hong Kong Courts, is 16; in 2010 Mr. Justice Geoffrey Ma gave a very clear guideline:

> On the basis of the Court's reasoning in *Leung* v *Secretary for Justice* that buggery was to be equated to sexual intercourse, so it had to follow by analogy that inasmuch as ss. 123 and 124 of the Crimes Ordinance dealt with unlawful sexual intercourse with underage girls (of less than 13 and 16 respectively), these provisions (and the sentences set out therein) applied equally to buggery with boys.[16]

Gross indecency: Section 118H says that, a man who (a) commits an act of gross indecency with a man under the age of 21; or (b) being under the age of 21 commits an act of gross indecency with another man, shall be guilty of an offence. But *Leung William Roy* v *Secretary for Justice*,[17] also decided that this section has violated the Basic Law and the Bill of Rights Ordinance, and is hence unconstitutional. Section 146 does not allow any person who commits an act of gross indecency with or towards a child under the age of 16, or who incites a child under 16 to commit such an act with or towards him or her or another.

7.2.1 Evidence: Rules on Corroboration and Past Sexual History

The rules stating that a judge should warn the jury with regard to uncorroborated evidence given (1) by a child (person age under 14)[18] or (2) the victim of sexual

---

[15] The Sub-committee on Review of Sexual Offences was set up in July 2006, with initial terms of reference: 'To review the common and statute law governing sexual and related offences under Part XII of the Crimes Ordinance (Cap 200) and the common and statute law governing incest under Part VI of the Ordinance, and to recommend such changes in the law as may be thought appropriate.' (Law Reform Commission of Hong Kong, *Consultation Paper: Interim Report on Sex Offender Register* Hong Kong: Law Reform Commission of Hong Kong, 2008, para 1) The terms of reference were expanded in October 2006 and are: 'To review the common and statute law governing sexual and related offences under Part XII of the Crimes Ordinance (Cap 200) and the common and statute law governing incest under Part VI of the Ordinance, including the sentences applicable to those offences, to consider whether a scheme for the registration of offenders convicted of such offences should be established, and to recommend such changes in the law as may be appropriate.' (Law Reform Commission of Hong Kong, *Sexual Offences Records Checks for Child-related Work: Interim Proposals* Hong Kong: Law Reform Commission of Hong Kong, 2010, para 1) Please also note that Section 118D is also under reviewed. The Sub-committee issued their final report, titled *Review of Substantive Sexual Offences*, in 2019. A number of significant reform suggestions were made. For more details, please see Chap. 8.

[16] *HKSAR* v *Chow Yuen-fai* [2010] 1 HKLRD 354, para 32.

[17] [2005] 1 HKLRD 657.

[18] Section 4(1), Evidence Ordinance (Cap 8, LHK).

offences have been cancelled. [19] In *HKSAR* v *Herder Johnathon Phillip*,[20] the defendant still tried to argue that the magistrate failed to consider the uncorroborated evidence that was given by a seven-year-old complainant. The judge extended this principle to trial without jury and said:

> Of course by virtue of the repeal of the statutory requirement for corroboration of the unsworn evidence of children and the operation of Sections 4A and 4B of the Evidence Ordinance, corroboration was not required and no warning as to the danger of convicting without corroboration was required.[21]
>
> [I]t needed no further frills or talk of corroboration or support.[22]

Also, unless there is a leave of a judge, evidence in relation to the complainant's past sexual history (besides those in relation to the defendant) should not be raised during a trial of rape and indecent assault.[23]

7.2.2 *Sentencing*[24]

In the case of rape, the following are aggravating factors:[25]

[19] Section 4A and Section 4B, Evidence Ordinance (Cap 8, LHK).

[20] [2005] HKEC 1063.

[21] [2005] HKEC 1063, para 8.

[22] [2005] HKEC 1063, para 9.

[23] Section 154, Crimes Ordinance. Another point worth noting is: An offence allegedly committed over a period of time based on evidence of multiple 'uncharged acts' that happened during the said period of time and at the same venue, might be very unfair to the defendant, as s/he would not be able to defend her/himself. In *HKSAR* v *Chu Chi-wah* [2010] 4 HKLRD 691, Mr. Justice Yeung explained: 'The prosecution alleged that within these periods of time, besides the sexual intercourse specified in the individual charges, there were many other incidents of sexual intercourse between the applicant and X. According to the prosecution, in any one of the periods of time referred to by the charges, the applicant did many other "uncharged acts", the exact number of which is not known. Owing to the fact that the offences and many other "uncharged acts" took place within the same place and the same periods of time, and under the same circumstances, the acts specified in the charges cannot be separated or differentiated from the many "uncharged acts" at all.

This handling method has two major defects: (a) It may lead to unfairness to the defendant, because the defence cannot distinguish which acts are the acts referred to in the charges and which acts are "uncharged acts", and therefore may encounter difficulties when preparing its defence; (b) It will also be difficult for the trial judge to give directions to the jury as to these "uncharged acts".' ([2010] 4 HKLRD 691, para 79, 80. Please see also *HKSAR* v *Kwok Hing Tony* [2010] 3 LRD 769).

[24] For details of the sentencing with regard to each offence, please see Appendix 2 of this chapter.

[25] The list is not exhaustive. *Secretary for Justice* v *Leung Yuet-hung* [2014] 3 HKLRD 304.

(1) The victim is either very old or *very young*,[26] if the age difference between the defendant and the victim is substantial, whether they were on good terms or in a romantic relationship is not a mitigation factor;[27] (emphasis added)
(2) Rape of *a child* or a victim who is especially vulnerable because of physical frailty, mental, impairment or disorder or learning disability;[28] (emphasis added)
(3) The defendant was openly preying on women in a public place;[29]
(4) The victim was abducted,[30] the offender adopts the victim and holds the victim captive;[31]
(5) There was further degradation of the victim beyond the offence of rape;[32]
(6) This was a concerted rape by more than one man. It was in vernacular terms 'a gang rape';[33]
(7) The victim will plainly have been traumatized having at the time of these offences been a virgin and by reason of her cultural background and religion she regarded herself understandably as having been 'ruined';[34]
(8) Failure to use a condom and ejaculate inside the victim, thus subjecting the victim to the risk of sexually transmitted disease and pregnancy;[35]
(9) Violence is used over and above the force necessary to commit the rape,[36] e.g. a weapon is used to frighten or wound the victim,[37] or the usage of drugs to overcome victim's resistance;[38]
(10) The rape is repeated,[39] i.e. the court will consider the number of occasions the offences were committed and the duration of the offences;[40]
(11) The rape has been carefully planned;[41]

---

[26] *R* v *Billam* [1986] 1 WLR 349; *IIKSAR* v *Hui Ka-sang* [2000] 2 HKLRD 718.

[27] *HKSAR* v *Yip Chi-shing* [2013] HKDC 1123, para 28.

[28] *HKSAR* v *Cheung Tsz-hong* HCCC 379/2017.

[29] *HKSAR* v *Habid Ahsan & Shah Amtiyaz Hussain* CACC 211/2002.

[30] *HKSAR* v *Habid Ahsan & Shah Amtiyaz Hussain* CACC 211/2002; *HKSAR* v *Cheung Tsz-hong* HCCC 379/2017.

[31] *HKSAR* v *Cheung Tsz-hong* HCCC 379/2017.

[32] *HKSAR* v *Habid Ahsan & Shah Amtiyaz Hussain* CACC 211/2002.

[33] *HKSAR* v *Habid Ahsan & Shah Amtiyaz Hussain* CACC 211/2002; *HKSAR* v *Cheung Tsz-hong* HCCC 379/2017.

[34] *HKSAR* v *Habid Ahsan & Shah Amtiyaz Hussain* CACC 211/2002.

[35] *HKSAR* v *Chow Kam-wah* HCCC80/2010.

[36] *HKSAR* v *Cheung Tsz-hong* HCCC 379/2017.

[37] *R* v *Billam* [1986] 1 WLR 349; *HKSAR* v *Hui Ka-sang* [2000] 2 HKLRD 718; *HKSAR* v *Cheung Tsz-hong* HCCC 379/2017.

[38] *Mahal Harpreet Singh* v *HKSAR* [2011] HKCA 458, para 21.

[39] *R* v *Billam* [1986] 1 WLR 349; *HKSAR* v *Hui Ka-sang* [2000] 2 HKLRD 718; HKSAR v Cheung Tsz-hong HCCC 379/2017.

[40] *HKSAR* v *Lee Hon-wah* [2011] 4 HKLRD 319.

[41] *R* v *Billam* [1986] 1 WLR 349; *HKSAR* v *Hui Ka-sang* [2000] 2 HKLRD 718; *HKSAR* v *Cheung Tsz-hong* HCCC 379/2017.

(12) The defendant has previous convictions for rape or other serious offences of a violent or sexual kind (e.g. a pedophile);[42] the chance of re-offending will also be considered;[43]
(13) The victim was subjected to further sexual indignities or perversions (e.g. photo taking or video taking);[44]
(14) The effect upon the victim, whether physical or mental, is of special seriousness;[45]
(15) The offender is in a position of responsibility towards the victim;[46]
(16) Racially aggravated rape and other cases where the victim had been targeted because of his or her membership of a vulnerable minority. For example, homophobic rape;[47]
(17) Possible impact on the victim's family members;[48]
(18) Presence of children;[49]
(19) Repeated rape in the course of one attack including cases where the same victim has been both vaginally and anally raped;[50]
(20) Raped by a man who is knowingly suffering from a life threatening sexually transmittable disease; whether or not he had told the victim of his condition or whether or not this disease was actually transmitted, and;[51]
(21) Other local factors:[52] 'One of them is that this [i.e. Hong Kong] is a crowded city, which is a safe city by international standards, and its residents have come to expect and are entitled to expect an environment in which it is safe for a female to walk about alone and at night. The fact of an attack in such circumstances must aggravate the sentence.'[53]

It is, however, important to note that young defendants can be given greater discount in sentencing;[54] and if the victim, unsolicited, seeks to 'persuade the court to exercise mercy or leniency in a wholly unsolicited, but principled manner, it would be

[42] *R* v *Billam* [1986] 1 WLR 349; *HKSAR* v *Hui Ka-sang* [2000] 2 HKLRD 718; *HKSAR* v *Cheung Tsz-hong* HCCC 379/2017.

[43] *HKSAR* v *Cheung Tsz-hong* HCCC 379/2017.

[44] *R* v *Billam* [1986] 1 WLR 349; *HKSAR* v *Hui Ka-sang* [2000] 2 HKLRD 718; *HKSAR* v *Cheung Tsz-hong* HCCC 379/2017; *HKSAR* v *Lee Hon-wah* [2011] 4 HKLRD 319.

[45] *R* v *Billam* [1986] 1 WLR 349; *HKSAR* v *Hui Ka-sang* [2000] 2 HKLRD 718; *HKSAR* v *Cheung Tsz-hong* HCCC 379/2017.

[46] *HKSAR* v *Cheung Tsz-hong* HCCC 379/2017.

[47] *HKSAR* v *Cheung Tsz-hong* HCCC 379/2017.

[48] *HKSAR* v *Lee Hon-wah* [2011] 4 HKLRD 319.

[49] *Mahal Harpreet Singh* v *HKSAR* [2011] HKCA 458, para 21.

[50] *HKSAR* v *Cheung Tsz-hong* HCCC 379/2017.

[51] *HKSAR* v *Cheung Tsz-hong* HCCC 379/2017.

[52] *Secretary for Justice* v *Lau Yun-leung* [1999] 3 HKLRD 289.

[53] *HKSAR* v *Chan Wing-tung* [2014] HKCA 247, para 36.

[54] *Chan Lai-sing & Lai Kwan-shing* (unreported), cited in *HKSAR* v *Cheung Tsz-hong* HCCC 379/2017.

wholly wrong for the court not to pay some regard to it.'[55] In cases related to unlawful sexual intercourse with a woman under 16, there are no real sentencing guidelines as such cases cover many possible factual circumstances.[56] Also, in cases related to indecent conduct towards a child under 16, there is no sentencing guideline.[57]

In relation to cases of indecent assault and buggery where a child is involved, the following are the aggravating factors in deciding the sentencing:[58]

(1) Protection of *children* is the prime target of the law;[59]
(2) Breach of trust (e.g. the incident happened between patient and doctor);[60]
(3) The risk of re-offending;
(4) The fact of repetitive offending;[61]
(5) Repeated course of conduct;
(6) The defendant is a sexual predator;
(7) Physical harm to the victim;
(8) Not wearing a condom; and
(9) Victims are targeted due to her/his membership to a vulnerable group.[62]

In the contexts of incest or indecent assault where a child was involved and the perpetrator is a parent or someone standing in the position of a parent, the following aggravating factors, as stated by Mr. Justice Robert Tang, in *Secretary for Justice* v *Chau Chi-yan*,[63] would be taken into account when deciding a sentence:

(1) *The younger the victim is, the more serious the crime would be.* (emphasis added)
(2) If there is evidence showing that the victim has suffered physically or psychologically from the incident.
(3) If the incident has continued frequently over a long period of time.
(4) If the incident has been accompanied by perversions, like buggery.
(5) If the victim has become pregnant because the perpetrator failed to take any contraceptive measures.
(6) If the perpetrator has committed similar offences against more than one victim.

Mr. Justice Tang also lists five mitigating factors:

[55] *R* v *Sung Chin-pang* [1995] 2 HKC 352, para 12.

[56] *HKSAR* v *Lam Yip-sing* [2001] HKEC 818.

[57] *HKSAR* v *KKF* DCCC897/2008.

[58] *HKSAR* v *Chow Yuen-fai* [2010] 1 HKLRD 354, para 39. The court would also take into account any aggravating factors listed in the rape case. *HKSAR* v *Ching Ka-lun* DCCC 6013/15, para 26.

[59] *HKSAR* v *HMC* DCCC 166/2018, para 19.

[60] *HKSAR* v *Chan Ching-ho* [2003] 3 HKLRD 476.

[61] *HKSAR* v *Cheung Kwok-yip Peter* [2014] HKCFI 1107.

[62] *HKSAR* v *Cheung Tsz-hong* HCCC 379/2017.

[63] [2009] 5 HKLRD 230, para 14. According to *HKSAR v Fung Ting-fai* [2022] HKDC 709, if the defendant feels regret is also considered by the court.

(1) Guilty plea.
(2) If there was genuine affection towards the victim on the part of the perpetrator.
(3) If the girl has previous sexual experience.[64]
(4) If the girl proactively seduced the perpetrator.
(5) If a shorter term of imprisonment will be beneficial to the family.

Another mitigating factor is: The defendant believed that the victim was aged above 16 when the incident happened and that there was nothing to suggest the contrary.[65]

In summary, in the cases of rape and intercourse with an underage woman, the age difference between the perpetrator and victim is deemed an aggravating factor: The bigger the difference is, the more severe the sentencing is. And, in relation to indecent assault and buggery where a child was involved, the exact age of the younger party is an aggravating factor. In sum, the Law Lords assume that age difference is equivalent to the difference in power where the innocent child will be exploited and abused, so the perpetuator should be punished more severely.

7.2.3 Proposals of the Hong Kong Law Reform Commission

Establishment of Sexual Offenders Cross Check for Child-related Work: The suggestion in fact first came from the judiciary. In *HKSAR* v *Kam Wing-yin*,[66] Mr. Justice Stuart-Moore wrote:

> We also recommend that consideration be given to the establishment in Hong Kong of a register in which those convicted of paedophile crimes are recorded on a formal basis and prevented, so far as it is practicable to do so, from working in close proximity to children.[67]

After releasing the *Consultation Paper: Interim Report on a Sex Offender Register* in July 2008, the Sub-committee, in February 2010, issued *the Sexual Offences Records Checks for Child-related Work: Interim Proposals*. The following are the major recommendations made by the Sub-committee:

(1) A scheme should be established by which the criminal conviction records for sexual offences of persons who undertake child-related work and work relating to mentally incapacitated persons[68] can be checked.

---

[64] Section 154, Crimes Ordinance (Cap 200, LHK).

[65] *HKSAR* v *Lam Yee-mong* DCCC 571/2010.

[66] [2006] HKEC 1314.

[67] [2006] HKEC 1314, paras 35–39.

[68] 'Child-related work' means jobs where the usual duties involve, or are likely to involve, contact with a child or children (i.e. people aged under 18). 'Work relating to mentally incapacitated persons' means work where the usual duties involve, or are likely to involve, contact with a mentally incapacitated person (Law Reform Commission of Hong Kong, *Sexual Offences Records Checks for Child-related Work: Interim Proposals* Hong Kong: Law Reform Commission of Hong Kong, 2010, Recommendation 2).

(2) Employers of persons involved in child-related work or mentally incapacitated persons-related work should be allowed to check whether an employee has any previous convictions for sexual offences. The check is, however, not mandatory.
(3) The proposed scheme should apply to both existing and prospective employees.
(4) The proposed scheme should reveal only a list of particular sexual offences.[69]

Abolishment of the Common Law Presumption that a Boy under 14 is Incapable of Sexual Intercourse: The Sub-committee published the *Report: The Common Law Presumption that a Boy under 14 is Incapable of Sexual Intercourse*[70] in December 2010. In that report, the Sub-committee suggested that the presumption should be replaced by a rebuttable presumption, which says: In the case where a boy between the ages of 10 and 14 is put in trial, the prosecution would have to 'prove beyond reasonable doubt that the boy knew his actions were seriously wrong.'

The Final Report on the Review of Substantive Sexual Offences: The Sub-committee, in the report, recommends:

(1) Creation of a legal definition of consent, which would put the emphasis on free and voluntary agreement and the capacity to make consent.
(2) Replacement of rape with a newly created offence 'sexual penetration without consent' and 'sexual assault'.
(3) Application of absolute liability to offences involving children between 13 and 16.
(4) Introduction of an offence which could make sexual activity in the presence of children illegal.
(5) Introduction of an offence of causing or inciting a child under 13 to engage in sexual activity.
(6) Introduction of offences of causing a child under 13 and under 16 to look at a sexual image; the purpose of which is to obtain sexual gratification, humiliating, distressing and/or alarming the child.
(7) Since either adult or children can commit offences which are related to underage victims, the age of offenders should no longer be mentioned in law.
(8) No marital defense is allowed in offences involving children.
(9) All consensual sexual activities involving people between 13 and 16 must be criminalized.
(10) Retainment of incest as an offence.

There are other recommendations made in relation to people with mental problems, bestiality and cancellation of a number of offences which involve same-sex

[69] Please see Appendix 3 of this chapter. On 30 May 2022, Hong Kong Law Reform Commission suggested that the system should extend to cover all existing employees, self-employed persons and volunteers.

[70] Law Reform Commission of Hong Kong, *Report: The Common Law Presumption that a Boy under 14 is Incapable of Sexual Intercourse* (Hong Kong: Law Reform Commission of Hong Kong, 2010), at para 25.

erotic activities.[71] For the purpose of this chapter, the focus of discussion is applied to points 3–9. Points 1 and 2 will be further investigated in Chap. 8.

7.3 The Child in Criminal Law Controlling Sexual Assault: Is a Child Subject Essentially Innocent?

Hong Kong criminal law concerning children is constructed and interpreted with reference to an important assumption: The child is invariably innocent and thus cannot give valid consent, so s/he needs legal protection and control. Put more accurately, the law in Hong Kong 'sets out to prevent the majority of children from making decisions about their experience'.[72] As Mr. Justice Stock puts it:

> It should go without saying that children are particularly innocent members of society. It is too easy for those who would prey on their *naiveté* and trust to succeed, for children are *by nature* trusting and the deliberate invasion of a child's *innocence* by an act of sexual abuse bears a repulsive character of its own and must be treated accordingly.[73] (emphasis added)

Mr. Justice Tang further advocated that this underlying presumption is particularly true in the era of the internet and thus the law has to adopt an increasingly patronizing position as parents may not understand the actual risks:

> Parents often do not realize just how much at risk their children may be to predators who can locate them in chat rooms on the Internet and encourage them to engage in sexual banter and bragging for their own ends, including for the ultimate purpose of obtaining sexual intercourse.[74]

Although a child may look so innocent and needing to be controlled (and protected) by law, there is no consistent and unified definition of 'child' in the legal context of Hong Kong. Generally speaking, adult means a person 18 or over: According to Section 3 of Interpretation and General Clauses Ordinance, (Cap 1,

---

[71] For details, please see *The Final Report on Review of Substantive Sexual Offences*, available at: https://www.hkreform.gov.hk/en/docs/rsubstantive_sexual_offences_e.pdf (visited 6 Nov 2020).

[72] Lind (1988), at 84.

[73] *HKSAR* v *Kong Yun-chiu* [2007] 4 HKC 391, para 11. In *Secretary for Justice* v *Man Kwong-choi* CAAR 8/2007, Mr. Justice Ma (the then Chief Judge of High Court and the former Chief Justice) also wrote: 'The aim of PCPO [Prevention of Child Pornography Ordinance, (Cap 579, LHK)] is principally the protection of children from being exploited and abused for the purpose of pornography.' (para 9)

[74] *HKSAR* v *Lau Chi-cheung* [2008] HKEC 691, para 4, In fact, law in Hong Kong nowadays seems also to take care of the parents of the victims in cases of child sexual abuse, as they are, in the view of the courts, haunted by the trauma. Mr. Justice Stocks writes: 'Parents of child victims will almost certainly be haunted by images of what has been done to the child and, in addition, will nurture a deep sense of guilt either for having entrusted the child to the company of someone who breaches that trust or, in other cases, for having left the child unguarded for the odd moment' (*HKSAR* v *Kong Yun-chiu* [2007] HKEC 1419, para 11).

LHK) 'infant' and 'minor' means a person who has not attained the age of 18; Section 2(1) of Age of Majority (Related Provisions) Ordinance (Cap 410, LHK) also writes: '[A] person shall attain full age on attaining the age of 18 years'.

However, in the context of sexual offences, the age of majority is irrelevant. Based on our discussion above, the age of consent is not the same as the age of majority and is different in different cases for different genders. There are offences against 'Incest by women of or over 16', 'Intercourse with girls under 13'[75] and 'Intercourse with girls under 16';[76] all hence implying that the full age of consent for women is 16. It also means that there is an absence of age of consent for males in the case of opposite sex vaginal intercourse. However, there is an age of consent in the case of male with male anal intercourse: Section 118C of Crimes Ordinance, which is ruled unconstitutional, still states that, in the case of male with male anal intercourse, the age of consent is 21;[77] however, the de facto age of consent in male with male buggery at this moment should be 16.

With regard to the age of criminal responsibility: There is a longstanding criminal law assumption that males under 14 are incapable of having sexual intercourse,[78] while the age of criminal responsibility is 10.[79] It should, however, note that the Sub-committee has already proposed to lower the age of sexual capacity from 14 to 10.

In sum, the age of consent for females in the case of opposite sex vaginal intercourse is 16; the de facto age of consent for (both opposite sex or male with male) anal intercourse is also 16. The 'maturity' age of male in cases of sexual offences is, at this moment, 14. Under the present law, a woman cannot commit the offence of rape herself, so the age of being able to commit rape and unlawful sexual intercourse does not apply to women.

7.4 Deleuzian Perspective on the (Child) Subject: Becoming Forever Goes On

We then take the age of consent/sexual capacity as the line of boundary between a child and adult in cases of sexual offences. In the strata created by (criminal) law, an adult is of course assumed to be mature and rational, able to make decisions and consent to sexual activities; while children are 'by definition, minors', and they 'can't speak for themselves'.[80] The critical question therefore is: Why is there such a

[75] Section 123, Crimes Ordinance.

[76] Section 124, Crimes Ordinance.

[77] Section 118D, Crimes Ordinance states that the age of consent for woman in case of opposite sex buggery is 21.

[78] [1892] 2 QB 600, at 601.

[79] Section 3, Juvenile Offenders Ordinance (Cap 226, LHK).

[80] Fourner (2019), at 114.

universal unrebuttable presumption that a child is always innocent and cannot make any decision in relation to sexual activities?

Any notions of philosophy which insist on re-developing a transcendental metaphysics of identity, like adult and child, are criticized by Gilles Deleuze. He associates such aims with 'stultifying, hierarchical regime of representation, to which he opposes the powerful, creative potential of difference'.[81] The theories devised by Gilles Deleuze (and Félix Guattari) thus try to provide spaces within strata of identity politics, including the hierarchical binaries of Child–Innocent vs Adult–Mature.

Identity, according to Deleuze, is a product of connections, disconnections and reconnections, which are parts of a process titled 'machine'.[82]Machines are driven by different assemblages which are formulated by two sorts of lines—molar lines of social force (including law courts, law making organizations, prison and law schools) and molecular lines of desire[83] (including sexual desire and related affects).[84] Deleuze argues that the molar lines always want to capture the molecular lines, which provide the energy for the exercise of assemblage, and fix an identity. Different molar lines relate to each other and produce a society of control, where a person with an identity is submitted to a non-stop modulation.[85] This is exemplified by criminal law controlling child sexual assault (a kind of machine), by which the sexual desire of fe/male children (molecular line) has been consistently put under the control (scrutiny/ignorance) of legal institutions and numerous cases (the molar lines)—the consent and the will of child, usually, could not be taken as a defence and are neglected—this is how law fixates the 'child' identity with innocence and hence subordinate to adulthood, and thus reconfirms the illusory formula of 'Children → (Teenager →) Adult'. Children thus need to be shepherded and protected. Law is only part of this modulation, which includes continuous learning and assessment (the medical profession and psychology, for example, besides law). Under this modulation, child sexual desire and conduct is constantly monitored by the fabric web of professionals (which is rhizomatic and not hierarchical) that is dispersed across the time and space of (child's) life.[86]

---

[81] Watson (2008), at 197, 198.

[82] As Claire Colebrook says: A machine is 'nothing more than its connections'. (Colebrook 2002b, at 56).

[83] According to Deleuze, while the social forces are always rigid, desire flows freely and preexists the human. As Claire Colebrook writes: 'Life is a flow of desire.' (Colebrook 2002b, at 142). Please also see May (2005), at 135.

[84] Deleuze & Guattari (1984), Jun (2009). It seems desire is the key driver of the machine: 'It is axiomatic for Deleuze and Guattari that no technical machine can exist without the prior investment of desire.' (Buchanan 2008a, at 17).

[85] Rose (2000).

[86] Kevin Haggerty and Richard Ericson argue that the body in the contemporary assemblage (a stative form) are broken down into pure information flow, monitored and analyzed. A good example will be the sexual offender registration system, where criminal records and career choices of sexual offenders are recorded and updated constantly. See Haggerty & Ericson (2000).

When assemblages look stable and identities (e.g. child and adult) becoming fixed, a virtual system of powerful hegemony is created.[87] Desire is codified and socialized by molar lines, usually via repetitive and different prohibitions and exclusions[88]—through non-stop different codification, certain qualities are read as marks of some individual essence that precedes and controls the lines of desire.[89] In the continuing interaction between child and (criminal) law, through the repetitive applications and interpretations of legal principles and provisions in different cases (e.g. the child cannot consent to any sexual activities or is not capable of having sexual intercourse)—the irrationality, immaturity, incapability of penetration and consenting/sexual inability and weakness are codified as the marks of children of different and relevant ages and genders—this is territorialization.

Territorialization is not nonetheless the end—if molar lines of social forces are rhizomatic and thus lack an origin or a centre, and molecular lines cannot be predicted, then identity can only be multiple and conflicting;[90] and repetition is never a repeat of the same (intersections of lines), but is also capable of producing of new (intersections of) different lines.[91]Molecular lines of desire, however, cannot be eternally controlled and overridden by molar lines of social force: Lines are always multiple and contested—there are always simultaneously different/new types of desire and social forces;[92] so, (diversified) machines, driven by different lines, can connect, disconnect and reconnect with other machines; i.e. machines are always fluid and dynamic.[93] In short, identity, formatted and controlled by interactions of lines, is on one hand, not free floating and relative;[94] and on the other, not completely fixed and essential.[95] Identities (including child and adult), to Deleuze, cannot be monolithic and are hence always complicated, folded and will never be completely unfolded.[96] In other words, no one can be pure, but unique. That explains why there are different principles of fe/male children in relation to age and consent in sexual offences cases. The best example is the suggestion put forward by the Sub-committee in regard to the age of male sexual capability—the reason underlying the proposal is that there have been many recent court cases showing that the existing assumption (i.e. only males over 14 are sexually capable) is just unrealistic—are there any cases where males under 14 penetrated the female victim without consent? According to the present law, the perpetrators in such cases cannot be prosecuted for the offence of rape.[97] This

87 Haggerty & Ericson (2000), at 609.

88 Buchanan (2008a), at 22; Žižek (2004), at 12.

89 Colebrook (2002a), at 45.

90 Linstead & Pullen (2006).

91 Žižek (2004), at 12.

92 Winslade (2009), at 336, 337.

93 Jun (2009), at 351.

94 Winslade (2009), at 336.

95 May (2005), at 125.

96 Rajchman (2000), at 60.

97 Tsang, Phyllis, 'Boys under 14 can rape, panel says', *South China Morning Post*, 14 Dec 2010, at EDT 3.

sort of unexpected and accidental legal encounter forces the law to reflect: It already shows that males under any certain age cannot be generalized, although biological function is related to ageing; and setting up an age assumption in regard to sexual ability is doomed to failure.[98]

It is hence not surprising that Deleuze advocates that identity is always 'becoming'. Becoming (including sensory becoming and absolute becoming),[99] which, as Levi Bryant said, in short, creates contradictions and oppositions.[100] Since becoming is a line-bloc (e.g. the zone between adults and children), and the effects of sensory becoming (the non-stop changing of definitions of the age of majority) and absolute becoming (the challenge of adult/children binarism) are always re-occurring, double and conflicting phenomena will always happen—thus manufacturing differences and multiplicities, and thus challenging the hegemony.[101] It is impossible to imagine that every man at the age of 10/14 will have the same level of biological capacity; wo/men at the age of 13/16 will share the same standard of im/maturity; and wo/men in different eras share the same scale and schedule of biological and psychological development; otherwise, the old common law presumption of male child sexual ability would not be challenged by controversial cases, and the Sub-committee would not have tabled its proposal. Contradictions among child subjects clearly exist: If the underage victims of sexual offences are always irrational and immature, then why did the law delete the assumption of corroboration for evidence provided by children? As John Rajchman rightly puts it: '[Multiplicities] means that we never wholly divide up into any "pure" species, races, even genders'.[102]

7.4.1 Body Without Age and Sex Organ: De-Ageing as a Resistance Strategy

Repetitive creation of the new and transformation, argued by Ian Buchanan, is fuelled by the lines of desire: Desire sows the seeds of resistance and revolution as it always tries to elude the coding imposed by the lines of social forces.[103] This is why Buchanan called lines of desire 'powerful' and 'liberatory'.[104] These lines of desire, which are 'stimuli in its own right',[105] come from people's own responses to the given context and lines of social force'[106] Desire, therefore, is productive.[107]

[98] Lefebvre (2008), at 58; De Sutter (2012), at 5.

[99] For further discussion of becoming, please see Chap. 4.

[100] Bryant (2008), at 58.

[101] Faber (2011), at 13; Silberstein (2006), at 150.

[102] Rajchman (2000), at 609.

[103] Buchanan (2008b), at 45.

[104] Buchanan (2008b), at 22.

[105] Buchanan (2008b), at 47.

[106] Deleuze (1995), at 33.

[107] Goodley (2007), at 147.

Because of unpredictable momentum, lines of desire, territorialization and fixation of identities/bodies is never complete, and the body cannot be a rigidly-ordered entity, but a 'Body without Organs' (BwO hereafter).[108] BwO signifies resistance to the notion of the territorialized body that comes with a whole package of organized and hierarchized organs, and is a metaphor for the shifting, interconnected, constantly moving and constructed body.[109] The concept of BwO, which initiates becoming,[110] does not mean there is an absolute absence of co-ordinated body parts, but that there is always something more—there can be different co-ordinations between body parts and there can be different interactions between body parts and reality/environment.[111] Becoming, motivated by BwO, therefore, manufactures points of undecidability.[112] Using BwO as the lens of scrutiny, we can then ask: Why does age (physical development) correlate with maturity (mental development)? If the correlation between age and maturity does not exist, then why do two people of the same age but different mental development have to be controlled by the same rule? Does sexual desire always grow with physical/sexual ability? Can sexual desire always be controlled by maturity? If so, why?

Desire, as pointed by Todd May, 'provide[s] the material that will be actualized' into temporary identities/bodies.[113] It is clear that children of the same age do not share the same pattern of desire/body and/or affect, which rightly challenges all the assumptions underlying the law controlling child sexual abuse: How a person's affect grows, develops and takes effect has no essential connection with one's age (and sex organs).

In other words, according to Deleuzian logic, identity is not always necessary—it is therefore impossible to territorialize the definition of child; childhood is only a conceptual persona which does not signify an actual person, but is a set of personalities that a child is supposed to embody.[114] Hence, in the context of child sexual assault, awkward results always occur: If a woman aged 15 consented to have vaginal intercourse with a man aged 14; under the present law, the former is deemed to be a victim, and the latter may be labeled as a 'child sex predator' and put on the sexual offenders register. Law in fact notices this: That is why genuine affection between the parties can be a factor of mitigation in sentencing (*Secretary for Justice* v *Chau Chi-yan,* per Mr. Justice Tang). Hence, why does the law still have to insist on fixing a prima facie relationship between age and criminal law? The De-ageing of our laws is especially productive and positive if the aim of law is to protect the victims from being

[108] Goodley (2007), at 153.

[109] Goodley (2009), at 267.

[110] As Ian Buchanan argues: '[T]he body without organs has two phases: an initial phase of construction and a subsequent phase of making things circulate.' (Buchanan 2021, at 196). In other words, BwO is a non-stop transformation.

[111] May (2005).

[112] Zehavi (2019), at 58.

[113] May (2005), at 137.

[114] Bohlmann & Hickey-Moody, (2019), at 7.

abused, in terms of physical/psychological state and power im/balance, which has no pregiven and presumed connections with age. Deleuzian philosophy successfully sensitizes us towards the non-essential and unnatural connection between age/body and power/maturity; since there is no consistent but conflicting levels of maturity among people of the same age, and there is no fixed and universal correlation between age and power/maturity, then it is in fact impossible to conclude that child is always 'naive' and 'innocent'. Age territorialization is exactly one of the problems underlying the proposal made by the Sub-committee with regard to the sexual offenders register: If the suggested mechanism aims to protect victims of sexual abuse, then why does it only claim to protect children, especially when the logic 'child = innocent' is only a virtuality and is always subjected to challenge and subversion? Is the Sub-committee assuming that adult victims cannot be innocent and only child victims are harmed?

If we disconnect age (and related identities, child and adult) in the law against sexual assault, then offences 'intercourse with underage women' and 'indecent conduct towards child under 16' should be reduced to 'rape' and 'indecent assault'; and the age of consent/sexual ability in the context of sexual assault should be cancelled.

John Winslade agrees that in order to construct a new line of flight and a different notion of subjectivation, a perspective outside of the experience can help.[115] Looking back through history, we can find that De-ageing is nothing new: It had happened in Imperial China, where (Orthodox) Confucianism and (Orthodox) Daoism played an important role in the formation of Han-Chinese 汉族华人 culture: The former emphasizes the hierarchical harmony of humans and developed the famous three cardinal guides (i.e. Emperor guides ministers, father guides sons, and husband guides wife) and five constant virtues (i.e. benevolence between father and son, righteousness between Emperor and ministers, differences between husband and wife, hierarchy between elder brother and younger brother, and fidelity between friends); the latter also stresses the importance of the harmony between heavenly order (TIAN Dao 天道) and human order (REN Dao 人道).[116] When analyzing the two schools of philosophy in detail, we can find that an isolated personhood (e.g. wo/men, non-adult) does not exist, but the positions in the social network—so there is no independent wo/man but wife and husband (minister and Emperor); no independent child and adult, but son and father. In other words, the child as a concept with reference to a particular age was not at all important in traditional China.[117]

Please note that the definition of child, unlike what is considered as common or normal knowledge nowadays, did not always rely purely on age, but body height: According to *Zhou Rituals* 周礼, 'Seven feet is age 20; and six feet means age 15' (trans., original: 七尺谓年二十, 六尺谓年十五). Also, while the concept of minor may have had an influence and been a consideration in relation to the format of trial and sentencing/punishment, it did not affect criminal responsibility; i.e. whether one

[115] Winslade (2009), at 341.

[116] For more discussion on Han-Chinese tradition, please see Part 1.

[117] Liao (2008), at 129.

was criminally guilty had nothing to do with her/his age.[118] According to the Han-Chinese Buddhist school of Vinaya-Discipline (Nan-shan School 南山宗), whether one is liable when a rule or regulation is violated does not simply depend on her/his age, but whether the wrongdoer accepts and understands the prevailing rules and regulations.[119] There was traditionally no regulation on the age of consent, criminal responsibility and/or sexual capacity. Only in the Qing 清 Code was there introduced a specific regulation on rape against a female child: Males having sexual intercourse with a woman under 12 shall be guilty of rape (奸幼女十二岁以下者虽和同强论); and, raping a female under 10 and causing her death, and raping a female under 10 shall incur the death penalty (强奸十二岁以下幼女因而致死及将未至十岁之幼女诱去强行奸污者照光棍例斩决).

What we can learn from the history of Imperial China are: (1) The definition of child is not universal, and a correlation between age and childhood is not always essential; (2) There was De-ageing.[120]

7.5 Further Legal Reform: De-Ageing as a Starting Point

The perspective developed from a Deleuzian philosophical perspective on the child subject can be employed to critically examine the whole set of child laws in Hong Kong. Questions like the following can be asked: Why do we have to set an age limit on the consumption of cigarettes, alcohol, pornography and films? If the age of consent in the case of sexual conduct can be challenged, should we not also ask why the law needs to set an age requirement on marriage? Shall we also review the weight the courts nowadays accord to the views of parties under 18 in custody cases? Should the concept of a ruling being in 'the best interests of the children', surely the most important principle underpinning family law, be reviewed—why would people above 18 have the power and status to decide what lies in the best interests of people under 18? Are all adults mature and rational enough to make such a decision? Are all non-adults not mature and rational enough to make a decision regarding their own self interest? And the most important question is: Before enacting any law relating to a child's rights and interests, should not law makers unlearn their privileges, and let the young people speak and also listen to their voices?

In the Japanese film 'Confession' 告白 (2010, awarded Picture of the Year and Screenplay of the Year in the 2011 Japan Academy Prize), two male Grade Seven students killed the only daughter of their female class teacher, a single mother who

---

[118] The only exception is Han 汉 Dynasty (206 BC–220), which once stated that the age of criminal responsibility is 10. *Year Two Regulation* 二年律令 writes: The person who is guilty but is under 10, exempted from being responsible' (*trans., original*: 有罪年不盈十岁, 除).

[119] Chen (2009). For more discussion on Han-Chinese Buddhist school of Vinaya-Discipline, please see Chap. 2.

[120] A question remains: Why do we have to import a foreign concept? For more discussion, see Part 1.

had just divorced her HIV-positive husband. But the two students will not be prosecuted according to the law in Japan as when the incident happened, they were below the age of criminal responsibility—age 14.[121] The class teacher therefore deployed a very well planned revenge, by which the two students killed their mothers respectively, without seeking assistance from the law.[122] The movie sensitized the audience, including me, to the possible subversion of the normal and natural boundary we draw between the child subject and adulthood—the former being innocent and naïve and the latter nurturing (and not torturing) the former. The most shocking and revealing insight is the status and functioning of the law in the formation and production of subjects—unless the law constantly confesses its insufficiencies and shortcomings when using age as a mark of distinction among human subjects, and unless the law is constantly reviewed and challenged, similar tragedies will only be repeated.

Appendix 1: Offences with Extra-Territorial Effect

According to Section 153P of the Crimes Ordinance, where a person who is a permanent resident of Hong Kong or usually resides in Hong Kong, has committed an offence listed in Schedule 2 outside Hong Kong, and the victim is under 16, or under 13 for offences under Section 123 (Intercourse with Underage Women) or Section 140 (Sex Work), that person shall be guilty of those offences—unless the person can prove that there is a marital relationship between the person and the complainant, or that the complainant consented to the sexual act. The offences listed in Schedule 2 include:

Section 118 Rape

Section 118A Non-consensual buggery

Section 118B Assault with intent to commit buggery

Section 118C Homosexual buggery with or by man under 21

Section 118D Buggery with girl under 21

Section 118F Homosexual buggery committed otherwise than in private

Section 118G Procuring others to commit homosexual buggery

Section 118H Gross indecency with or by man under 21

Section 118J Gross indecency by man with man otherwise than in private

Section 118K Procuring gross indecency by man with man

Section 119 Procurement by threats

Section 120 Procurement by false pretences

Section 121 Administering drugs to obtain or facilitate unlawful sexual act

Section 122 Indecent assault

Section 123 Intercourse with girl under 13

Section 124 Intercourse with girl under 16

---

[121] Article 41, Criminal Penal Code of Japan.

[122] For details of the movie, please see http://kokuhaku-shimasu.jp/index.html (visited 8 Feb 2011).

Section 126 Abduction of unmarried girl under 16

Section 130 Control over persons for purpose of unlawful sexual intercourse or prostitution

Section 132 Procurement of girl under 21

Section 134 Detention for intercourse or in vice establishment

Section 135 Causing or encouraging prostitution of, intercourse with, or indecent assault on, girl or boy under 16

Section 140 Permitting girl or boy under 13 to resort to or be on premises or vessel for intercourse

Section 141 Permitting young person to resort to or be on premises or vessel for intercourse, prostitution, buggery or homosexual act

Section 146 Indecent conduct towards child under 16.

Appendix 2: Summary of Criminal Offences and Related Penalties

Offences	Related statutory provisions	Maximum penalty
Incest	Section 47, Crimes Ordinance	20 year imprisonment
	Section 48, Crimes Ordinance	14 year imprisonment
Rape	Section 118, Crimes Ordinance	Life imprisonment
Intercourse with underage woman	Section 123, Crimes Ordinance	Life imprisonment
	Section 124, Crimes Ordinance	5 year imprisonment
Indecent assault	Section 122, Crimes Ordinance	10 year imprisonment
Indecent conduct towards child under 16	Section 146, Crimes Ordinance	10 year imprisonment
Abduction	Section 126, Crimes Ordinance	10 year imprisonment
	Section 127, Crimes Ordinance	7 year imprisonment
Procurement	Section 132, Crimes Ordinance	5 year imprisonment
	Section 135, Crimes Ordinance	10 year imprisonment
	Section 138A(1)(a), Crimes Ordinance (The person depicted in pornography is under 16)	$3,000,000 fine + 10 year imprisonment
	Section 138A(1)(b), Crimes Ordinance (The person depicted in pornography is under 18 but 16 or above)	$1,000,000 fine + 5 year imprisonment
Sex work	Section 140, Crimes Ordinance	Life imprisonment
	Section 141, Crimes Ordinance	14 year imprisonment
Buggery	Section 118A, Crimes Ordinance	Life imprisonment

(continued)

(continued)

Offences	Related statutory provisions	Maximum penalty
	Section 118C, Crimes Ordinance	Life imprisonment
	Section 118D, Crimes Ordinance	Life imprisonment
Gross indecency	Section 118H, Crimes Ordinance	2 year imprisonment
	Section 146, Crimes Ordinance	10 year imprisonment

Appendix 3: Offences which can be Checked According to the Proposed Sexual Offenders Registry

Crimes Ordinance

Section 47	Incest by men
Section 48	Incest by women of or over 16
Section 118	Rape
Section 118A	Non-consensual buggery
Section 118B	Assault with intent to commit buggery
Section 118C	Homosexual buggery with or by a man under 21 (only if the victim was under 16)
Section 118D	Buggery with a girl under 21 (only if the victim was under 16)
Section 118E	Buggery with a mentally incapacitated person
Section 118G	Procuring others to commit homosexual buggery (only if to procure a victim under 16)
Section 118H	Gross indecency with or by a man under 21 (only if the victim was under 16)
Section 118I	Gross indecency by a man with a male mentally incapacitated person
Section 119	Procurement of an unlawful sexual act by threats or intimidation
Section 120	Procurement of an unlawful sexual act by false pretences
Section 121	Administering drugs to obtain or facilitate an unlawful sexual act
Section 122	Indecent assault
Section 123	Sexual intercourse with a girl under 13 (only if the offender was 18 or above)
Section 124	Sexual intercourse with a girl under 16 (only if the offender was 18 or above)
Section 125	Sexual intercourse with a mentally incapacitated person
Section 126	Abduction of an unmarried girl under 16
Section 127	Abduction of an unmarried girl under 18 for sexual intercourse
Section 128	Abduction of a mentally incapacitated person from parent or guardian for sexual act

(continued)

(continued)

Section 129	Trafficking in persons to or from Hong Kong for the purpose of prostitution
Section 130	Control over persons for the purpose of unlawful sexual intercourse or prostitution
Section 132	Procurement of girl under 21
Section 133	Procurement of a mentally incapacitated person to have unlawful sexual intercourse
Section 134	Detention for intercourse or in a vice establishment
Section 135	Causing or encouraging prostitution of, intercourse with, or indecent assault on, a girl or boy under 16
Section 136	Causing or encouraging prostitution of a mentally incapacitated person
Section 138A	Use, procurement or offer of persons under 18 for making pornography or for live pornographic performances
Section 140	Permitting a girl or boy under 13 to resort to or be on premises or vessel for intercourse
Section 141	Permitting a young person to resort to or be on premises or vessel for intercourse, prostitution, buggery or homosexual act (only if the victim was under 16 and the offender was 18 or above)
Section 142	Permitting a mentally incapacitated person to resort to or be on premises or vessel for intercourse, prostitution or homosexual act
Section 146	Indecent conduct towards a child under 16

Prevention of Child Pornography Ordinance

Section 3	Offences relating to child pornography

Related Inchoate Offences

• Inciting another to commit any of the above offences
• Aiding, abetting, counselling or procuring the commission of any of the above offences
• Conspiracy to commit any of the above offences
• Attempting to commit any of the above offences

References

Bohlmann, Markus & Hickey-Moody, Anna, 'Introduction' in Markus Bohlmann & Anna Hickey-Moody, (eds), *Deleuze and Children* (Edinburgh: Edinburgh University Press, 2019), 1–12.

Bryant, Levi, *Difference and Givenness: Deleuze's Transcendental Empiricism and the Ontology of Immanence* (United States of America: Northwestern University Press, 2008).

Buchanan, Ian, 'Power, Theory and Praxis' in Ian Buchanan & Nicholas Thoburn, (eds), *Deleuze and Politics* (Edinburgh: Edinburgh University Press, 2008a), 13–34.

Buchanan, Ian, *Deleuze and Guattari's Anti-Oedipus* (London & New York: Continuum, 2008b).
Buchanan, Ian, *The Incomplete Project of Schizoanalysis* (Edinburgh: Edinburgh University Press, 2021).
Chen, Hung-hsueh, 'The study of Research Value and the Underlying Legal theory of Vinaya' (trans., original: 『戒律』研究价值及其法理思维探析), (2009) *Collections of College Students Thesis Relating to Buddhism (trans., original 大专学生佛学论文集)*, 1–24.
Colebrook, Claire, *Understanding Deleuze* (Australia: Allen and Unwin, 2002a).
Colebrook, Claire, *Gilles Deleuze* (London & New York: Routledge, 2002b).
De Sutter, Laurent & McGee, Kyle, 'Introduction' in Laurent De Sutter & Kyle McGee, (eds), *Deleuze and Law* (Edinburgh: Edinburgh University Press, 2012), 1–14.
Deleuze, Gilles, *Negotiations* (New York: Columbia University Press, 1995).
Deleuze, Gilles & Guattari, Félix, *Anti-Oedipus* (London: Continuum, 1984).
Faber, Roland, 'Introduction: Negotiating Becoming' in Roland Faber & Andrea Stephenson, (eds), *Secrets of Becoming* (New York: Ford University Press, 2011), 1–52.
Fourner, Mat, 'Just Tell Them I'm a Chipmunk' in Markus Bohlmann & Anna Hickey-Moody, (eds), *Deleuze and Children* (Edinburgh: Edinburgh University Press, 2019), 110–127.
Goodley, Dan, 'Becoming rhizomatic parents: Deleuze, Guattari and disabled babies' (2007) 22(2) *Disability and Society*, 145–160.
Goodley, Dan, 'Bringing the Psyche back into Disability Studies: The Case of the Body with/out Organs' (2009) 3(3) *Journal of Literary & Cultural Disability Studies*, 257–272.
Haggerty, Kevin & Ericson, Richard, 'The surveillant assemblage' (2000) 51 (4) *British Journal of Sociology*, 605–622.
Jun, Nathan, 'Deleuze and Normativity' (2009) 53(4) *Philosophy Today*, 347–358.
Lefebvre, Alexandre, *The Image of Law: Deleuze, Bergson, Spinoza* (Stanford, United States of America: Stanford University Press, 2008).
Liao, Xiao-ping, 'Filial Piety and the Moral Situation of Minors in Chinese Culture' (2008) 32(4) *Journal of Xiangtan University (Philosophy and Social Sciences)*, 129–134.
Lind, Craig, 'Law, Childhood Innocence and Sexuality' in Les Moran, Daniel Monk & Sarah Beresford, (eds), *Legal Queeries* (London & New York: Cassell, 1988).
Linstead, Stephen & Pullen, Alison, 'Gender as multiplicity: Desire, displacement, difference and dispersion' (2006) 59(9) *Human Relations* 1287–1311.
May, Todd, *Gilles Deleuze: An Introduction* (Cambridge: Cambridge University Press, 2005).
Rajchman, John, *The Deleuze Connections* (London: MIT Press, 2000).
Rose, Nikolas, 'Government and Control', (2000) 40 *Brit J. Criminol*, 321–339.
Silberstein, Laurence, 'Becoming Israeli/Israeli Becomings' in Ian Buchanan & Adrian Parr, (eds), *Deleuze and the Contemporary World* (Edinburgh: Edinburgh University Press, 2006), 146–160.
Watson, Janell, 'Theorising European Ethnic Politics with Deleuze and Guattari' in Ian Buchanan & Nicholas Thoburn, (eds), *Deleuze and Politics* (Edinburgh: Edinburgh University Press, 2008), 196–218.
Winslade, John, 'Tracing Lines of Flight: Implications of the Work of Gilles Deleuze for Narrative Practice' (2009) 48(3) *Family Process*, 332–346.
Zehavi, Ohad, 'Undoing the Parent-Function' in Markus Bohlmann & Anna Hickey-Moody, (eds), *Deleuze and Children* (Edinburgh: Edinburgh University Press, 2019), 47–63.
Žižek, Slavoj, *Organs without Bodies: On Deleuze and Consequences* (London & New York: Routledge, 2004).

Chapter 8
Deterritorializing Sexuality, Act(less)ing Justice: Žižekian/Deleuzian/Lao Zi's Perspective on Hong Kong Law Reform on Sexual Offences

8.1 Proposal of the Hong Kong Law Reform Commission

The ripple effect caused by the landmark case *Leung Roy William* v *Secretary for Justice* (2004)[1] has been far-reaching and significant in its impact: In 2006, the Hong Kong Law Reform Commission set up the Sexual Offences Sub-Committee ('the Sub-Committee' hereafter); in the next four years, the Sub-Committee issued a series of reports and consultation papers: (1) *Interim Proposals on a Sex Offender Register—Consultation Paper* (2008); (2) *Sexual Offences Records Checks for Child-related Work: Interim Proposals* (2010); and (3) *The Common Law Presumption that a Boy under 14 is Incapable of Sexual Intercourse: Report* (2010). One of the most important outcomes was a consultation paper, titled *Rape and Other Non-consensual Sexual Offences* (*Consultation Paper* hereafter), which was published in September 2012. Recommendation 1 of the *Consultation Paper* declared that (1) Respect for sexual autonomy; (2) Protective Principle; (3) Gender Neutrality; and (4) Avoidance of distinctions based on sexual orientation are the guiding principles behind other recommendations,[2] which include:[3]

(1) The creation of a statutory definition of 'consent' to sexual activity which reflects the need for 'freely and voluntarily agreement' to the sexual activity and the capacity to consent;
(2) A newly-defined offence of rape which can be committed against a person of either sex and covers penile penetration of the vagina, anus or mouth;

This chapter is derived in part from an article published in *Reconstruction* (2015).

[1] HCAL 160/2004. The court in this case decided that the restriction on male-with-male buggery violated the Basic Law, the mini-constitution of Hong Kong.

[2] Other guiding principles are: Clarity of law and adherence to the International Covenant on Civil and Political Rights (ICCPR) and the Hong Kong Bill of Rights Ordinance (Cap 383, LHK).

[3] *Rape and other non-consensual sexual offences*, The Law Reform Commission, available at: http://www.hkreform.gov.hk/en/publications/rape.htm (visited 1 Nov 2013).

M.-C. Chiu, *Transforming the Hong Kong Legal Machine*,
https://doi.org/10.1007/978-981-19-1272-6_8

(3) A reformed mental element with regard to the issue of 'consent', moving away from a focus simply on the subjective belief of the accused as to whether the complainant consented, to a mixed test of subjectivity and objectivity. Currently, if an accused subjectively holds a genuine belief that the complainant consented, the accused is entitled to be acquitted even if that belief was unreasonable;
(4) The abolition of the offence of 'non-consensual buggery', so that the conduct which is the subject of such an offence would be covered in future by the gender neutral offence of rape;
(5) The creation of a new offence of 'sexual assault by penetration' to cater for the more serious forms of conduct, not constituting rape, and currently covered by the offence of 'indecent assault';
(6) Substituting the offence of 'indecent assault' with a new offence of 'sexual assault' focusing on conduct which is 'sexual' rather than 'indecent', with a proposed definition of 'sexual';
(7) 'Under-the-skirt photography' should, amongst other intentional acts of a sexual nature, constitute 'sexual assault';[4] and
(8) The abolition of the offence of procuring another to do an unlawful sexual act by the use of threats or intimidation (Section 119, Crimes Ordinance Cap 200, LHK) and the creation of the offence of 'causing a person to engage in sexual activity without consent', emphasizing the protection of one's sexual autonomy.'

On 5 December 2019, the Sub-Committee released *The Final Report on the Review of Substantive Sexual Offences* (*Final Report* hereafter). Recommendations made include the following:[5]

(1) The Sub-Committee reconfirms its earlier recommendation in relation to consent.
(2) Replace 'rape' with 'sexual penetration without consent', a newly created offence, which is gender neutral and will cover penetration of mouth, anus and vagina.
(3) 'Indecent assault' shall be replaced by 'sexual assault', another newly created offence, which 'should be constituted by a person who, without the consent of another person (the complainant) and without a reasonable belief that the latter consents, intentionally does any of the following things: (a) Touches[6] the complainant where the touching is sexual; (b) Ejaculates semen onto the complainant; (c) Emits urine, saliva or any other bodily fluid onto the complainant sexually.'[7]

[4] This suggestion is accepted by Hong Kong Legislative Council in 2021.

[5] Recommendations that are related to children are discussed in Chap. 7.

[6] 'Touching' includes 'touching through anything', in particular, touching that 'amounts to penetration.' Please see Final Recommendation 17, *the Final report on Review of Substantive Sexual Offences*, available at: https://www.hkreform.gov.hk/en/docs/rsubstantive_sexual_offences_se.pdf (visited 6 Nov 2020).

[7] Final Recommendation 18, *the Final report on Review of Substantive Sexual Offences*, available at: https://www.hkreform.gov.hk/en/docs/rsubstantive_sexual_offences_se.pdf (visited 6 Nov 2020).

(4) 'Sexual' will be defined by the reasonable person test; i.e. the following test shall be adopted: '(a) whatever its circumstances or any person's purpose in relation to it, it is because of its nature sexual, or (b) because of its circumstances or the purpose of any person in relation to it (or both), it is sexual.'[8]

(5) Non-consensual upskirt-photography, that should be applicable to both female and male (not limited to natural gender), shall be made an offence.

(6) A uniform age of consent (age 16) shall be introduced.

In sum, the Sub-Committee proposes to (1) redefine consent in the rape law machine, and (2) replace the current sexual assault offences with a series of new offences. I have discussed the problems related to consent elsewhere, arguing that consent does not simply mean agreement (e.g. agreement to sexual intercourse under psychological influence).[9] When analyzing the reasons and justifications underlying the recommendations, we can therefore critically ask: Why do we have to distinguish between penetration, assault (including ejaculation of semen, urine and saliva, and touching); if the law, as claimed by the Sub-Committee, seeks to protect the sexual autonomy (or body) of victims and the seriousness of the harm? In short, can the proposal re-create justice? What is justice? And, in the genre/milieu of gender/sexual politics, what is the connection between justice and (sexual) desire? Can desire re-manufacture justice? In this chapter, I will investigate the above questions from the respective philosophical perspectives of Slavoj Žižek, Gilles Deleuze and Lao Zi 老子, examining how they help construct and elaborate the dialogue between desire and social order/machines (including law and justice), and whether the first two theories, originated and developed overseas, can be effectively transplanted into the cultural context of Hong Kong, a predominately Han-Chinese 汉族华人 society.

Let us start with the Žižekian theorem.

8.2 Žižekian Jouissance on Desire and Law: Acting Justice

As elaborated in Chap. 6, desire in human subjects motivates the exercise of Lacanian fantasy; and only by being translated into the symbolic language of fantasy, can desire be represented and assessed by the human subject.[10] As a product of Symbolic Order, fantasy cannot be omnipotent—like the Master Signifier, fantasy has its shortcomings; when human subjects notify the weaknesses of fantasy, fantasy can be subverted and the Master Signifier challenged.[11] This notification cannot come from the Symbolic Order; the alert must come from the Real via jouissance—the repetitive illegitimate pleasure, though it cannot be understood rationally by human

[8] Final Recommendation 15, *the Final report on Review of Substantive Sexual Offences*, available at: https://www.hkreform.gov.hk/en/docs/rsubstantive_sexual_offences_se.pdf (visited 6 Nov 2020).

[9] For details, please refer to Chiu (2015).

[10] Peng (2019), at 3, 133.

[11] Chen (2019), at 75.

subjects, is there for them; and it signals the limit or the impotency of symbolic power. Sexual offences, non-consensual actions violating the autonomy of others' bodies, show how this machine works: The reoccurrence of an offence, driven by desire, on one hand, breaches the legal structure, however, on the other hand, it (as jouissance) reinforces male domination and derived gender roles (Symbolic Order and fantasy), which underlie the development of law and related judgments, and reconstitute human subjectivities.

The dilemma is: When a symbolic self is trying very hard to fulfil its desire, s/he does not know what the Big Other exactly desires of her/him—this explains why people can never exhaust or understand completely what a society expects from wo/men. In other words, a person, even after submitting herself/himself totally to the current law in Hong Kong, would still not fully understand the legal definition of 'sexual'. Although the *Consultation Paper* and the *Final Report* suggest that the reasonable person test should be adopted in deciding what 'sexual' means, and the law would consider the circumstances in contention, people's purposes and the nature (of the activity) when making its decision, the key question—'what is desire?'—is left unanswered. Is sexuality a kind of desire? Why should the court's decision replace and be more accurate than the perpetrator's subjective motive and intention? In *R* v *George*,[12] for instance, although the defendant admitted that removing a shoe from a female's foot gave him sexual gratification, the court still considered that action itself not sexual.

The machinic (re)constitution of the human is a becoming, which is a result of dis/re/connections of different machines, so humans tend to be indecisive about what they and others desire, which is never stable and fixed (e.g. social expectations regarding gender roles, gender dialogue and the law controlling sexual/assault are always changing and debatable).[13] The subject (including human, law and justice), like desire, is thus always decentred and unstable.[14]

8.2.1 Is Justice Always a Fantasy?

Due to the power of the Master Signifier, fantasy succeeds in quilting different floating signifiers, human subjects and the common sense world while the existing discrepancies are ignored.[15] In the context of gender/sexual politics, justice can be the fantasy that propels and drives the legal system—Rawlsian justice, which preambles and tries to attain equality and protection of the powerless, problematizing patriarchal heterosexism. Nonetheless, such a notion of justice, as argued by Rawlsians, can be fulfilled through the machine of law (another area of heterosexist male domination)—in this way, Rawlsian justice can be allowed and accepted by law, but only when it

[12] [1956] Crim LR 52.

[13] Vighi & Feldner (2010), at 39.

[14] Žižek (2006), at 42.

[15] Liu (2011), at 53.

does not challenge the Master Signifier of the machine—the phallus. The Hong Kong rape law reform proposal is one of the best illustrations of this—it certainly puts more emphasis on penile penetration.[16]

Fantasy, simply put, fends off the possible invasion of residual pleasure, which is being left in the Real by the incomplete symbolic castration, to common sense reality. In the context of the rape law reform proposal, what Žižekian philosophy shows us is that the proposal's justice, which starts with equality—Rawlsian justice—would only end up inflicting more pain, as it fails to problematize and challenge the male domination underlying the development of the legal system. For example, in order to maintain fairness in a trial, where the rights of a male defendant have to be respected and observed, the names of the female victim (as a witness in such trials) is not normally kept confidential from the media, and the victims, when appearing as a court witness, sometimes fail to apply for the use of a screen, so as to preserve their anonymity, thus submitting themselves to a 'second rape'.[17]The above phenomenon is not mentioned at all in the *Consultation Paper* and the *Final Report*.

Certainly, due to the jouissance machine, even though it seems everyone understands that the proposal cannot completely transform the current male-dominating socio-legal culture, the proposal and related recommendations will, very probably, be accepted and followed—not because there is no choice, but because society feels insecure if the Master Signifier of socio-legal structure, i.e. the phallus, is challenged. The proposal and possible acceptance of rape law reform is natural and essential, as law, and rape, are both the products of a misogynist socio-legal structure, a phallic product; a genuine reform, by which heterosexist masculinity and related violence are subverted and politicized, could only take place if there is a new Master Signifier.[18]

8.2.2 Žižekian Justice: To Act, Not to Be Instructed to Enjoy

Law, being part of the Symbolic Order, requires support and needs confirmation from the superego otherwise it cannot exert its influence.[19] The superego hence acts as the ultimate enforcer and promoter of society's laws, morals and codes of acceptable behavior and good conduct.[20] Under current gender-sexuality politics, whether a person wants to lead a life of good lady or gentleman does not matter, but laws and

---

[16] It is further evidenced by the *Sentencing and Related Matters in the Review of Sexual Offences: A Consultation Paper*, released by the Sub-committee on 12 November 2020. It suggested that the maximum penalty for penetrative sexual activity without consent should be life imprisonment, while the maximum penalty of non-penetrative sexual activity without consent should be 10 years' imprisonment.

[17] 'Being raped and then forced to experience trauma' (trans., original: 被强奸还要自揭伤疤), *Apple Daily*, 18 Mar 2011. Available at: http://hk.apple.nextmedia.com/news/art/20110318/15087320 (visited 1 May 2014).

[18] Žižek (2013).

[19] Žižek (1994), at 54.

[20] Kul-Want & Piero (2011), at 71.

customs, with the superego, would instruct her/him to enjoy being a straight wo/men, even against his/her desire.

According to Žižek, justice can only be constructed if people are awakened from their fantasy.[21] This does not simply mean the repeal of old laws and/or enactment of new laws (as the *Consultation Paper* is proposing), because that would fail to challenge or destabilize the superego and thus can only mark a further entrenchment of the existing Symbolic Order. In the matrix of the Hong Kong rape law reform proposal, the definition of 'sexual', the re-definition of 'rape', and the introduction of sexual assaults, as elaborated above, while not subverting the patriarchal order do further submit the constitution of subjectivity to the power of (phallocentric-patriarchal) sexuality. So, the *Consultation Paper* and the *Final Report* cannot help us to escape or subvert the patriarchal (socio-legal) system, which not only takes part in provoking sexual assault, but further instructs us to live within a patriarchal society. Žižekians will argue, in the context of the rape law reform proposal, that justice would only be possible if humans are prepared to give up their existing concepts of ideal and fixed identity, which are the products of the socio-legal superego, and challenge the Master Signifier (i.e. the Phallus).[22]

The abandonment of these concepts of identity could be achieved by an act, initiated, ironically, by jouissance—according to Jacques Lacan and Žižek—fantasy never looks for any scarless harmony during the quilting between different signifiers, and between human subjects and common sense world—scars, left by the conflicts, are the channels by which jouissance appears to re-instate and destabilize (via the act) the power of fantasy and the Master Signifer. A relevant and valid strategy of acting is thus Foucauldian Desexualization. The ideology of Desexualization was proposed by Michel Foucault in Volume 1 of the *History of Sexuality.*[23] In that ground-breaking book, Foucault describes social and historical discourse as a field of struggle where powers circulate; and sexualities do not exist as a pre-given, but are reproduced by multiple and conflicting interactions of power.[24] Foucault effectively argues that sexuality has been historically deployed throughout Euro-American society through the operation of power/knowledge networks, including legal mechanisms and psychoanalysis.[25]

Desexualization not only means anti-discrimination or cancellation of gender/sexuality stereotyping, but the acceptance of multiple sexual desires; in other words, the liberation of different desires. The Desexualization of law, therefore, 'means sexuality (not sexual action, such as rape) under all circumstances should not be subjected to any legal regulations; i.e. law should accept and tolerate the multiplicities of sexuality.'[26] In other words, the phallus should cease to be the essential guiding philosophy of the legal system in Hong Kong.

---

[21] For details, please see Chap. 6.

[22] Kul-Want & Piero (2011), at 118.

[23] Foucault (1978).

[24] Foucault (1978), at 157.

[25] Black (1988), at 51.

[26] Chiu (2015).

Looking back at the *Final Report*, the suggestion to (re)define 'sexual' (Recommendation 15) by using the traditional 'reasonable person' test, where a particular subjecthood is manufactured under a heterosexist patriarchy, simply goes against the ideology of Desexualization. Adopting the standard of the reasonable person when fixing the definition of 'sexual', in the machine of patriarchal heterosexism, would directly make penile penetration prevail, and degrade other sexualities and sexual orientations, hence reinstating the phallus as the Master Signifier. Further, according to Foucault's notion of Desexualization, rape or sexual assault would be reduced to mere bodily assault. Such an offence would not be related to any particular organ (e.g. anus, penis or vagina). Through Desexualization, the existing hegemony (male domination) and the status of the phallus is problematized and challenged.

An act, in short, rejects or suspends the Symbolic Order by breaking all the conventions; thus the symbolic instructions and superego orders become ineffective. The act, in the context of rape law reform, means a continual and very painful challenge to definitions such as rape and 'sexual' and a subversion of legal tradition, which is predicated upon a heterosexist script of life:

> [I]t is only through an act that I effectively assume the big Other's inexistence, that is, I enact the impossible, namely what appears as impossible within the coordinates of the existing sociosymbolic order.[27]

An act creates a breakthrough and a discourse by which a new common sense world and a new Master Signifier[28] can be produced (though an act never proposes any new Master Signifier).[29] Desexualization of the law—i.e. the reduction of sexual offences to common bodily assaults, which I discussed above—would hence make sexuality/products of the phallus cease to be the key signifier; and although it does not propose the creation of any new signifier, it creates an opportunity for the production of new signifiers, or even for us to rethink whether a Master Signifier is essential in the manufacture of the subject or justice.

In other words, an act expands the possibility to create an innovative Symbolic Order and can also recreate history, so that when a new order is created, it appears as if it was already there.[30] Žižek, in *Event*, summarizes the effect of an act:

> This eventual moment [i.e. the act] is the moment when the signifier – a physical form that represents meaning – falls into the signified, into what it means, when the signifier becomes part of the object it designates...[31]
>
> Such a signifying reversal (the imposition of a Master-Signifier) is not simply external to the designated thing: what it does to the thing is to provide it with an *additional unknowable feature* which appears as the hidden origin of its properties. (emphasis added)[32]

---

[27] Žižek (2004), at 510.

[28] A Master Signifier 'is an empty signifier which has no signified content, and which unifies a field of meaning precisely through this very lack or inconsistency.' (Wood 2012, at 8).

[29] Kay (2003), at 5; Wood (2012), at 30.

[30] Wood (2012), at 15.

[31] Žižek (2014), at 136.

[32] Žižek (2014), at 139.

Žižek argues that justice can be temporarily achieved through suspending the Big Other, so that everyone can be her/his own self. However, the Žižekian act, which does not expect anything, cannot guarantee any success.[33]

Žižekian philosophy, in sum, proposes a reflective and constitutive paradigm of justice. If the Rawlsian procedure sets the foundation for creating justice, then the Žižekian framework creates the constant initiative which repetitively challenges the discrimination created by the nonstop re/territorialization of identity. This echoes with the Deleuzian definition of 'revolution' (initiated by line of flight): 'Revolution occurs through making *additions* to the script, bringing in unexpected amendments by borrowing strategies from elsewhere.' (emphasis added).[34]

8.3 The Deleuzian Machine of Justice: Becoming the Powerless in the Legal-Sexual Machine

The Deleuzian line of flight always connects with desire. According to Deleuze, desire is the greatest power of life and change,[35] which is applicable in all contexts and relations:

> When desire is present, however, it exists as a process that changes the connections and social relations of society, transgressing all fixed boundaries. Desire is revolutionary in essence, not because it wants revolution, nor because it may be provocative to express liberated sexuality, but because it affects and changes every established order of society.[36]

Deleuzian desire is, in short, always positive and productive[37]—simultaneously different/new types of desire are formulated and created by different machinic assemblages;[38] multiple desires in turn formulate and create (new) machinic assemblages, which then produce different machines. A machine can connect, disconnect and reconnect with other machines; one machine can never be reduced to any singular connection, i.e. machines are always fluid and dynamic.[39] Deleuzian desire, with this power and energy, hence plays a vital role in the creation of subjects, concepts and identities:

---

[33] Devenney (2007), at 56.

[34] Goodchild (1996), at 2. Guattari and Rolnik provide further elaboration of the concept: 'The attempt at social control on a world scale through the production of subjectivity clashes with considerable factors of resistance from processes of permanent differentiation that I would call "molecular revolution".' (Guattari & Rolnik 2008, at 61).

[35] De Bolle (2010), at 8.

[36] Goodchild (1996), at 74.

[37] Goodley (2007), at 147. Desire, to Deleuze, means the state of impulses and drives. Smith (2012), at 182.

[38] Winslade (2009), at 336, 337. Crockett (2013), at 61.

[39] Jun (2009), at 351.

> [E]very machine functions as a break in the flow in relation to the machine to which it is connected, but at the same time is also a flow itself, or the production of a flow, in relation to the machine connected to it.'

The creation of subjects, concepts and identities, which come from the desire that fuels deterritorialization (which then creates affect and thus action; i.e. the lines of flight), can easily take place at the weaker margin or edge of a rhizomatic web of social forces.[40] Deterritorialization can be translated and fulfilled in the existing social force machine/assemblages.[41]

Deterritorialization, according to Deleuze (and Félix Guattari), can produce a social space where immanent relations, which 'instead of acting out roles given to them by some real or imaginary third party in the role of a transcendent scriptwriter, are capable of shaping, affecting, and changing any mediating factors just as easily as these can shape the relations', are manufactured.[42] Deleuze thus advocates that every concept/identity (including law and justice), especially the powerless (e.g. the rape victims), is always a 'becoming', not a simple one-stop process.[43] Crockett further argues that 'Deleuze rejects internal relations of property because of his critique of identity; if beings lack identity, then they lack proper parts and thus internal relations'.[44] So becoming, as Levi Bryant indicates, always contains contradictions and oppositions;[45] lines of flight always take off at the same time when de/territorialization, with the fuel of different and multiple desires, challenges the existing territorialized and layered domination. Thus, any effort to stabilize a subject is doomed to be a failure, and an identity or a concept is always becoming.

Deterritorialization, initiated by desire, can be conducted proactively and strategically. This is where the machine of emergent law, deterritorialization in the legal machine, is developed: As Jamie Murray argued, emergent law, initiated and maintained by a molecular line of desire, can certainly overcome the codification and fixation of legal principles which are territorialized by the existing legal machine, and can be accommodated and incorporated within the current socially-dominant

---

[40] Sutton & Martin-Jones (2008), at 6; Rizzo (2012). According to Philip Goodchild, 'Lines of flight escape from machinic functioning and social subjection by functioning as cutting edges of deterritorialization that continually change the nature of the entire machine.' (Goodchild 1996, at 170).

[41] Murray (2013), at 48.

[42] Goodchild (1996), at 3.

[43] Deleuze (1995), at 173; Lorraine (2011), at 76; Rizzo (2012), at 54. As Roland Faber explains: '[T]he event of becoming is the process by which nothing that happens is, in its subjective/objective moments, a predicate of an underlying substrate; rather, that which becomes repeats and alters patterns, structures, or modes of existence in order to become what it seems to be from the outset, but only is by re-instantiating such patterns in new events.' (Faber 2011, at 13. Please note that the repetition in this context is not a 'repetition of the Same', but a 'repetition of differences', which is hidden under the former. (Crockett 2013, at 30).

[44] Crockett (2013), at 17.

[45] Bryant (2008), at 58.

structure. Murray believes that only through this machine of emergent law, can new and ground-breaking legal principles and court cases be produced, by lawyers who, though trained by the existing legal machine, understand those social conflicts and problems which are not dealt with by the existing legal machine (*Leung Roy William* v *Secretary for Justice*[46] is a good and effective illustration). Emergent law, in short, is a channel, which can effectively direct desires to challenge mainstream social forces:

> In emergent law, desire, justice and schizo law replace molar law, and emergent law develops as a practice of desire, justice and the creation of concepts of legality. Emergent law is a machine of desire and justice.[47]

Applying Murray's interpretation of Deleuzian legal philosophy in analyzing the Hong Kong rape law reform, multiple sexual desires (including SM, homosexuality, etc.) could initiate and formulate effective different lines of flight, in terms of new law proposals (e.g. Bills) and court cases (like *Leung Roy William* v *Secretary for Justice*).[48] The existing legal control/territorialization on gender identities, sexual orientation and sexual activities can thus be challenged. As argued by Murray, such changes can only come from lawyers, or legally trained people, including, of course, the Hong Kong Law Reform Commission.

Another good example of deterritorialization is the concept of 'Body without Organs' (BwO hereafter): because of energy brought by lines of desire, the body can never be a rigidly regulated entity, but only a BwO.[49] A BwO is the way by which the body, once territorialized (under the schema of the Oedipal complex), can be decoded. The BwO, which is a platform where becoming starts,[50] is also a revolution, which aims to challenge any attempt to territorialize the (Fe/Male, Trans) body.[51] The BwO can, put simply, help us escape from 'stratified forms of being'.[52] The concept is best summarized by Simone Bignall:

> A body is therefore defined not only by shifts in the consistency of its internal relations but more particularly by the affection these relations produce…the body is an extensive entity that is comprised of elemental parts, combined in particular configurations according to the ways in which they affect one another.[53]

The body is thus a matrix of assemblages constructed with other bodies in a milieu. Further, using the Deleuzian concepts of deterritorialization, emergent law and BwO as lenses to critically analyze the recommendations made by the *Consultation Paper* and the *Final Report*, by which the scope of the rape offence is extended from sole penile penetration of the vagina to penile penetration of vagina (artificially

---

[46] HCAL 160/2004.

[47] Murray (2013), at 149.

[48] HCAL 160/2004.

[49] Rajchman (2000), at 153.

[50] Faber (2011), at 13.

[51] Rajchman (2000), at 267.

[52] Beckman (2013), at 104.

[53] Bignall (2010), at 83, 84.

created), anus (both naturally born and artificially created) or mouth, we can then ask: Is the rape law reform proposal an emergent law, initiated by lawyers who privilege male domination and celebrate the significance of the male sex organ? Why does law have to re-glorify the status of the penis and make penile penetration a different offence? Why do we have to prioritize a certain and particular organ (like the vagina and penis) in defining and fixing a sexual/gender identity? Is it a natural result of the heterosexist legal machine where opposite-sex sexual intercourse (and possible natural reproduction) is privileged? Or, is the law reform proposal simply a re/territorialization of gender politics?

As elaborated by Ian Buchanan, Deleuzian desire is the origin of revolution as it always tries to problematize the coding imposed by lines of social forces.[54] Deleuzian desire-based justice hence means the release of multiple desires, through which all 'attempts to ground any reasoning, rationale, or logic on some object measure' would be destroyed and torn off.[55] The exercise of desire, however, is never a free flow, but is influenced by the molar social force. Thus, the line of flight is always a zig-zag action.[56] In other words, Deleuzian justice can only be created when becoming and deterritorialization happen, and where all fixed and territorialized layers and connections are broken by lines of desire; as Goodchild puts it:

> [W]hen deterritorialized, a desire leaves behind the constant nature given by its previous strata in order to cross a boundary and becomes something entirely different.[57]

Using a Deleuzian perspective, in the machine of the rape reform proposal in Hong Kong, not only will sexual desire of heterosexuals, male and female, be respected, but different formats of sexual activities/desires should and must also be considered by the new rape law proposal. In other words, again we have to ask: Why does the law have to differentiate between rape and other sexual assaults, as proposed by the *Consultation Paper* and the *Final Report*?

8.3.1 *Deleuzian Justice = Desexualizing Law?*

Deleuzian justice is a kind of becoming, created by multiple and different desires; in the words of Alexandre Lefebvre, desire makes law creative.[58] In the case of the Hong Kong rape law reform proposal, a Deleuzian will argue that different desires (for example, different sexualities and multiple sexual orientations) have successfully initiated the drive (another new desire) to revise and improve existing forms of social cooperation between institutions and among people of different gender/sexual identities, for example, through the revision of rape law/sexual offences (and perhaps

---

54 Buchanan (2008), at 45.

55 Capeheart & Milovanovic, (2007), at 125.

56 Braidotti (2006).

57 Goodchild (1996), at 146.

58 Lefebvre (2008).

the Sex Discrimination Ordinance Cap 480, LHK). What Deleuzians are looking and striving for is, as I argued above, a total deterritorialization of sexuality, since sexuality (in law machine) is nowadays imprisoned; as Frida Beckmann argues:

> In interpretations of Deleuze, sexuality has tended to be positioned alongside territorialized forms of the body, and thereby as a force that closes rather than opens the body to what is capable of.[59]

Desexualization is the way sexuality can be deterritorialized.[60] Deleuze himself does not use the exact term in this context, but his co-author Guattari did insist that: 'Desire, if allowed to open up to the world rather than be repressed by it, is no longer destructive…but creative.'[61] Benjamin Noys, another Deleuzian, also argues that only when sexuality is not codified, can new formats between the self and the other exist.[62] It will not be surprising that Deleuze would also support Desexualization. Desexualization of law, where, as argued above, no offences would be linked with a particular organ (vagina, anus or penis), thus debonding the machine created by connections between organs (penis and vagina/anus/mouth); and sexual identities/gender identities/sexuality/sexual orientation/formats of sexual activities would no longer be territorialized with violations of bodily autonomy. This strategy can therefore create an opportunity whereby the cultural imaginary, in relation to desire and the body, is critically cross-examined and the need to devise law which can go beyond normative standards is acknowledged. What Desexualization re-manufactures is the right to desire, through which all bodies have the right to 'exercise discretion and preference in forming and transforming the situations and associations that constitute their identity'.[63]

[59] Beckman (2013), at 6.

[60] It may be argued that not only do Foucault and Deleuze not share the same understanding of sexuality and desire, but Deleuze also criticizes Foucault for not constructing a mature resistance strategy. However, as pointed out by Beckman, when it comes to the constitution of subjectivity, Foucauldian analysis of desire is 'akin' to the way Deleuze and Guattari see it. Beckman (2013), at 21, 22, 25.

[61] Beckman (2013), at 7.

[62] Noys (2008).

[63] Bignall (2010), at 99.

8.4 Lao Zi's yi[64]/Justice Beyond Desire: The 'Actionless-ness' of Natural Cosmology

Lao Zi, like Žižek and Deleuze, exposed the impossibility of universal metaphysics. According to Lao Zi, a profound scholar of Daoism (a school of philosophy developed in Imperial China), Dao is the origin of the universe, including humanity, law and society.[65] To quote Lao Zi:

> All-pervading is the Great Dao! It may be found on the left hand and on the right.
>
> All things depend on it for their production, which it gives to them, not one refusing obedience to it.
>
> (trans., original: 大道氾兮, 其可左右。万物恃之以生而不辞。)[66]

Hsien-hao Liao further elaborates, Dao is 'both an immanence that underlies all beings and the source of all becomings. The relationship between the Tao [Dao] and the world can be summarized as: If people in influential positions attain Tao [Dao], the world will become of itself.'[67]

In short, Dao continues to exist through the exercise of the material world. Xiaobing Fei writes that Dao observes and understands universe and life instinctively and objectively, since Dao, as Lao Zi advocates, can go beyond desire and needs.[68] (Self-centric) Desire (e.g. fame and power), to Lao Zi, is damaging: Not only does overindulging in materialistic desire fulfillment enhance greed and accelerate deterioration, such an attitude also instructs all human subjects to follow and obey a particular self-created value judgement and underlining perspective, and thus ignores and suppresses differences: 'Let the hearing (of the ears) rest with the ears. Let the mind rest in the verification (of the rightness of what is in the will)'[69] (trans., original: 听止于耳, 心止于符。). This leads to the growth of over-insistences and forbids any kind of challenge and innovation.[70] In fact, Daoists argue that humans should aim at engaging with Dao and surpassing all kinds of desire:

---

[64] yi 义 is generally used as the translation for 'Justice' in a Han-Chinese context. The inter-relationship between Justice and yi is further elaborated in Chap. 1 and below.

[65] Fei (2013), at 4, 75.

[66] Verse 34, *Lao Zi*, available at: https://ctext.org/zhuangzi/adjustment-of-controversies (visited 6 Nov 2020).

[67] Liao, Hsien-Hao, 'Becoming Gad, and Dog: Taoist *You*, Deleuzian Nomadism and *God, Man, Dog*', Paper presented in Conference on Deleuze's Cultural Encounters with the New Humanities, organized by Hong Kong Shue Yan University, Utrecht University (9–12 Jun 2014), at 3.

[68] Fei (2013), at 5, 132.

[69] Verse 2, Man in the World, Associated with Other Men人间世, *Chuang Zi* 莊子, available at: https://ctext.org/zhuangzi/adjustment-of-controversies (visited 4 Nov 2020).

[70] Wang (2018), at 6.

> He who devotes himself to learning (seeks) from day to day to increase (his knowledge); he who devotes himself to the Tao [i.e. Dao] (seeks) from day to day to diminish (his doing). He diminishes it and again diminishes it, till he arrives at doing nothing (on purpose). Having arrived at this point of non-action, there is nothing which he does not do.[71] (trans., original: 为学日益, 为道日损,损之又损, 以至于无为,无为而无不为。)

However, (Orthodox) Daoism also understands that desire is the driver for all kinds of movement, progress and innovation. From a Laozian perspective, desire, however, has to be controlled before being surpassed.[72] By controlling desire, the ruling authority (including legislature and judiciary) can, hopefully, transcend all self-interest and insistence.

In the eyes of Daoism, law, as a language discourse within Symbolic Order that is created and used by the ruling authorities, is constituted in the format of binarism. Human subjects hence are all living in the legal matrix which is made up of multiple hierarchal differences.[73] Due to rapid social development, law is becoming complicated, and so is the related control based on binarism. Every human subject hence has to invariably determine her/his respective discursive positions in multiple dichotomies, and develop her/his self-centric desire and interest. What Daoism aims to do is to assist human subjects to go beyond this matrix; because only by doing so, can everyone return to Dao. While this does not mean a complete abandonment of the legal system, it does require us to reject the either-or perspective which is underlining the current legal development. In other words, law and yi/justice, transformed by Daoism, can be an assemblage that controls desire.

How can we omit the either-or perspective and go beyond self-centric desire? The answer, according to *The Great and Most Honoured Master* 大宗师, written by another significant Daoist, Chuang Zi 莊子, is by sitting and forgetting 坐忘. Sitting and forgetting has three parts: Dissolution of body parts 堕肢体, discarding of perceptive organs 黜聪明, and leaving material form and saying farewell to knowledge 离形去知. It in fact means going beyond the physical self and unlearning the language (including law), feel the (pre-social and pre-linguistic) self and start the interaction between both. Shi-san Lai further suggests an interchange strategy: Let one step into others' shoes and imagine what would happen to her/him afterwards.[74] Through doing so, human subjects can feel Dao, a feeling which is not distorted by language and the related binarism.[75] The description put forward by Chuang Zi looks abstract; however, in fact, it merely encourages the production of space within the current Symbolic Order, where the fossilized binarism can be problematized, so we can feel and talk to our respective selves and let different subjects have a dialogue with each other.[76]

---

[71] Verse 48, *Lao Zi,* available at: https://ctext.org/dao-de-jing (visited 17 Dec 2020).

[72] Fei (2013), at 283.

[73] Lai (2011), 254.

[74] Lai (2013), at 499. For more discussion on this process from perspectives of Confucianism and Rawlsian Justice, please see Chaps. 3 and 4.

[75] Lai (2011), at 306.

[76] Lai (2019), at 331.

Daoist yi/justice, according to Chuang Zi's *Levelling All Things* 齐物论, hence has two themes: (1) Representing the equality of every object on earth; and (2) going beyond binarism: 'Heaven, Earth, and I were produced together, and all things and I are *one*.'[77] (emphasis added. trans., original: 天地与我并生, 而万物与我为一。) 'One', in this context, does not mean unification or essentiality, but, due to unlimited interaction among different objects (not only human subjects), the universe and every subject is thus becoming one continuum. Simply put, only when human subjects, after abandoning self-centric desire and over-insistency, can feel with others to be on an equal footing, the hegemony relying on binarism can be dissolved; and differences in the universe will be accepted and respected:[78] 'As soon as one finds this pivot [of Dao], he stands in the centre of the ring (of thought), where he can respond without end to the changing views; without end to those affirming, and without end to those denying.'[79] (trans., original: 枢始得其环中, 以应无穷。是亦一无穷, 非亦一无穷也。) Due to the unlimited interaction between differences, new subjects and concepts can be produced.

In the linguistic/law machine of gender/sexual politics, according to the philosophical perspectives of Lao Zi and Chuang Zi, no one should exploit or impose any perspective on others, and everyone should respect the differences among people and the singularities of others.[80] Looking at the Hong Kong rape law reform proposal, a Daoist would argue that we should not impose any hegemony (i.e. misogynist or heterosexist socio-legal structure), however implicitly, by privileging the offence of rape (penile penetration) over other new offences. Also, the proposal, if accepted and passed by the legislature, would further re-strengthen the male hegemony, by making the penis/phallus a privileged and more powerful body organ/Master Signifier, and reinstating the patriarchal social machine through the establishment of new offences. Such a proposal does not work for the betterment of the powerless (i.e. the victims of sexual assault).

8.4.1 Actionless-ness: A Daoist Perspective on Law and yi/Justice

It is not surprising that Lao Zi argues that socio-political chaos is caused by the over-whelming self-centric desire of the ruling authorities. As an antidote to this situation, Lao Zi created the principle of actionless-ness 无为. While action 为 means any implementation that is initiated by a self-centric desire, a drive that assumes

77 Verse 9, *Levelling All Things* 齐物论, available at: https://ctext.org/zhuangzi/adjustment-of-controversies (visited 3 Nov 2020).

78 Lai (2013), at 145.

79 Verse 5, *Levelling All Things* 齐物论, available at: https://ctext.org/zhuangzi/adjustment-of-controversies (visited 3 Nov 2020).

80 Wang (2004), at 144.

universal subjecthood;[81] actionless-ness is, prima facie, the limitation of power and avoidance of power abuse, where self-centric desire and self-hood are absent:[82] 'He who knows other men is discerning; he who knows himself is intelligent. He who overcomes others is strong; he who overcomes himself is mighty.'[83] (trans., original: 知人者智, 自知者明。胜人者有力, 自胜者强。).

According to the principle of actionless-ness, as the ruling authorities are no longer self-centred, they (in fact, all human subjects), when facing new challenges, cannot rely on experiences but only reflections; and from those reflections, innovative ideas are generated, constructing a breakthrough and solving the imminent crisis.[84] Furthermore, actionless-ness, together with sitting and forgetting, destroys self-centric desires, goes beyond either-or binarism, and refuses to impose any particular set of values (e.g. heterosexist socio-legal structures) on others.[85]

Actionless-ness does not mean 'not doing anything', but rather meticulous planning, extensive consultation, the aesthetic exercise of power and no unnecessary laws; so, the populace do not feel the interference of the ruling class:[86] 'Abstaining from speech marks him who is obeying the spontaneity of his nature.'[87] (trans., original: 希言自然) In the machine of actionless politics, the starting point is going beyond self-centric desire;[88] when engaging with interchanging strategies, rulers should be able to stand and think from others' perspectives and understand that policy should not be made and implemented to disturb the lives of the populace: 'The Dao in its regular course does nothing (for the sake of doing it), and so there is nothing which it does not do.'[89] (trans., original: 道常无为而无不为。) Put simply, law cannot be over-complicated,[90] or abolish or extinguish natural instincts. Lao Zi strongly advocated that '[i]n the kingdom the multiplication of prohibitive enactments increases the poverty of the people' (trans., original: 天下多忌讳, 而民弥贫。).[91] People

[81] Verse 22, *Lao Zi,* available at: https://ctext.org/dao-de-jing (visited 3 Nov 2020).

[82] Lee (2010), at 54, 263.

[83] Verse 33, *Lao Zi,* available at: https://ctext.org/dao-de-jing (visited 3 Nov 2020).

[84] Xia (2016), at 149.

[85] Lai (2013), at 462.

[86] Xia (2016), at 191.

[87] Verse 23, *Lao Zi,* available at: https://ctext.org/dao-de-jing (visited 3 Nov 2020).

[88] Lee (2010), at 142.

[89] Verse 37, *Lao Zi,* available at: https://ctext.org/dao-de-jing (visited 3 Nov 2020).

[90] Fei (2013), at 166.

therefore, according to Liao, should therefore 'relinquish the goal-oriented or destination-bound mindset…and "settle oneself in one action". For only then can they see "the unadorned nature of things".'[92]

Embedding the Daoist theory of actionless-ness in investigating the rape law reform proposal, we can then argue that creating more and more offences (like sexual offences with penetration and sexual assault) only makes the law unnecessarily complicated, and glorifies further phallocentric heterosexism. Daoists would also agree with the strategy of Desexualization, by which law can be made simpler, by not privileging a particular set of ideologies and related hegemonies, like the phallocentric patriarchal socio-legal structure—all sexual offences would be reduced to bodily assault, where sex, sexuality or either gender (and sexuality) would not be hegemonized.

8.5 Engaging Foreign Concepts with Hong Kong Culture: Where Are the Sim*u*larities?

The remaining question is: If there is an indigenous platform for re-constructing yi/justice, why do we still need foreign support? As discussed in Part 1, the machine of transcultural sim*u*larity, developed by Hsiao-hung Chang, can offer us an efficient and functional paradigm to conduct such a transplantation.

Chang, using the Deleuzian theory of simulacrum, politicizes the binarisms of real/origin and fake/replica. Chang argues that a genuine and authentic original culture has never existed, and that there are zones of possible similarities between cultures, i.e. simulacra. According to Chang, cultural interaction can be taken as the sim*u*larity between cultures—there are similarities, and simulations can occur between cultures. According to Chang, the zone of sim*u*larity is a virtual product, where infiltration between cultures can be proactively directed.[93] In Daoism, Dao is also a theoretical space which functions comparably with the zone of sim*u*larity where different values can be accommodated. Lao Zi emphasized that Dao can go beyond the unending chain of dichotomies (out/inside, straight/non-straight) which relies on strict mutual exclusiveness and otherization.[94] In Lao Zi's words, while the common sense world is full of different value judgments, Dao is value-free, cannot be fixed and is fluid, multiple and full of energy and possibilities of changing. It is in this context that Yu-kwan Ng argues that, as Dao does not have any essential or monolithic nature, it can accommodate different perspectives:

---

[91] Verse 57, *Lao Zi*, available at: https://ctext.org/dao-de-jing (visited 3 Nov 2020).

[92] Liao, Hsien-Hao, 'Becoming Gad, and Dog: Taoist *You*, Deleuzian Nomadism and *God, Man, Dog*', Paper presented in a Conference on Deleuze's Cultural Encounters with the New Humanities, organized by Hong Kong Shue Yan University, Utrecht University (9–12 Jun 2014), at 4.

[93] Chiu (2008).

[94] Verse 2, *Lao Zi*, available at: https://ctext.org/dao-de-jing (visited 17 Dec 2020). See also Fei (2013), at 106.

> If we are going to adapt the Western ideology of democracy, I am afraid that we need to use the Daoist perspective of relaxation and openness…Daoism is different (from Confucianism), it is a philosophy which does not insist itself or offer any particular perspective…it provides the largest spiritual space for different philosophies to engage; this is its most obvious and precious characteristic. (trans.)[95] (trans., original: 我们要吸纳西方的民主思想，恐怕要借助道家的冲虚的、开放的怀抱……道家便不同，它是最没有主见与成见的一种思想……它能提供最大的精神空间，让不同的思想能游息其中，这是它的最大特色。)

Dao therefore constructs and provides the platform/matching points through which Han-Chinese culture can engage with Deleuzian and Žižekian concepts of Justice.

Juxtaposing the theories of Žižek, Deleuze and Lao Zi, a number of commonalities can be located and constituted: (1) The existence of a monolithic transcendence, which certainly suppresses and constitutes peripheral powerlessness, creates and produces injustice; every theory provides its own analysis of why it exists: Žižekians allege that ideology wants to maintain Symbolic Order (by allowing and controlling fantasy); Deleuzians argue that social forces always try to sustain complete and ever-lasting territorialization, masking any differences; and (Orthodox) Daoists believe that anything which goes against Dao and fails to accommodate different desires, allow self-centred desire to grow and over-insistence to result. (2) Monolithic transcendence will be definitely challenged, by either a Žižekian production of a new Master Signifier (i.e. Žižekian act), Deleuzian deterritorialization, or forever changing Dao, which aims at transforming self-centered desire into desire to work for the betterment of humankind. (3) Desire motivates changes and subversion—Žižekian act, which offers an opportunity to construct a new Master Signifier, is ignited by desire; Deleuzian desire is always productive; and the Daoist notion of desire, if not self-centred, can work for the betterment of humankind.

In the context of the Hong Kong rape law reform proposal, we can then argue that the recommendations made cannot meet the criteria of the justice theories proposed by Žižek, Deleuze or Lao Zi. The recommendations are trying to territorialize gender identities with certain attributes (glorifying the significance of the male penis by setting up the offence of sexual penetration without consent) and failing to challenge the existing powerful Master Signifier (i.e. the phallus) (again by the setting up of the new offence of sexual assault by penetration), and finally, the proposal makes the law unnecessarily complicated (the new offence of sexual assault). The solution, as I have consistently advocated, is the Desexualization of crime, initiated and motivated by multiple (sexual) desires and the desire to change. Legal Desexualization can revoke any blind attachment to any hegemonic attachment, and re-accommodate multiple and the never ending creation of desires into everyday life. It means, in short, reducing rape to bodily assault and accepting different sexualities. This solution problematizes

[95] Ng (1998), at 1–2.

the phallus as the ultimate universal signifier (i.e. Žižekian act), deterritorializes assault from the politics of sexuality, simplifies the existing law and therefore allows it to accommodate and accept different sexual desires (i.e. no matter whether the unconsented sexual activities in question involve people of same sex, a different sex or a third sex/transgender/transsexual).

I need to reemphasize that Desexualization, like any recommendation or suggestion, is not a once-and-for-all pathway to constructing justice—for as Deleuzians argue, re/deterritorialization will always occur, or as Žižekians accept, a new Master Signifier will emerge, or as Daoists believe, Dao is always changing and floating, so new problems will definitely occur, and the definition of a better being is always debatable. The fight against assault and for justice never ends; but as Žižek writes: 'Now the struggle is still going on, and this for me is the true hope…My point is that there's still a lot of hope, but hope is always mixed with danger.'[96]

References

Beckman, Frida, *Between Desire and Pleasure: A Deleuzian Theory of Sexuality* (Edinburgh: Edinburgh University Press, 2013).

Bignall, Simone, 'Affective Assemblages: Ethics beyond Enjoyment' in Simone Bignall & Paul Patton, (eds), *Deleuze and the Postcolonial* (Edinburgh: Edinburgh University Press, 2010).

Black, Joel, 'Taking the sex out of sexuality: Foucault's failed history' in David Lamour, Paul Allen Miller & Charles Platte, (eds), *Rethinking Sexuality: Foucault and Classical Antiquity* (Princeton: Princeton University Press, 1988), 42–60.

Braidotti, Rosi, *Transpositions* (Cambridge: Polity, 2006).

Bryant, Levi, *Difference and Givenness: Deleuze's Transcendental Empiricism and the Ontology of Immanence* (United States of America: Northwestern University Press, 2008).

Buchanan, Ian, *Deleuze and Guattari's Anti-Oedipus* (London & New York: Continuum, 2008).

Capeheart, Loretta & Milovanovic, Dragon, *Social Justice: Theories, Issues and Movements* (United States of America: Rutgers University Press, 2007).

Chen, Jian, *From Ideology to Moral Law* (GuangZhou: JiNan University, 2019).

Chiu, Man-chung, 'A Hybrid of Harmony and Resistance at the Margin: Legal Discourse of Gender/Sexual Justice in Hong Kong, PR China (2008) 35 *Journal of Social Sciences* 179–201.

Chiu, Man-chung, *Eros of Law – Postcolonial Han-Chinese Erotic Politics and Legal Discourse* (Hong Kong: Red Publish, 2015).

Chu, Yiu-wai, *Otherness Machine? Essays on Postcolonial Hong Kong Culture* (Hong Kong: Youth Literary, 1998).

Crockett, Clayton, *Deleuze Beyond Badiou* (New York: Columbia University Press, 2013).

De Bolle, Leen (ed), *Deleuze and Psychoanalysis* (Leuven, Belgium: Leuven University Press, 2010).

Deleuze, Gilles, *Negotiations* (New York: Columbia University Press, 1995).

Devenney, Mark, 'Žižek's Passion for the Real' in Paul Bowman & Richard Stamp, (eds), *The Truth of Žižek* (London & New York: Continuum, 2007), 45–60.

Faber, Roland, 'Introduction: Negotiating Becoming' in Roland Faber & Andrea Stephenson, (eds), *Secrets of Becoming* (New York: Ford University Press, 2011), 1–52.

Fei, Xiao-bing, *Research on Legal Perspective of Lao Zi (trans., original: (老子)法观念探微)* (BeiJing: China University of Politics and Law Press, 2013).

[96] Žižek (2013), at 92.

Foucault, Michel, *The History of Sexuality, Vol 1* (New York: Vintage, 1978).
Goodchild, Philip, *Deleuze and Guattari: An Introduction to the Politics of Desire* (London: Sage, 1996).
Goodley, Dan, 'Becoming rhizomatic parents: Deleuze, Guattari and disabled babies' (2007) 22(2) *Disability and Society* 145–160.
Guattari, Félix & Rolnik, Suely, *Molecular Revolution in Brazil* (New York, United States of America: Semotext(e), 2008).
Jun, Nathan, 'Deleuze and Normativity' (2009) 53(4) *Philosophy Today* 347–358.
Kay, Sarah, *Žižek: A Critical Introduction* (Oxford & Cambridge: Polity, 2003), at 5.
Kul-Want, Christopher & Piero, *Introducing Žižek* (Malta: Gutenberg Press, 2011).
Lai, Shi-san (trans., original: 赖锡三), *Contemporary Neo-Taoism (trans., original: 当代新道家)* (TaiPei: National Taiwan University Press, 2011).
Lai, Shi-san (trans., original: 赖锡三), *On Taoist Intellectuals: The Critique of Power and Cultural Revitalization in Zhuangzi (trans., original: 道家型的知识分子论: 庄子的权力批判与文化更新)* (TaiPei: National Taiwan University Press, 2013).
Lai, Shi-san (trans., original: 赖锡三), *Zhuangzi's Intercultural Weaving: Nature, Qi, and Body ((trans., original: 〈庄子〉的跨文化编织: 自然. 气化. 身体)* (TaiPei: National Taiwan University Press, 2019).
Lee, Tseng (trans., original: 李增), *Philosophy of Lao Zi's Dao (trans., original: 老子道之哲学)* (TaiPei: TonSan 唐山, 2010).
Lefebvre, Alexandre, *The Image of Law: Deleuze, Bergson, Spinoza* (Stanford, Stanford University Press, 2008).
Liu, Shi-heng, *Unbreakable Phantasm: Research on Slavoj Žižek's Ideological Theory (trans., original: 难以摆脱的幻象缠绕-齐泽克意识形态理论研究)* (BeiJing: Intellectual Property Publishing House, 2011).
Lorraine, Tamsin, *Deleuze and Guattari's Immanent Ethics* (New York: State University of New York Press, 2011).
Murray, Jamie, *Deleuze & Guattari: Emergent Law* (New York: Routledge, 2013).
Ng, Yu-kwan, *Contemporary Analysis of Lao-Chuang Philosophy* (TaiPei: WenJin 文津, 1998).
Noys, Benjamin, '"The End of the Monarchy of Sex": Sexuality and Contemporary Nihilism' (2008) 25(5) *Theory, Culture & Society* 104–22.
Peng, Jun-Guo (trans., original: 彭均国), *Desire Society: the Research on Slavoj Zižek's Thought of Ideological Function* (BeiJing: People's Publishing House, 2019).
Rajchman, John, *The Deleuze Connections* (London: MIT Press, 2000).
Rizzo, Teresa, *Deleuze and Film: A Feminist Introduction* (New York: Continuum, 2012).
Smith, Daniel, *Essays on Deleuze* (Edinburgh: Edinburgh University Press, 2012).
Sutton, Damian & Martin-Jones, David, *Deleuze Reframed* (London: I B Tauris, 2008).
Vighi, Fabio & Feldner, Heiko, 'From subject to politics: The Žižekian field today' (2010) 3(1) *Subjectivity* 31–52.
Wang, Qing-jie, *Heidegger and a Hermeneutical Interpretation of Confucianism and Daoism* (BeiJing: RenMin University Press, 2004).
Wang, Pang-hsiung (trans., original: 王邦雄), *Seven Lectures on Chuang Zi (trans., original: 庄子七讲)* (TaiPei: Yuan-Liou 远流, 2018).
Winslade, John, 'Tracing Lines of flight: Implications of the Work of Gilles Deleuze for Narrative Practice' (2009) 48(3) *Family Process* 332–346.
Wood, Kelsey, *Žižek: A Reader's Guide* (United Kingdom: Wiley-Blackwell, 2012).
Xia, Hai (trans., original: 夏海), *Lao Zi and Philosophy (trans., original: 老子与哲学)* (BeiJing: Joint Publishing, 2016).
Žižek, Slavoj, *Metastases of Enjoyment* (London: Verso, 1994).

Žižek, Slavoj, 'From Politics to Biopolitics…and Back' (2004) 103 (2/3) *The South Atlantic Quarterly* 501–521.
Žižek, Slavoj, *How to Read Lacan* (London & New York: W. W. Norton & Co, 2006).
Žižek, Slavoj, *Demanding the Impossible* (Cambridge: Indigo, 2013).
Žižek, Slavoj, *Event* (London: Penguin, 2014).

List of Cases

M.-C. Chiu, *Transforming the Hong Kong Legal Machine*,
https://doi.org/10.1007/978-981-19-1272-6

List of Legislation

M.-C. Chiu, *Transforming the Hong Kong Legal Machine*,
https://doi.org/10.1007/978-981-19-1272-6

Index

M.-C. Chiu, *Transforming the Hong Kong Legal Machine*,
https://doi.org/10.1007/978-981-19-1272-6

MIX
Papier aus verantwortungsvollen Quellen
Paper from responsible sources
FSC® C105338

If you have any concerns about our products,
you can contact us on
ProductSafety@springernature.com

In case Publisher is established outside the EU,
the EU authorized representative is:
Springer Nature Customer Service Center GmbH
Europaplatz 3, 69115 Heidelberg, Germany

Printed by Libri Plureos GmbH
in Hamburg, Germany